On The

PSYCHOLOGY OF WOMEN

A Survey of Empirical Studies

On the
PSYCHOLOGY OF WOMEN
A Survey of Empirical Studies

(First Edition, Fourth Printing)

By

JULIA A. SHERMAN, Ph.D.

Madison, Wisconsin

Formerly

Minneapolis Clinic of Psychiatry and Neurology

Minneapolis, Minnesota

Consultant, Professional Service Corps

Los Angeles, California

CHARLES C THOMAS · PUBLISHER

Springfield · Illinois · U.S.A.

12319

Published and Distributed Throughout the World by

CHARLES C THOMAS PUBLISHER
Bannerstone House
301-327 East Lawrence Avenue, Springfield, Illinois, U.S.A.

This book is protected by copyright. No part of it may be reproduced in any manner without written permission from the publisher.

1971, by CHARLES C THOMAS • PUBLISHER

ISBN 0-398-01744-1 (cloth)
ISBN 0-398-02762-5 (paper)
Library of Congress Catalog Card Number: 77-149194

First Edition, 1971
First Edition, Second Printing, 1973
First Edition, Third Printing, 1974
First Edition, Fourth Printing, 1975

With THOMAS BOOKS careful attention is given to all details of manufacturing and design. It is the Publisher's desire to present books that are satisfactory as to their physical qualities and artistic possibilities and appropriate for their particular use. THOMAS BOOKS will be true to those laws of quality that assure a good name and good will.

Printed in the United States of America
00-2

To

Stanley G. Payne

PREFACE

THE PURPOSE of this book is to provide information concerning the psychology of women. A strongly empirical approach to the topic has been taken, since there is little consensus of expert opinion and since no other examination of the objective psychological data of the female life cycle has heretofore been available. In many instances, data is meager and of poor quality; the reader is warned against easy generalizations. Conclusions found in this book must be regarded as tentative assessments of the current status of the evidence. The data is often presented in sufficient detail so that with the help of the bibliography, the reader may form his own conclusions. It is hoped that this review may serve as a constructive catalyst to further research in this neglected area (Carlson and Carlson, 1960). Opinions are many; facts are few. The reader unenthusiastic for the empirical density of the text may gain a fair idea of the book's contents by perusal of the summaries at the end of each chapter and at the end of the book.

A word of explanation regarding choice of emphasis would seem to be necessary. Freud's theory of female development was chosen for close scrutiny because it still appears to be the single most influential theory on the topic. This is particularly unfortunate, since scant support for Freud's hypotheses of *female* development was found. However, the findings cited should not be viewed as a rejection of Freud's theory of male development or of other aspects of his theory.

The biological emphasis of the book developed from the following factors: (a) the psychology of certain biological events is uniquely and irrefutably feminine, (b) many books emphasize feminine social problems, but almost none examines the biological life cycle, (c) mind-altering drugs and psychological side effects of the "Pill" pose the question of what alterations result from naturally occurring chemical changes, and (d) the psychology of reproduction is of strategic importance not merely to women but also to the production of healthy babies. The emphasis on the biological should not be construed as a denial of the importance of social factors in the psychology of both women and men.

Nearly every topic considered has proven to be controversial. I have tried to be even-handed and fair in evaluating the issues, and I would request that the reader cast aside his preconceived ideas and let the data lead him to his conclusions.

My sincere thanks to Paul Meehl who criticized an earlier version of the manuscript, to Albert Heilbrun, Jr., who criticized sections of Chapter 5, and to Donald O. Price who offered advice from the point of view of a gynecologist and obstetrician. I am much indebted to Boyd McCandless who generously took time from his busy schedule to give the manuscript a thorough going over. My husband, Stanley Payne, offered helpful suggestions, moral support, and the indispensable cooperation which made this book possible. Needless to say I alone am responsible for any remaining errors and for the views expressed.

JULIA A. SHERMAN

CONTENTS

12319

On The

PSYCHOLOGY OF WOMEN

A Survey of Empirical Studies

Chapter 1

BIOLOGY OF SEX DIFFERENCES

In these days of "his" pants for her too, shaggy hair, and unisex styles, many people seriously question whether there is a specific psychology of women. Some people even question whether the sexes are very different biologically from one another. Unfortunately, answers to these questions are obscured by propagandistic writings. Some writers have minimized or even denied sex differences, presumably in the hope of furthering social and political equality for women. Others have written in defense of a traditional position, glorifying the "natural" role of women. An accurate assessment of the question will require careful avoidance of the frequent biases involved.

This chapter will present a brief overview of biological aspects of sex differences, such as the influence of chromosomes and hormones and the nature of embryonic development. In addition, a variety of the more important physical sex differences will be discussed. Additional material on later physical sex differences will appear in the chapter on adolescence, and biobehavioral hormone influences will be discussed as they become pertinent through the life cycle.

CHROMOSOMAL SEX DIFFERENCES

Sex differences are apparent from the very beginning of life. Of the twenty-three pairs of chromosomes which determine human inheritance, one pair controls sexual development. In the case of females, the two chromosomes are similar to each other and by scientific convention are designated XX. The corresponding male pair, XY, might more descriptively be represented by Xy since there is about five per cent less genetic material in Y than in X and since the genes on X and Y do not seem to be parallel to each other. The Y chromosome may contain material which has no counterpart in X. The exact contents of Y are unknown, though it is now accepted that they are responsible for male development. The older notion that it is the lack of a second X chromosome, not the presence of a Y chromosome, that determines male development is clearly incorrect. Females are females because they lack whatever it is in Y that is responsible for male development (Childs, 1965). The inherited sex of an individual affects all the cells in his body, not just his sex organs. All the cells in the entire body of a female are different from those of any chromosomal male.

FEMALE GENETIC ADVANTAGE

It has been proposed that the female has a genetic advantage in that she has more genetic material and a second stand-in chromosome which might be able to take over or outweigh the function of a defective chromosome. A widely accepted theory, the Lyon hypothesis, holds that only one X chromosome is operant in each cell, which one being a random matter. The cells of the female body would thus be a mosaic of cells, some with one X chromosome being active, others with the second X chromosome active. If this is true, it would decrease the female genetic advantage considerably but not entirely (Childs, 1965). In any case, there is no question that genetic flaws and sex-linked disorders are more common in males. The greater incidence of color blindness and hemophilia in males appears to result from the relative lack of protection of a second, stand-in chromosome. Genetic advantage has also been proposed as the explanation of the fact that the death rate of women is less than that of men in every decade of life. With few exceptions, every disease and disorder is a less common cause of death in women than in men (Childs, 1965; Scheinfeld, 1944). Women show greater resistance to infection, perhaps due to the advantage of heterozygosity of the immune mechanism (Washburn, Medearis, and Childs, 1965). Girls are less thrown off their growth curves by malnutrition than boys. They appear better canalized in growth, not merely better able to withstand adverse conditions (Tanner, 1962).

The old stereotype of the weaker female is clearly correct, however, in the case of muscular strength, since females are not so strong as males. Androgenic (male) hormones* are responsible for a difference in male metabolism of nitrogen, leading to greater development in musculature (Money, 1961). Given the positive relationship between androgens and sex drive (see Chapter 8), it seems the intuitive female practice of judging a potential mate by his musculature is not far amiss. Other possible examples of the frailty of women are that, even excluding indispositions related to menstruation and childbirth, women are sick about 20 per cent more often than men (Scheinfeld, 1944). Peterson (1964) reports, however, that when relevant variables are controlled, women actually lose fewer work days because of illness than men, possibly because their illnesses tend to be less severe. Certainly women are much more vulnerable than men at certain times of reproductive stress.

HORMONES

After the chromosome, the hormone is the most influential biological factor in developing sex differences. Endocrinology is a science in its infancy; the interrelationships among the hormones and the effects of certain ones are not clearly understood. It is now possible to measure the level of at least some hormones in the blood, which presumably permits greater accuracy in estimating their effect on important tissues than did the method of measuring the end products of hormone metabolism as they occurred in the urine. There is considerable disagreement, however, about the best way of measuring hormones and when to use which measure. The effect of hormones varies with the amount, the age of the organism, the types of previous hormonal influences, and even the previous history of the organism. The hormones themselves are chemically unstable and once in the body may change to

*Hormones have been rather misleadingly tagged as either male or female sex hormones. This is misleading because neither "male" nor "female" hormones are limited to their respective sexes. Women produce androgens and men produce estrogens. The normal hormone balance, of course, is in the direction of the sex-typical hormones. Furthermore, sexuality is only one bodily function affected by "sex" hormones, and sexuality is by no means directly determined by them. It should also be noted that there are several chemically similar compounds which are sometimes called androgens or estrogens or simply androgen and estrogen.

other compounds, possibly with quite different effects. Furthermore, the same hormone may affect male and female cells somewhat differently, since the cells themselves are fundamentally different. One might think of it as parts of a gear fitting together. The chemicals of the male hormones mesh more easily with the chemicals in the male cell than in the female cell. It is clear that hormonal changes are effected at the cellular level, possibly by altering cellular genetic function but in any case, by somehow influencing enzyme action in the cell (Hechter and Halkerston, 1965).

Children produce small amounts of androgens and estrogens. Sex differences in production of hormones accelerates drastically at puberty, and although androgens are also increased in females, androgens in males eventually reach a level twice that of females. In girls, estrogen production increases at about age eleven and begins to take a cyclic form about eighteen months before menarche (Hamburg and Lunde, 1966). Many parents needlessly worry about a masculine-looking girl or a feminine-looking boy who will be completely changed by hormonal influences during puberty. In early years, it is difficult to predict the eventual development of secondary sex characteristics, since these depend on hormones which are not produced in quantity until later.

The pituitary gland used to be characterized as the master gland, since it was believed to be responsible for control of a large part of the hormone system. Now there is little question that the pituitary gland itself is subject to control by the hypothalamus and thus potentially under the influence of the higher centers of the brain. Conversely, concentrations of hormones have been found in the brain, providing biological evidence of a way in which hormones could influence the brain (Hamburg and Lunde, 1966). These findings help to point up possible mechanisms of mutual mind-body influence.*

*The problem of mind-body relations continues to confuse and confound psychologists. Feigl (1958) provides perhaps the most enlightening discussion of the problem. He supports an identity thesis which hypothesizes that what is experienced by the mind is identical with the object of knowledge as described by molar behavior theory and this in turn is identical with what the science of neurophysiology will eventually be able to describe. Such identity is ultimately to be empirically justified.

EMBRYONIC DEVELOPMENT

Accumulative evidence indicates that the basic pattern of embryonic structural development is female in form. Male differentiation apparently occurs under the influence of androgenic hormones, possibly from the fetal testes (Goy, 1968; Money, 1965a; Whalen, 1968). In other words, without the intervention of these androgenic hormones, female structure will automatically develop. The following account of embryonic development is adapted from Diamond (1968). Until the sixth or seventh week, the human fetus contains neither testes nor ovaries but indifferent gonads. At this time, two systems of primitive ducts also exist in the fetus; these are the Müllerian duct system which can give rise to oviducts, uterus, and upper vagina, and the Wolffian duct system which normally gives rise to the epididymides, vas deferens, and seminal vesicles. Normally, genotype determines direction of development of the primitive gonads. Individuals carrying XX chromosomes develop ovaries; those with XY chromosomes develop testes. Once the gonad differentiates, it induces direction to the development of the two pairs of genital duct structures. An as yet unidentified fetal morphogenic testicular substance induces masculine development of the Wolffian duct and inhibits development of the Müllerian duct system. The ovary does not elaborate a substance inducing development of the Müllerian duct system and regression of the Wolffian ducts. These effects result from the absence of the fetal testicular substance. Similar, but not identical, processes are at work on the external genitalia. Prior to sex differentiation, an indifferent genital tubercle exists and remains undifferentiated until about the end of the third month. These sexually bipotential structures are differentiated as female genitalia unless stimulated by testicular, adrenal, maternal, or exogenous androgens. Ordinarily in the male, the tubercle elongates and a cleft forms on the underside; the elongation continues and the cleft closes, forming the penis. In the female, it does not grow longer, and the cleft deepens. The cleft eventually results in the vagina, while the part that in the male developed into a penis becomes the clitoris.

The similar embryonic beginning of the two sexes was one of

the bits of data that inspired Freud's theory of bisexuality. It was also one of the reasons he considered clitoral excitation masculine. (It is also true that in the female, this tissue produces male-like growth in response to androgenic hormones.) Until recently, it was not understood that the lower part of the vagina and the urethra, as well as the clitoris, develop from the analogous embryonic tissues that form the penis. However, since part of the vagina also develops from "masculine" tissues, it is obvious that it makes little sense to label clitoral (as opposed to vaginal) excitation as masculine. Freud's theory of bisexuality is discussed further in Chapter 3.

PHYSICAL SEX DIFFERENCES

There are a great number of physical differences between the sexes. Sex differences exist for almost every physical variable, and they increase with maturation (Anastasi, 1958). Sex differences range widely and manifest themselves in curious ways. At birth, females more frequently have a second finger longer than the fourth finger, and the male forearm is longer than that of the female (Tanner, 1962). Girls have proportionately less muscle and more fat than boys from birth on (Garn, 1957, 1958). At birth, they weigh about 5 per cent less than boys; by age twenty, they weigh about 20 per cent less. They are 1 to 2 per cent shorter than boys throughout most of childhood, becoming 10 per cent shorter by age twenty (Anastasi, 1958). As has already been mentioned, females have less muscular strength at all ages, roughly 10 per cent less at age seven and 50 to 60 per cent less at age eighteen. In the early years, hand grip may be the only measure to show a decided sex difference (Tanner, 1962). Girls are also slower and less well coordinated, except for fine hand movement in which they develop greater skill and dexterity. As infants, they tend to be more sedentary and sleep more (Scheinfeld, 1944). They show less restless, vigorous overt activity from at least age two on (Anastasi, 1958). Their vital capacity—the total volume of air expelled after maximal inhalation—is less. This factor, important in sustained energy output, is 7 per cent less in girls and 35 per cent less in women. Even equating body size and activity level, adult women in the normal state have a lower metabolism, that is, produce less energy, than men. They therefore require less food per pound as many a housewife ruefully knows.

Mechanisms of maintaining bodily stability, the homeostatic mechanisms, apparently operate within wider limits in the female than in the male. In women, there is more marked physiological reaction to stress but a quicker recovery (Sontag, 1947). Sometimes this works to the female advantage, as in the case of reaction to temperature change. Women have a greater capacity to speed up or slow down metabolism in order to produce more or less heat and thus can adjust more easily to temperature extremes (Scheinfeld, 1944).

Ellis (1908) discussed sex differences in the brain, and the topic is still of interest. Differences are reported in the external appearance of the brain (Connolly, 1950). Sex differences, apparently arising at adolescence, have been found in electroencephalogram recordings of the brain (Ellis and Last, 1953; Henry, 1944; Smith, 1954). Lansdell (1962, 1964) found differences between the sexes in their reaction to unilateral neurosurgery. He notes that the right vein of Trolard is larger than the left in girls but not in boys. He concluded that sex of the patient is a factor in the laterality of cerebral function.

SENSORY DIFFERENCES

There are some differences in the senses. Vision is similar in the sexes except that males more frequently have vision defects. However, Garai and Scheinfeld (1968) concluded that males have superior vision and prefer visual stimulation, while females prefer auditory stimulation. Females can apparently hear high tones better (Anastasi, 1949; Tanner, 1962), and at least part of the time, they have a superior sense of smell. Sense of smell is apparently dependent on estrogen, and hence women have a superior sense of smell. Moreover, olfactory acuity varies cyclically with the monthly variation in estrogen production (Money, 1965a). The most dramatic increase in acuity comes in early pregnancy. An acute olfactory sense no doubt aids the female in her reputation of being more fastidious and discriminating, but the fact that sometimes she notices a smell and sometimes she does not may be confusing for her husband. The superior taste acuity of women is apparently attributable to the fact that they smoke less than men. It is interesting to note that 66 per cent of a sample of women studied showed an increase in taste sensitivity *during* the menstrual period (Kaplan, 1968). For some subjects dramatic reliable increases were found. Thus while the estrogen drop decreases the sense of smell during the menstrual period, for many women the sense of taste increases. Even this brief and selective resume of the more physical sex differences will allow the imaginative reader to grasp the inherent possibilities for misunderstanding between the sexes.

RATE OF MATURATION

One of the most important sex differences is yet to be discussed —the very pronounced difference in the rate of physical maturation. This difference begins before birth, in that ossification of the skeletal system proceeds more rapidly in females than in males. Female bones begin to harden one to two months before the same bones harden in the male, and the process is also finished one to two months earlier. On the average, the female child is born after a shorter gestation period than the male child, though estimates of how much earlier vary from several days to only a half day (Levine, 1966). Permanent dentition also proceeds more rapidly in females than in males. The rate of female acceleration in skeletal maturity increases, so that by age five she is a year ahead of the male and two years ahead at age thirteen. Because of this difference in maturational rate, girls are larger than boys in practically all dimensions from ages $10\frac{1}{2}$ to 13 when the effects of the boys' later growth spurt begin to be noticeable. Girls also stop growing earlier; on the average, girls reach 98 per cent of their final height by $16\frac{1}{2}$, boys by $17\frac{3}{4}$ (Tanner, 1962). Males, however, are ahead in sexual behavior and in attaining fertility (Siecus, 1970). Differences in the rate of physical maturation make it difficult to know how to compare the sexes fairly before they reach physical maturity.

SUMMARY

Each sex has its own special physical assets and liabilities. The principal female liability of less muscular strength is not ordinarily a handicap in a civilized, mechanized society. Even among primitive societies, less difference is found between the roles and status of the sexes in those cultures which place less premium on superior strength and motor skills. Examples of such cultures are sedentary, agrarian cultures and those that do not depend on hunting large animals (Barry, Bacon, and Child, 1957). There is nothing in the biological evidence to prevent women from taking a role of equality in a civilized society. On the other hand, a review of the evidence leaves no doubt that human males and females, while sharing much in common biologically, are fundamentally different from the beginning. These differences normally become more pronounced as maturity is reached. Certainly there are biological differences, but are there psychological differences? If so, how early do they appear?

Chapter 2

PSYCHOLOGICAL SEX DIFFERENCES

WHETHER there are psychological sex differences has long been hotly debated. The controversy rages most strongly outside the psychological discipline. Within the profession, psychological sex differences are acknowledged and considerable agreement is found among the several reviews of this extensive literature (Anastasi, 1949, 1958; Garai and Scheinfeld, 1968; Maccoby, 1966a; Piret, 1965; Terman and Tyler, 1954; Tyler, 1965). A thorough review of studies of psychological sex differences will not be repeated here. This chapter will present a summary of psychological sex differences and an examination of several key issues in more detail. These topics encompass sex differences in analytical ability, dependency, aggression, and emotionality.

THE NATURE - NURTURE PROBLEM

Discussion of sex differences has generally floundered on the nature-nurture oversimplification. Causation of any psychological phenomenon is usually the result not of one factor but of multiple factors. Furthermore, the factors and their relative importance often differ from individual to individual. So far as the nature-nurture controversy specifically is concerned, it has now become clear that the argument also cannot be meaningfully phrased in these terms because they are not mutually exclusive (Lorenz, 1965). In many instances, an inborn tendency will only manifest itself under proper environmental circumstances. Sometimes an innate influence is shown in the fact that a given behavior may be more readily elicited. That is, the same stimulus produces an effect in one organism but not in the other until the stimulus intensity is increased in some way. An innate cause may be involved but not in any simple manner. Thus both nature and nurture usually play a role in producing behavior. Where the state of evidence permits, an effort will be made to delineate the probable character of causation.

METHODOLOGICAL PROBLEMS

Most reports of sex differences come from studies which were not specifically designed to study this factor. As a result, there are frequently so many uncontrolled variables that it is very difficult to attribute the finding to sex per se. For example, comparisons of groups of high school students are misleading, since more unachieving males have dropped out of the sample. Thus girls are compared with a more select male population. Even comparisons between matched groups of children are ambiguous because of the sex difference in maturational rates. However, it is questionable to assume, as did Garai and Scheinfeld (1968), that for this reason males are *really* superior when no statistically significant sex difference is found between groups of equal age. Different physical aspects—teeth, bones, fertility, types of coordination—mature at different comparative rates and even though "mental" and "physical" maturation can not reasonably be regarded as wholly unrelated, it is also true that neither does there appear to be any one single timetable of maturation (Bayley, 1956).

Sex of subject is an obvious and popular variable, and there are many routine computer grindouts of sex differences involving thousands of subjects. Not only are many variables pertinent to sex uncontrolled in these studies, but in addition, these findings are particularly subject to misconstruction because of failure to understand the paradoxical effect of large numbers of subjects (Lykken, 1968; Meehl, 1967). It has frequently been supposed that a statistically significant difference between large numbers of subjects is more likely to represent a true difference than if the number of subjects were small. This is not necessarily the case, since the mean difference necessary to attain statistical significance is drastically reduced with very large numbers. The statistical significance of the finding will not guarantee it psychological relavance. In addition to uncontrolled variables, experimenter bias or lack of construct validity may rob the findings of their apparent validity. Most psychological sex differences are small average differences; the sex distributions of nearly all traits overlap very considerably. In a practical sense, this means that even if, on the average, females are more verbally facile than males, for example, this information will be of little help in predicting how individual males or females will perform.

SUMMARY OF PSYCHOLOGICAL SEX DIFFERENCES

The previously cited reviews have been in general agreement that females are less physically active and more sedentary from birth onward. They are more verbally precocious and more fluent verbally. Girls have fewer speech and reading problems. Males have keener perception in some kinds of spatial tasks and in general excel females in areas of mathematical problem solving, geometry, science, engineering, and tasks requiring mechanical aptitude. Women are superior in tasks requiring fine hand movements and in clerical skills. Females have a slower reaction time. Maccoby (1966b) pointed out that the correlations between intellectual performance and personality differences seem to be different for boys and girls. She concluded that impulsiveness is a negative factor for boys, while it is less negative or even positive for girls. Anxiety, however, has a substantially negative influence on measures of aptitude or achievement for girls and women, while correlations for boys are low negative, zero, or positive. Aggressiveness appears to be more of an inhibitor and less a facilitator for intellectual development among boys than among girls.

Older girls and women are more dependent, conforming, and less willing to take risks, while males are more physically aggressive than females, beginning at an early age. Women murder less and commit suicide less. Adult males are more dominant. Girls and women show more fearfulness and obtain higher scores on inventories of anxiety.

Males greatly excel females in athletic ability and have a greater preference for strenuous outdoor activities. Females show more interest in other people from an early age and have more pity for those in misfortune; they are more religious. Men are more professionally ambitious and achieve more. Ellis (1908) credited women with being more politically capable, but this has not been a subject of recent study.

Bennett and Cohen (1959) studied the responses of a sample

of 1,300 individuals from ages fifteen to sixty-four. The subjects were asked to select from three hundred words those words which described them best and least. Bennett and Cohen concluded that there was extreme similarity between male and female thinking. The average correlation between the sexes was .90. In their view, female thinking formed the mold, while masculinity consisted of being somewhat less feminine. They found male thinking was less intense, more oriented to the self, more concerned with achievement, and less concerned with love and friendship. Males found more value in rough-and-tumble competition, while females preferred autonomy in a friendly, pleasant environment.

The Bennett and Cohen study accentuates the fact that the sexes are very similar to each other, a fact that must not be forgotten as we focus on sex differences. Most differences, except in athletics and to a lesser extent in mechanical aptitude, are small average differences. The distribution of scores on most measures overlap considerably. Material concerning sex differences in conscience and in sexuality will appear in later chapters.

SEX DIFFERENCES IN INTELLECTUAL FUNCTIONING

Belief in the innate, general inferiority of female intelligence has long since been discredited, but the belief is quite persistent, even among college students (Fernberger, 1948). The issue is far from dead. The question now typically takes other forms and discussion is often so muted that it is difficult to decipher the author's opinion. The basic reason for continued concern about this question is the fact that male intellectual achievement continues to surpass female achievement (Dodge, 1966; Maccoby, 1963). American females with doctorates, however, do make scholarly contributions (Astin, 1969), and the myriads of differences in the roles and experiences of the two sexes still make fair comparisons very difficult. Epstein (1970), for example, points out some of these problems.

The question has traditionally been posed as to why there are so few women geniuses. Various explanations have been advanced, aside from obvious genetic possibilities. The hypothesis that males show greater variability than females and thus would have both more geniuses and more mental defectives in their ranks has not been disproven, though Tyler (1965) concluded that the evidence does not strongly support it. The importance of two points seem largely neglected. First, genius is a high-status position determined by social value judgments. Men and women differ in values and male values are dominant in our culture (Smith, 1962). Second, performance is affected by many other factors besides intellectual ability, such as emotional factors, health, free time, energy, and education. Furthermore, for genius to result, these factors have to be maximally combined. Genius is a rare event; the probability of getting the maximal combination drops drastically when large numbers of women are not educated, do not have free time to pursue their interests, or waste their energies floundering about in role confusion and cultural resistance to pursuit of their work and interests. They encounter all these handicaps in addition to those which face the male potential geniuses.

Crandall (1967) reviewed material relevant to sex differences in achievement motivation. She found that females were not more unrealistic in assessing their abilities compared to males; the sexes simply err equally in opposite directions. She concluded that from elementary school to college, girls tend to underestimate their ability, while boys tend to overestimate. That boys may be more highly motivated was suggested by the fact that although girls and boys seem equal in amount of effort, boys returned more to unfinished tasks than girls. Crandall also concluded that there are indications that boys and girls achieve for different reasons. Girls seemed more motivated by approval and affiliative motives than simply need for achievement. In contrast to Crandall's conclusions, however, Stein (1969) found that praise resulted in significantly more achievement in both boys and girls. Girls were no more dependent on external praise than boys. The question of why women have not intellectually achieved as much as men cannot be answered in any way definitively convincing to individuals of all viewpoints. In this chapter, perhaps some light will be shed on important variables for further investigation.

Some Possible Female Advantages in Intellectual Development

In certain ways, females would seem to be given advantages for intellectual development. Fewer girls suffer brain injury at birth (Knoblock and Pasamanick, 1963), and it has been suggested but not established that girls are less fragile in their intellectual development as well as in their physical growth. This conclusion was inferred from the fact that intelligence in girls, unlike boys, developed nearly unaffected by maternal behavior and was also unrelated to characteristics of the girls' own personalities (Bayley, 1967; Bayley and Schaefer, 1964).

Girls appear to have a head start in development, and some have thought that an acceleration in mental maturity parallels the female acceleration in some aspects of physical maturity. Anastasi (1949) doubted that this could be the case, and it does not appear that there is any single developmental timetable controlling both physical and mental growth (Bayley, 1956). On the other hand, Tanner (1961) concluded that compared to other children the same age, physically advanced children show a small but consistent superiority in mental age. Ljung (1965) concluded that the results of his investigation gave a general mental growth pattern in good agreement with the physical growth pattern. Maccoby (1963) points out that faster physical growth may be correlated with faster maturation of certain motor and perceptual abilities that underlie intellectual performance. Performance of these early tasks does not predict eventual intellectual level very well, and an accelerated start does not necessarily imply anything about ultimate levels of intellectual achievement. Nonetheless, it is of interest to examine in what ways girls show precocious development.

Girls learn bowel and bladder control earlier and dress themselves earlier (White House Conference, 1936). In drawing a man, Gesell (1940) found that girls included more details than boys; they were better at drawing a circle at eighteen months and two years, but there were no differences in drawing a cross. From ages two to six, girls counted higher and erred less (Buckingham and MacLatchy, 1930; Gesell, 1940). During ages five to nine, a group of girls matched for age, IQ, and socioeconomic status with a group of boys were found to be more mature in their responses to a variety of tests including the Rorschach (Ames and Ilg, 1964). Ljung (1965) found that girls showed a clear tendency to a faster general mental growth rate. Except in some items of gross motor activity and strength, where there are differences between the sexes, they favor females. One gains the impression that little girls are more competent than little boys of the same age. The difference becomes even more pronounced when we consider verbal development.

Girls are verbally precocious when compared with boys (Kagan, 1969a). Mead also found this to be the case in all cultures she had observed (Mead, 1958). Moreover, verbal skill seems to be more important in the eventual intellectual functioning of females (McCall, 1955). Verbal precocity in the first year correlated with IQ up to thirty-six years of age for females but not for males (Bayley, 1967). Girls begin to talk somewhat earlier than boys, to make sentences earlier, to use a greater number of words, and to show superior articulation. At twenty-four months, McCarthy (1943) found 78 per cent of girls' speech comprehensible compared to only 49 percent of boys' speech. The boys did not entirely catch up until age four. This would imply that girls can communicate effectively earlier than boys. Women do not retain their verbal superiority in all areas, but even as adults they show superior verbal fluency (Tyler, 1965). McCall (1955) points out that males catch up with females in most verbal skills and eventually become well-rounded intellectually, while females tend to rely heavily on their verbal skill. It might also be noted that the early verbal skill of girls "bends the twig" more to problem solution through social communication. This could be relevant to the greater development of sociability and dependence in females. However, even at six months, girls have been reported to look at faces more than boys (Lewis, Kagan, and Kalafat, 1969). Girls show more interest in other people as early as age two (Goodenough, 1957), and they tend to be more affectionate and sociable (Bach, 1945), a finding which extends cross-culturally (D'Andrade, 1966). Evidence regarding dependency in females will be considered later in this chapter.

In addition to verbal precocity, at least in the United States there is evidence that girls are advanced in a variety of ways relevant to development of reading skills (Sapir, 1966). Girls learn to read earlier than boys (Anderson, Hughes, and Dixon, 1957), and in the first grade are superior in reading readiness and reading achievement (Balow, 1963).

All these findings, especially those of Ljung (1965), suggest the tentative conclusion that there is a mental acceleration in girls paralleling the general physical acceleration of their growth. Possibly these advantages stood women in good stead in the beginning of civilization. Beard (1931) supposes that women originated culture and civilized men. Is it for nothing that the Greek deity for wisdom was a woman, Athena?

The Mental Shutdown Question

The other side of the advantage of the more rapid rate of maturation of some physical and possibly mental qualities is the question of whether the early decline of physical growth in women is paralleled by an early end to mental growth, perhaps a premature end. This idea was considered by Ellis (1908), more fully developed by Marañon (1932), and more recently expressed in the article of Garai and Scheinfeld (1968). The implication is that a less complex level of intellectual development is reached in the female. Marañon advanced the argument that since a slower rate of maturation is known to be related to greater development of intellectual capacity in cross-species comparisons, by analogy, human males would be expected to show greater intellectual development than females. It should be noted that this idea is not wholly consistent with the fact that human males become fertile earlier than females (SIECUS, 1970). Marañon viewed the female as an underdeveloped male physically and mentally. When chromosomal sex differences were interpreted to mean that males were males because they lacked a second X chromosome, Marañon's view seemed incongruent with biological fact. Furthermore, the evidence showed no general difference between the sexes in intelligence (Anastasi, 1958; Tyler, 1965), and Anastasi (1949) made the point that there had been a general lack of correlation in humans between physical and mental variables. All these facts and interpretations weighed heavily in discounting Marañon's view.

However, as discussed in the first chapter, recent findings indicate that without the influence of male hormones, a genetic male will develop external female genitalia. Thus an aspect of maleness has been shown to be a further development of a basic female prototype. Furthermore, girls do show evidence of a faster rate of mental development compared to boys (Ljung, 1965). Maccoby (1966b) concluded that boys may show greater intellectual gain than girls during the high school years and that during late adolescence and adulthood, changes in intelligence somewhat favor men. Garai and Scheinfeld (1968) came to an even firmer conclusion of the same kind. However, the matter is not settled, and two recent studies do not support this view. Lunneborg (1969) and Droege (1967) have found that in an atmosphere of continuing education, male and female high school and college students show equal intellectual growth. Lunneborg (1969) comments that the next step is to check whether equal growth continues *without* education. Indeed the whole question of the effects on women of lack of intellectual stimulation and frustration of competence motivation would seem to deserve much more study. At the turn of the century, Breuer and Freud (1957) pointed to these factors as important in developing the mental disturbance of the famous and historic case of Anna O.

Another development in the controversy about female intellectual ability has been the shift from the contention of general female intellectual inferiority to inferiority in specific abilities such as abstract reasoning and analytical ability. In fact abstract reasoning is the very area in which Garai and Scheinfeld (1968) indicate that males, but not females, continue to grow. These authors arrived at a broad conclusion of male superiority in abstract and logical thinking. In support of this view, they concluded that males are superior in vocabulary, verbal comprehension, and verbal reasoning. However, the more extensive Oetzel (1966) bibliography lists six findings that females are superior in vocabulary, three that males are superior, and eleven in which there are no statistically significant differences. In the two adult studies cited, women are superior. Among the studies of verbal reasoning listed, males were superior in three studies, females were superior in two studies, and no difference was found in a sixth study. Theiner (1965) also found no overall sex difference in abstract thought. Among the studies Oetzel lists relevant to abstract thought, females were superior in three studies, males were superior in two studies, and no difference was found in three studies. In spite of the weight of the evidence in favor of females, one widely quoted study supporting a contrary view should be mentioned. Kostick (1954) found that males were superior to females in deductive reasoning, even in solving home economics problems. On the whole, however, a broad conclusion of male superiority in reasoning and in abstraction that includes the verbal area appears unjustified at this time.

Since the vast majority of the studies which support the view that women have inferior analytical ability come from studies involving nonverbal, especially spatial tasks, it will be well to look at this research more closely.

Analytical Cognitive Approach (Field Independence)

A large body of evidence has been amassed showing a small, average sex difference in cognitive approach. It is important to note that this sex difference is not always found (Berry, 1966; Farr, 1969; Immergluck and Mearini, 1969; MacArthur, 1967; Witkin, 1949). Males are said to have an analytical (field-independent) cognitive approach while females tend to show a global (field-dependent) cognitive approach (Witkin, Dyk, Faterson, Goodenough, and Karp, 1962; Witkin, Lewis, Hertzman, Machover, Meissner, and Wapner, 1954). Perceiving in an analytical, field-independent way is said to involve experiencing items as discrete from their backgrounds. It reflects ability to overcome the influence of an embedding context. For example, the most typical measures of field dependence are the Rod and Frame Test and the Embedded Figures Test. In the Rod and Frame Test, the subject attempts to position vertically an illuminated rod in a dark room. The rod is placed in a "frame" which may afford misleading cues. The field-independent subject does not rely on cues from the frame, but figures out verticality, probably on the basis of cues from his own body. The field-dependent subject relies more on the background context of the frame in making his judgment of verticality. In the Embedded Figures Test, the individual picks out "hidden figures" from a confusing context. Both these tests have a spatial character (Sherman, 1967) .* While they significantly relate to spatial factors, they did not significantly relate to the verbal area (Witkin, Dyk, Faterson, Goodenough, and Karp, 1962) . As already discussed, the weight of other evidence also does not support male superiority in verbal abstraction. In fact, males appear to be superior only on analytical cognitive tasks involving spatial perception. Use of the term "analytical cognitive approach" implies a generality which is by no means established. The term "analytical ability" which has also been used in reference to the same findings (Maccoby, 1966, Diamond, 1968) is even more misleading. It is recommended that these terms be discontinued in favor of the more neutral term "field independence." The real source of the sex difference may lie in the spatial character of the tasks and not in the analysis.

Sex Differences in Space Perception

Among those studying space perception, there has been considerable disagreement over how many space factors there are and what to call them. It has generally been concluded, however, that all the space factors are closely related (Michael, Guilford, Fruchter, and Zimmerman, 1957; Werdelin, 1961) . Reviews consistently conclude that males are superior in space perception (Anastasi, 1958; Fruchter, 1954; Sandström, 1953; Tyler, 1965; Werdelin, 1961) . Sex differences have been reported on all space factors, but Werdelin (1961) believes the sex difference may be limited to the visualization factor. This is the ability to grasp space relations as they change in space.

While the sex difference in field dependence may only pertain to those tasks involving spatial perception, skill in spatial perception potentially involves broad areas of learning. Male

*Not all the references and arguments relevant to this topic will be repeated here. The interested reader is referred to Sherman (1967) .

superior spatial skill may partly account for their known superior performance in aspects of geometry, mathematical problem solving, engineering, architecture, and the mathematical and physical sciences generally (Frandsen, 1969; Sherman, 1967). It should always be understood that when men are said to be superior in these areas, an average difference is referred to, usually a small average difference. Individual women may greatly excel in such tasks.

It should also be noted that spatial skill is not the only factor which may affect sex differences in these areas. Of particular interest is the fact that these tasks are generally accepted as masculine in our culture. Performance on problem-solving tasks correlated, for both sexes, with a measure of masculine sex-role identification (Milton, 1957). When sex-role identification was controlled by means of an analysis of covariance, performance differences between the sexes were reduced to insignificance. However, Farr (1969) did not find sex-role identification an important variable in problem solving. Carey (1955) significantly improved the performance of female, but not male, subjects on problem-solving tasks by means of a pep talk. The discussions emphasized the fact that it was socially acceptable to excel at problem solving. Stein and Smthells (1969), however, concluded that their data do not support the view that sex-role standards are *causal* to sex differences in intellectual performance.

Exactly at what age the sexes diverge in space perception is not entirely clear. While Zazzo (Tanner and Inhelder, 1958) reported sex differences as early as ages two to three, sex differences in space perception are not commonly found until the early school years (Maccoby, 1966b). During adolescence, a further and more decisive increment in the sex difference in space perception and cognitive approach apparently occurs (Fruchter, 1954; Gardner, Jackson, and Messick, 1960; Witkin, Lewis, Herzman, Machover, Meissner, and Wapner, 1954). Sandström and Lundberg (1956) reported the puzzling finding that women showed an absolute decline in performance of spatial localization tasks compared to girls. They consider these results entirely unexplained.

The causes of sex differences in space perception and field dependence have not been established. Witkin and his colleagues (1954) have attributed the difference in cognitive approach to cultural factors, though Witkin (1969) has not ruled out innate factors. Maccoby (1966b) has developed the position that field dependence may be attributed to the greater emotional dependency of females. Sherman (1967) emphasized the importance of differential practice in activities plausibly related to the development of spatial perception. These activities are blocks (Farrell, 1957), model construction, working with machines, aiming games and activities, and courses in mechanical drawing and analytical geometry. Mere activity, at least among children four to five, did not correlate with a measure of analytical cognitive approach (Maccoby, Dowley, Degerman, and Degerman, 1965). There is considerable evidence that practice improves spatial perception (Goldstein and Chance, 1965; Sherman, 1967).* More practice in cross-sex role activities is consistent with the active, tomboy background of women who do achieve intellectually (Maccoby, 1966b).

Piaget and his colleagues have been little interested in individual differences and have not focused much on sex differences in intellectual development. However, Piaget's frequent collaborator, Inhelder, commented on the sex difference in spatial perception in this way: "Those children who at all ages have much richer possibilities of manipulation and visual tactile exploration have, as a general rule, better spatial representation. The mental image in its spatial form seems originally to be the interiorization of movements of exploration. This is why we think that the differences observed between the performances of boys and girls are not only linked to sex but are due rather to the intervention of a number of causes, among others, sensory-motor exercise and the school and cultural 'climate.'" (Tanner and Inhelder, 1958, p. 63.)

---

*Witkin (1948) and Elliott and McMichael (1963) concluded that it was not possible to learn field independence, but the training methods they used were largely didactic, involved few actual trials of practice, and the subjects were not trained to the asymptote of their ability. Moreover, Witkin's female subjects actually improved their performance, but Witkin dismissed the finding as not indicating learning since the subjects reported that the correct response still seemed wrong. There is a Russian report of failure to improve spatial visualization with training, but it is difficult to evaluate the study adequately from the amount of information given (Rebus, 1965).

Lynn (1969a, 1969b) has developed an entirely different explanation of the sex difference in cognitive approach. His thesis is based on the notion that boys become superior in analysis because they must abstract their sex-role requirements from a complex array of data while girls need only copy their mothers. One finding that does not support Lynn's hypothesis was reported by Kohlberg and Zigler (1967). Contrary to their expectation, these authors did not find that cognitive development was more related to sex-role development in boys than in girls. Lynn has marshalled a great deal of evidence and argument in support of his view, but the data could be interpreted in other ways. He concludes that girls moderately distant (emotionally) from their mothers should show more field independence and greater ability in problem solving, but is this because these girls have more of a "problem" in learning their sex role? Can it even be assumed that girls learn their sex roles from their mothers? (See Chapters 4 and 5.) Perhaps girls moderately distant from their mothers are more field independent because they are more emotionally independent, as Maccoby (1966b) has suggested. Perhaps being more distant from their mothers, they spend more time doing things for themselves, exploring on their own, and hence develop more skill in performing spatial tasks and in spatial problem solving (Sherman, 1967). Lynn (1969a, 1969b) did not deal with alternative hypotheses.

Findings from genetic studies indicate that genetic factors need also to be considered as a possible cause, perhaps acting in combination with other factors. There is evidence that many fewer women may inherit the genetic qualities most likely to develop at least some kinds of spatial skill (Stafford, 1961). Stafford's research suggested that a recessive gene carried on the X chromosome is involved in spatial visualization. It remains to be seen whether further studies will confirm this finding.

Other findings suggesting a genetic basis for sex differences in spatial perception are that individuals with an XO chromosome pattern (only one X chromosome rather than the normal pattern of either an XX or XY pair of sex chromosomes) have shown a pronounced degree of space-form blindness (Money, 1964; Money, 1968; Shaffer, 1962). The space-form blindness of these individuals with Turner's syndrome may be a direct or indirect genetic effect, e.g. a result of hormonal disturbance. They have no normal gonads of either sex. Comparison of the intellectual functioning of untreated cases of Turner's syndrome with patients having primary amenorrhea from anorexia nervosa might prove interesting. It should be noted that the data from cases of Turner's syndrome are not consistent with Stafford's (1961) hypothesis that spatial visualization is a recessive characteristic carried on the X chromosome (Garron, 1969, 1970). If Stafford's hypothesis were correct, individuals with one X chromosome would be expected to show superior, not inferior, space perception. Clearly more research will be needed to resolve this question.

Another hypothesis proposed to account for some of the sex differences in cognitive abilities attributes them to sex differences in hormonal production (Broverman, Klaiber, Kobayashi, and Vogel, 1968). Broverman and his colleagues attempt to account for female superiority on tasks requiring relatively simple perceptual-motor associations and male superiority on inhibitory perceptual-restructuring tasks (including measures of field dependence) on the basis that estrogens are more potent activating agents than are androgens. The idea is that females have more difficulty inhibiting immediate, obvious, but incorrect reactions. Broverman (1969) reports evidence that gonadal hormones systematically affect cognitive processes in humans. They have found perceptual responses that cycle with the menstrual cycle and which are interrupted by birth control pills (Enovid®).

Other interesting findings in this area include the fact that children whose mothers received progestins or natural progesterone during pregnancy appear to be intellectually superior (Dalton, 1968; Ehrhardt and Money, 1967). Likewise, patients with the adrenogenital syndrome, a genetic disorder which causes excessive androgens, showed superior intellectual ability (Lewis, Money, and Epstein, 1968). It is too early to know exactly what conclusions about female intellectual functioning will be warranted from these various lines of investigation, but it is clear that genetic and physiological hypotheses cannot be ignored.

Implications for Education

The earlier maturity of prereading skills may, in part, account for the fact that girls have fewer problems in school, have better grades, have fewer reading and speech problems, and create less trouble for the teacher (Tyler, 1965). More boys than girls may receive premature instruction leading to undue frustration and discouragement. Other sex differences such as less willingness to obey and conform (Tyler, 1965) probably also contribute to the poorer adjustment of boys to school. Moreover, school tends to conflict with the male role. Female teachers reinforce feminine behavior in both boys and girls (Fagot and Patterson, 1969). The school is seen as a feminine environment (Kagan, 1964), and the requirement of conformity is more consistent with the female sex role than with the aggressive initiative expected of the male sex role. Boys are thus placed in a contradictory role-expectancy situation (Weinstein and Geisel, 1960).

However, the disadvantages of the educational system may not be so clearly on the male side as has been supposed. Enormous time and effort have been spent in training boys in their less sex-preferred ability, verbal skill. What would be the effect if such intensive training in spatial skills and problem solving were provided for girls? Boys are also provided with skilled cross-sex models —their mothers and teachers. Maccoby (1966) has commented upon the importance of cross-sex identification in maximal intellectual development for both males and females. Rarely, however, has thought been given to providing girls with cross-sex models. In short, while some boys may be pressured in verbal areas too early, and some boys may be put off by the feminine atmosphere, the whole structure of the educational system, activities, and content may be much more directed toward maximal male achievement than has been realized.

DEPENDENCY

Dependency has been a popular topic of research, though the evidence that it is a unitary and/or bipolar trait is equivocal (Hartup, 1963). On the whole, the evidence suggests that females, combining all ages, are more dependent, passive, and conforming than males (Kagan, 1964; Tyler, 1965). This evidence is mainly based on white, middle-class Americans, and therefore this conclusion is best limited to that group. It is instructive to look at the comparisons between the sexes age by age. Examining the Oetzel (1966) classified summary of sex differences, the weight of the evidence leans only slightly to greater dependency in girls no older than six. However, from age six to adulthood, females were significantly more dependent in all studies. Studies of conformity show a similar result. Douvan and Adelson (1966) found that even though girls date earlier and hold jobs earlier, between ages fourteen and sixteen, 93 per cent of girls compared to 78 per cent of boys spend some leisure time with their parents. The relative dependency of females appears to increase with age as a function of sex-role pressure. Kagan and Moss (1960, 1962) concluded that the stability of dependency (and aggression) appear to depend upon sex-role congruence; dependent girls became dependent women, while dependent boys did not become dependent men.

Sears (1963) found that measures of dependency intercorrelated better for preschool girls than for boys. The median correlation with total dependency was .45 for boys and .61 for girls. Nonetheless, the clustering of dependency measures did not seem sufficient to qualify it as a common or unitary trait. Mischel (1966) cited this sex difference in intercorrelations as evidence of a sex difference in patterns of sex-typed behavior. However, since this finding of higher intercorrelation among dependency measures for girls is opposite to that reported in the 1953 study (Sears, Whiting, Nowlis, and Sears, 1953), it is difficult to know how much weight to place on it.

In the 1963 Sears study, dependency in girls was correlated with maternal permissiveness for dependency and for sex. Different sorts of dependent behaviors, however, had different sorts of antecedent conditions. Negative attention seeking (a sort of misbehaving for attention) correlated with low demands and restrictions with high participation of the father in the girl's rearing. Seeking of reassurance correlated with high demands for achievement from both parents plus apparent sexual anxiety produced by the father's sexual permissiveness. The dependent behaviors of being near, touching and holding correlated with low demands and restrictions but without much father participation in child rearing. Positive attention seeking correlated with low maternal caretaking in infancy, as well as currently, and with a nonpermissive attitude toward aggression. Positive attention seeking was associated with mother's satisfaction with her daughter. Sears suggested that while dependency behavior in girls may be acceptable, congruent with sex-role and progressive, it may be regressive for boys and a sign of failure to develop independent behaviors. More extensive detailing of the results of previous studies of dependency will not be attempted here, since the findings are so inconsistent that few valid generalizations appear possible at this time (Yarrow, 1968).

Causes of Sex Difference in Dependence

Given the inconsistencies of the results already cited, the reader will appreciate that it is difficult to make reliable inferences regarding the causes of greater dependency in girls and women. The relationships appear complex (Lansky and McKay, 1969). A sex-role pressure influence has been demonstrated (Kagan and Moss, 1962). However, as Mischel (1966) pointed out, there is no definitive study showing that the sex difference in dependency may be attributed to differences in the way the sexes are reared. Goldberg and Lewis (1969) found a curvilinear relationship between dependency and maternal treatment. Mothers who touched their daughters much or little at six months had daughters who sought more contact at thirteen months. This finding gains additional support from the fact that it is precisely what would be predicted on the basis of clinical theory and experience. Individuals with very close maternal experiences would be expected to be more dependent, while rejected, harshly treated individuals would *also* be expected to be dependent, since their fear and insecurity would cause them to cling (Horney, 1939). (See Chapter 3 for evidence that girls are not wanted so much as boys.) An additional complexity is the fact that the timing of various maternal behaviors is probably also important to developing dependency, e.g. needed help would conduce security and ultimate

12319

independence, while unneeded help would be expected to increase dependence.

While single-cause explanations are more dramatic, it is clear that dependent behavior may be reached by more than one route. It may well be that if very early factors do not result "naturally" in sex-role congruent dependency behavior, more direct training will be instituted to achieve this effect. What follows is a sketch of multicausal effects which might well add up to greater dependency in females.

At very early ages, males received more maternal attention because they are more irritable and fussy. However, the attention did not seem to "pay off" for either mother or child, so that by three months fussing and maternal tending were correlated for girls, but not for boys (Moss, 1967). It would seem that girls, but not boys, are learning that fussing and interpersonal interaction are rewarding.

By the age of six months, girls notice faces more than boys (Lewis, Kagan, and Kalafat, 1966), and they are more interested in other people by the age of two (Goodenough, 1957). They begin to talk earlier and more articulately so that they have functional speech earlier than boys (McCarthy, 1943). Thus the twig may be bent to problem solution by interaction with other persons rather than with things.

During the preschool years, girls appear to receive less corporal punishment (Newson and Newson, 1968; Sear, Maccoby, and Levin, 1957). In other ways, however, it would appear that preschool boys are treated with greater care and consideration (Brun-Gulbrandsen, 1967; Kagan and Freemen, 1963). Since girls are less valued for themselves (see Chapter 3), being a "good girl" may assume more importance for them (Kohlberg, 1969). This would promote conforming, dependent behavior.

It is during the preschool years that the father might be expected to intervene differentially in the treatment of the two sexes (see Chapter 5). Fathers appear to be less tolerant of dependency in their sons than in their daughters, while the reverse is true of mothers (Rothbart and Maccoby, 1966). One would suppose that the father will intervene more strongly if he perceives his son becoming a "Mama's boy" than if his daughter appears too dependent. Since it is sticky and difficult for the mother to switch dependency behavior from herself, by herself, her attitude about dependency is probably not so important as the father's attitude. Thus the fact that fathers are less tolerant of dependent behavior in their boys may lead them to draw off their sons into more independent behavior. Mothers, especially perceiving the girl's greater ability to care for herself, may be less tolerant of dependency behavior from their daughters, but their efforts to enforce more independent behaviors may lead to feelings of rejection and an increase in insecurity-derived dependency behaviors instead.

Being on one's own could certainly lead to more independent behavior. One striking bit of information which thus far does not appear to have been systematically investigated is the frequent report of nursery school administrators that they have far more applications for boys than girls. This may suggest that mothers are more motivated to separate from sons than from daughters. Left to their own devices, however, a sample of male children did not move farther from the mother than female children (Rheingold and Eckerman, 1970). Echoes of these findings may be found in the monkey-mother studies.

In the rhesus monkey, separation from the mother and maternal ambivalence appears to be due to hormonal factors and behavioral changes in the infant (Harlow, Harlow, and Hansen, 1963). The infant changes from a reflex, clinging, cuddling individual to one that moves freely, squirms when held, inflicts physical discomfort, and reaches out physically and intellectually to the world around it. Hansen (1966) contends that punishment from the rhesus monkey mother plays an important role in the emancipation of her youngster. Mitchell (1968) found that mothers had more physical contact with female infants and kept them from running off more than males. Mothers of males withdrew from, played with, and presented to their infants more often than did mothers of females. Among the langurs observed in the field, Jay (1963) reported a bit of a battle between mother and child at weaning time. Male infants were reported to disturb the mother more and therefore were threatened and chased more than female infants.

One group of investigators has made a specific laboratory study of sex differences in the development of independence in the pig-tailed monkey (Jensen, Bobbitt, and Gordon, 1968). If anything, the mother was closer to the male child at a very early stage. However, after the first three weeks, mothers and sons were significantly more often apart and stayed apart longer. By the fifth week, mothers retained their sons less than daughters. Males were not more active in a gross way until fifteen weeks, so these differences were not merely the result of greater male activity. It appeared to the investigators that the mother was initiating the greater separation, but they were not sure if the males acted differently or to what the mothers were responding.

Among human children during the grade school years, there are consistent reports that girls receive more love and nurturance than boys (Bronfenbrenner, 1960a; Droppleman and Schaefer, 1963). During grade school years, a boy who is still behaving in a dependent manner would be expected to encounter increasing censure from parents, especially fathers, and from peers as well. In the fifth and sixth grades, a sample of girls with a high need for approval were among the most popular, while boys with high need for approval were among the least popular (Tulkin, Muller, and Conn, 1969). It seems likely that if a boy does not "naturally" come to show independent behavior, various environmental pressures will be applied to achieve that end. If a girl shows excessive dependent behavior, her father is less likely to help her develop independence, and if her mother becomes annoyed with her dependency, it may only increase.

Dependency as a Desirable Trait

While it has been frequently suggested that dependency is adaptive in women, there is increasing reason to question this concept. The stereotyped characteristics of femininity, including passive-dependent characteristics, have been rated by clinicians of both sexes as less mature, healthy, and socially competent than the stereotyped description of masculinity (Broverman, Broverman, Clarkson, Rosenkrantz, and Vogel, 1970). Maccoby (1963) wonders if it is really necessary for women to be so dependent in order to be "feminine." Cohen (1966) reported that the women who best fit the traditional ideal feminine personality of being passive and dependent were simply inadequate—as people, as sexual partners, as wives, as mothers. Inclusion of such built-in maladaptations in the feminine cultural ideal may account for many a discrepancy between the expected associations of femininity, good adjustment, and good mothering. For example, Locke (1951) found that *directorial* ability in the wife was significantly associated with happy as opposed to divorced marriages. A helpless wife makes for an unhappy husband and a disorganized family. The hysterical, passive, culturally feminine woman was the most frequent type among mothers of children brought to a child-guidance center (Marks, 1961). The topic of dependency recurs in later discussions of sex role, pregnancy, and motherhood.

AGGRESSION

The evidence is very clear that little girls and their mothers are less inclined to physical aggression.* The physical aggressiveness of boys is not necessarily malicious but may be just rough-and-tumble play. While significant differences in general aggressiveness are not always found between the sexes, when there are significant differences, they favor males. Among the thirty-two findings Oetzel (1966) cited having to do with preschool physical and verbal aggression in behavior and fantasy, girls exceeded boys at a statistically significant level in only one instance, a comparison involving verbal aggression in fantasy. Otherwise girls were not even more aggressive verbally. Dreams have been thought to be one of the purest measures of primitive drive states. Hall and Domhoff (1963a) found that the dreams of males under twelve showed more physical aggression than female dreams, but like a study of Mexican children (Siñán Dominguez Laws, 1965), they reported no overall sex difference in dream aggressiveness among children. Aggression-eliciting stimuli also appear to have different effects on men and women (Fischer, Kelm, and Rose, 1969).

*The sex difference in aggression which is apparently innately and hormonally based has been called "physical aggression." By this is meant aggressions which accentuate the use of large muscles, e.g. pummeling, but not pinching.

A variety of experimental studies published since the Oetzel (1966) review show that while females are not more aggressive than males, they may be just as aggressive under certain conditions, such as (a) modern as opposed to traditional home atmosphere (Minuchin, 1965), (b) when females are directly or indirectly given "permission" to aggress (especially nonphysical aggression) by the experimental situation (Leventhal and Shemberg, 1969; Mallick and McCandless, 1966), and/or (c) when measures include more indirect aggression (Feshbach, 1969).

Goodenough (1931) found that angry outbursts increased in both sexes until eighteen months of age and then a sharp decline occurred. She found no sex difference in angry outbursts before age two. While this data has been cited (Bandura and Walters, 1963a) to indicate that there is no innate difference in aggressiveness between the sexes, data for this point consisted only of parental reports of five female and six male infants. After age two, a marked sex difference was apparent with more angry outbursts shown by male children. Bandura and Walters (1963a) attribute increased aggressiveness in the male to parental and social pressure for sex-appropriate behavior. They concluded from their review of studies of the development of aggressiveness that the sex difference in aggressiveness is a joint outcome of social reinforcement and modeling processes.

The effect of culture in developing sex differences has been most strikingly illustrated by Mead's famous study, *Sex and Temperament in Three Primitive Societies* (1935). Among the Arapesh people of New Guinea, for example, she found both men and women to be gentle and nurturant, considering promotion of growth, be it children or yams, to be the greatest of values. In other tribes, she found different patterns—both sexes aggressive or even the females aggressive and the males passive. She concluded that human character is extremely malleable and greatly influenced by the culture.

Partially related to greater aggressiveness is the matter of dominant authority. Stressing the limits of cultural variation, Mead (1958) has made the point that there is no known society in which women are not subject to the authority of some male, whether it be a father, husband, or brother. Romney (1965, p. 212) also concluded, "It seems that in all societies, authority over household units is exercised predominantly by males rather than females." The matriarchy is a pure myth and has never existed, though there are many examples of cultures that trace lineage through the mother only (Mead, 1958). Mead has concluded that whatever is defined as important in a society tends to be in the hands of the men. If dressing dolls is considered of great importance in a given society, it is certain that men will do it. Mead has also stressed the point that cultural pressures can introduce strain when they are too much at odds with biological endowment. The Arapesh male, she felt, paid a price for his gentle nature (1955).

In a longitudinal study of normal children, Kagan and Moss (1962) found that a boy who was aggressive in his early years continued to be so as an adult, while aggressive girls did not become aggressive women. For the trait of dependency, the situation was exactly reversed. Dependent girls became dependent adults, while dependent boys changed as they approached adulthood. These findings are consistent with the fact that the sex differences in dependency become more pronounced with maturation (Oetzel, 1966), and the fact that Hall and Domhoff (1963a) found an increased sex difference in aggressiveness after age twelve. Kagan and Moss interpreted their finding as indicating the influence of sex-role expectations.

There is independent evidence that parents do have different ideas of what to expect from boys and girls. Parents of nursery school children expect boys to be more aggressive and girls to be more gentle, submissive, and affectionate (Kohn, 1959; Sears, Maccoby, and Levin, 1957). It might be argued that parental expectations are not causing the sex differences but merely reflecting a realistic and accurate knowledge of boy and girl behavior. This may be true, but these attitudes probably produce an effect themselves, a snowball effect, adding to any innate influences that exist. That the parents may contribute to sexual divergence in aggressiveness is suggested by the finding that the father's presence in the home increased physical expressions of aggression in three-year-old boys but not in girls (Sears, Pintler, and Sears, 1946). On the other hand, Bach (1945) found less doll-play aggression among children of both sexes whose fathers were absent from the home.

The argument that there is a cultural factor in sex differences in aggression and dependency is made even more convincing by the evidence concerning emotional conflict which Kagan and Moss (1962) obtained. They used measures of conflict based on tachistoscopic presentations of pictures depicting scenes of dependency and aggression. A tachistoscope is a machine that can present pictures for brief glimpses. As adults, males showed significantly higher thresholds (i.e., the picture had to be shown longer) for perceiving pictures of dependency, while women had more difficulty perceiving aggression. The authors concluded that under the influence of sex-role expectations, males repress dependency more and females repress aggression more. That is, females are permitted to be dependent but not permitted to be aggressive. The relative lack of general aggressiveness in women is apparently more extreme than would be expected from biological determinants alone, since it is achieved only at the cost of increased conflict and repression. Berkowitz (1962) has also concluded that females have more anxiety about aggression. Conflict about aggression is consistent with the findings of greater controlled rage, less overt aggression, and more covert hostility found in a large sample of American women (Bennett and Cohen, 1959).

While there is no doubt that differential learning is responsible for part of the sex difference in aggressiveness, it seems more prudent to conclude with Anastasi (1958) and with Berkowitz (1962) that the cause of the difference is partly biological and partly cultural. Garai (1970) stresses biological causation. One fact in support of the importance of a biological factor is that the greater aggressiveness of males occurs cross-culturally (D'Andrade, 1966). There are rare exceptions to this rule (Mead, 1935). It could, however, be argued that this merely represents cross-cultural adaptation to the greater strength and power of the male. Thus the greater physical aggressiveness of males would be an indirect result of biological differences.

Several factors, however, provide evidence of a more direct biological factor in the greater aggressiveness of males. Sex differences in physical aggressiveness can be discerned before there are pronounced differences in strength. Moreover, the higher male mammals are consistently more aggressive than the females (Hamburg and Lunde, 1966). In addition, since ancient times it has been known that castration will reduce aggressiveness in human males. Normal males produce about six times as much testosterone as women (Dorfman and Ungar, 1965). The complexity and pervasiveness of hormone effects, however, are only gradually being understood. For example, while male monkeys are more aggressive than female monkeys from infancy onward, alterations in the behavior of female monkeys have been brought about by prenatal administration of testosterone to the mother. The female monkeys were born pseudohermaphroditic with genital alterations such as hypertrophy of the clitoris. Observed under carefully controlled conditions, these females definitely showed more aggressive, masculine behavior than did normal females. It is important to note that this effect, measurable for at least three years postnatally, was brought about by a period of *prenatal* administration of male hormones (Hamburg and Lunde, 1966). These prenatal male hormones apparently changed the brain in some way, so that the female monkeys became more masculine and aggressive in behavior even though they no longer were receiving the male hormones. Similar effects have been reported among humans (Ehrhardt, Epstein, and Money, 1968; Money, 1968).

Another recent bit of evidence favoring an innate factor in determining greater male aggressiveness is the finding of superaggressive behavior in males with an extra Y chromosome (Casey, Street, Segall, and Blank, 1968; Nielsen, 1969). The overwhelming evidence of strong cultural and learning factors in the development of aggression does not logically rule out innate factors; it appears likely that they also have their role to play.

EMOTIONALITY

It has been asserted that females are more emotionally unstable than males and that this difference is discernible as early as the preschool years (Terman and Tyler, 1954). Some sex bias is suggested by the fact that what is meant by emotionality is anxiety and other psychic discomfort symptoms; undue physical or verbal aggression or tantrum behavior more characteristic of males is almost entirely excluded from consideration. Additional complexities of labeling are illustrated by the fact that the same underlying physiological state may be labeled in different ways, depending upon cognitive and contextual factors (Schacter, 1964). That is, underlying physiological states that may be labeled one way by males may be labeled another way by females.

Sex differences in emotionality (of the psychic discomfort variety) have been attributed partly to innate sources (Garai, 1970; Johnson and Terman, 1940). Some studies have shown greater autonomic reactivity to stress in females (Berry and Martin, 1957; Sontag, 1947), though other studies to be discussed later in this section have not (Wilson, 1966, 1967). In neonates, there are reports of greater female sensitivity to tactile stimulation (Bell and Costello, 1964) and possibly to pain (Lipsett and Levy, 1959). Bronson (1969), however, found no sex differences in the average degree of fearfulness on any measure at any age from one month to $8\frac{1}{2}$ years.

In addition to possibly greater physiological reactivity in the female system, Johnson and Terman (1940) stated that the greater hormonal changes in the female predispose them to greater emotional instability. Issues related to cyclical changes and psychobiology will be discussed in subsequent chapters; however, this factor would hardly account for greater instability of females beginning in nursery school years. Anastasi (1958) has argued that the data presented in behalf of innate causation are not entirely convincing.

Two major reactions to threat are fight and flight. Given the reluctance of American women to express aggressiveness, it would not be surprising to find flight more characteristic. Greater dependency also tends to make people more vulnerable to anxiety. A passive dependent attitude is apt to evoke anxiety, since the individual feels helpless and vulnerable, unable to act. Moreover, a dependent person, even when provoked to justifiable anger, may conceal his anger for fear of antagonizing the person upon whom he is dependent. In neurotic reactions, he may even become very anxious, fearing that his felt anger will show.

The evidence of greater female emotionality, anxiety, emotional instability, neuroticism, and the like cited by Oetzel (1966), Terman and Tyler (1954), and Johnson and Terman (1940) is massive but nearly always consists of evidence obtained from self-report questionnaires. Most of these do not have adequate safeguards for measuring test-taking attitude, and they most often have dealt with complaints relating to anxiety, worry, and low self esteem. Male social role expectations would appear to be more strongly biased against admission of fear, anxiety, or indeed any weakness. There is, in fact, some evidence that boys are more defensive than girls about admitting anxiety. Hill and Sarason (1966) conducted a longitudinal study of sex differences in anxiety. There was no significant sex difference in the first grade of school, but the difference increased with age. With age, boys also became significantly more defensive. Among children, Ruebush (1963) has concluded that defensiveness is a crucial variable in studies of anxiety and may account for the sex difference found. Among college students, Bendig (1959) found no significant difference between the sexes in covert anxiety but a significant difference in overt anxiety. There was significantly less difference between overt and covert anxiety scores in females than in males.

Approaching the problem in a different manner, Wilson (1966) found no significant galvanic skin response (GSR) difference (a physiological measure of anxiety) between the sexes in response to tachistoscopic phobic items, despite the fact that females scored higher than males on the Fear Survey Schedule. Wilson (1967) followed this up with a further study which found that the proportion of men to women admitting a particular fear was significantly related to its social acceptability. This suggests that the seemingly obvious sex difference in fearfulness may be more apparent than real. Women may merely be more willing to admit and display fearfulness while men are more strictly bound by convention to show bravery.

An apparent bit of contradictory data are the findings of a sex difference in avoidance conditioning, specifically in eyelid conditioning. Women conditioned better than men and individuals with a high anxiety level conditioned better than those with a low level of anxiety (Spence and Spence, 1966). The authors did not conclude, however, that women are more anxious than men generally but suggested the possibility that the dark, weird conditions of the experimental setting may arouse more anxiety in college girls than boys. That is to say, the true sex difference may not lie in ease of conditioning but in the anxiety produced by aspects of the experimental conditions which then increased conditionability.

Further reason for caution in accepting the conclusion that girls and women are more fearful and anxious than boys and men is found in the contrary results of the Rorschach studies. The Rorschach test consists of ten ink blots. The subject is asked to tell what each could be. The technique is designed to elicit more unconscious material and to bypass defense systems. It is much harder to disguise or evade telltale responses on the Rorschach test than on most questionnaires. Testing of cross-cultural samples with the Rorschach supports the conclusion that females are less anxious and better adjusted than males (D'Andrade, 1966). Weinlander (1966) and Phillips (1966) also report that American males score significantly higher on the anxiety measure of the Structured Objective Rorschach Test, though in the same sample, Phillips found that females scored significantly higher than males on the Taylor Manifest Anxiety Scale. The two anxiety measures, however, were not strongly related, as they correlated only .25 for males and .03 for females. (A correlation of .99 would represent a nearly perfect relationship.)

It should be pointed out that neuroticism or emotional instability is but one form of maladjustment, and other expressions of maladjustment, notably various addictions, suicide, and antisocial behaviors are found more frequently in men (Scheinfeld, 1944). The Eysencks (1969) found males higher in psychoticism, but lower in neuroticism. Furthermore, the Midtown Manhattan Study (Srole, Langner, Michael, Opler, and Rennie, 1962) found no overall difference in the psychological adjustment of the two sexes.* On the other hand, a study (Gurin, Veroff, and Feld,

*While comparison of the sexes in rates of psychiatric care in hospitals or outpatient facilities would be of potential interest, available data contain so many unknowns and confounded variables, that they did not appear worth citing.

1960) which interviewed a large representative sample of the stable American population over twenty-one, concluded that women's outlook on life was more negative and passive, more introspective and inwardly turned, and more sensitive in relation to others. Women also showed more distress. The authors were not sure whether women were really having more distress, were more aware of their distress, or merely more willing to admit it. The interview method does not get around the problem of differential defensiveness.

An example of early contrasting styles of maladaptation may be found in a study of the problems of normal children from age two to thirteen (Macfarland, Allen, and Honzik, 1954). The boys tended to show overactivity, attention-demanding behavior, jealousy, competitiveness, lying, selfishness, tantrums, and stealing. Girls were more prone to thumbsucking, being reserved, fussy with food, timid, shy, fearful, oversensitive, somber, and given to mood swings. Both the male tantrums and female mood swings suggest emotional instability, though of different emotions. The male style shows more aggressiveness and acts against other people, while the female style shows more fear and personal discontent.

There are three related but somewhat different issues discussed in this section. These are adjustment, stability, and fear. Are girls and women generally more maladjusted than boys and men? The answer to this question clearly appears to be No. Are they more emotionally unstable? Sex bias has been involved in the exclusion of angry, aggressive feelings in the interpretation of this question. It is also a more difficult question to answer, since it requires not merely measuring emotion but changes in emotion. While the fluctuating hormones of the adult female might have such an effect, there is no good evidence of an overall greater emotional instability in women. Most evidence cited in a discussion of emotional instability is really more appropriate to the question of sex differences in anxiety or fear and related symptoms. Girls and women show more fearfulness, especially on questionnaires, but this appears to be because they are less defensive about admitting and displaying their fear. Bronson (1969) did not find very young females more fearful than males. The exact contribution of innate factors in producing a sex difference in fearfulness is not clear.

SUMMARY

Even from this brief review of selected topics, it is apparent that the psychology of women is not the same as the psychology of men. Sex differences in behavior appear in neonates. The extent to which various of these differences are due to innate factors is largely unknown at this time. Probably the most convincing case for an important innate factor can be made for the sex difference in physical aggression. Cultural factors have been demonstrated to contribute to sex differences in intellect, dependence, aggression, and emotionality. However, evidence of cultural pressure is not sufficient evidence of total causation. Cultural institutions may themselves be formed partially to fit true biological differences. These institutions may then react on the conditions which created them in the first place, exaggerating or elaborating them (D'Andrade, 1966). An innate difference may form a core for ever-increasing layers of cultural accretion. Changes in cultural conditions may then render the institutional structure maladaptive. A society that had placed a premium on physical strength, once mechanized, may incongruously exclude women from many positions. On the other hand, if our civilization were to be erased today, factors relevant to primitive sex differences might readily reassert themselves. In any case, innate or not, a consideration of the psychology of women as distinct from the psychology of men appears not only justifiable but necessary.

Chapter 3

FREUDIAN THEORY OF FEMININE DEVELOPMENT

WHILE FREUD'S THEORY is passé in some circles, psychoanalytic theory continues to be influential and important in the helping professions and in the thinking of the literate public. In order not to exceed the scope of this book, however, it will be necessary to consider only Freud's specific hypotheses regarding the psychology of women. For the most part, hypotheses concerning men and concerning general aspects of Freud's theory will not be discussed.* In this chapter, there will be presented an overview of Freud's theory as it applies to the early psychological development of women. Major revisions and criticisms by other psychoanalysts will also be considered.† Freud's hypotheses about feminine development will then be examined in more detail, with special attention to the empirical evidence for them.

There are some difficulties in presenting Freud's views in a way satisfactory to all his followers. There are very few orthodox Freudian psychoanalysts in the world today; most people holding psychoanalytic views have modified them in some ways from Freud's original views. For example, Freud's emphasis on the biological and universal character of the psychosexual stages of development, e.g. the innate, inevitable Oedipus stage, was never taken seriously in the United States. Freud was much annoyed with this "watering down" of his theory (Jones, 1953). Not surprisingly Freud modified his own views from time to time. For example, in 1905 he appeared to equate femininity and passivity,

*Readers unacquainted with Freudian theory may find helpful the introductions provided by Hall (1954) and Hall and Lindzey (1957). A more general, and quite negative critique of Freudian theory of feminine psychology may be found in the work of Fisher (1957). An extensive resume of psychoanalytic views and some new viewpoints are contained in the work of Chassequet-Smirgel, Luquet-Parat, Grunberger, McDougall, Torok, and David (1970).

†The works of Deutsch will be discussed in Chapter 8; the work of Benedek is also presented in later chapters.

masculinity and activity (Freud, 1938a), while in 1933, he warned against precisely such equations (Freud, 1965). Later, too, he placed more emphasis on pre-Oedipal development (mother-daughter relationship), rather than focusing on the father-daughter relationship (Freud, 1950a). The changes and inconsistencies in Freud's writings give rise to various misunderstandings and complicate the task of evaluating his work.

Freud, himself did not always seem fully satisfied with his work on feminine psychology. Concluding his lecture, "Femininity," he said, "That is all I had to say to you about femininity. It is certainly incomplete and fragmentary and does not always sound friendly . . . . If you want to know more about femininity, enquire from your own experiences of life, or turn to the poets, or wait until science can give you deeper and more coherent information" (Freud, 1965, p. 135). There are other instances, however, when he vigorously defended his ideas of feminine development (Freud, 1950a, 1950b).

SEX IN FREUD'S THEORY

Sexuality is central to Freud's theory. A more thorough evaluation of female sexuality will be attempted in Chapter 8. Freud radically revised views of sexuality in that he saw sexuality as a powerful drive, striving for expression. Moreover, for Freud, sexuality began at birth and not at puberty (Freud, 1938a). These views, more or less accepted in scientific circles for many years (Kinsey, 1965; Sears, 1943), have now been challenged (Chodoff, 1966; Gagnon, 1967; Simon and Gagnon, 1969a, 1969b). Also, Freud considered human beings, as bisexual (1938a, 1962, 1965). In the sense that both males and females share certain embryonic beginnings, hormones, and the capability for the same behaviors, bisexuality is generally accepted (Ford and Beach, 1951); the differences between the sexes are considered more of a matter of balance than of mutual exclusiveness. An hypothesis of sexual neutrality without biological directionality to inherited sex has been advanced by Hampson and Hampson (1961), but it has been subjected to severe criticism (Diamond, 1965; Gagnon, 1967). Freud's concept of bisexuality has been sharply criticized by the psychoanalyst Rado (1965). The pressure of sexuality which permeates Freud's theory suggests that in the male there is a pressure to express femininity, and in the female there is a pressure to express masculinity. Freud's conception of bisexuality went far beyond the kind of bisexuality generally accepted among scientists.

Evidence of chromosomal and cellular sex differences plus the fact that normally sexual development progressively deviates in the direction of genetic sex suggests that the theory of bisexuality (if interpreted as either equal influence or pressure to express characteristics of the opposite sex) is misleading and that the theory of neutrality is inaccurate. For example, as discussed in the last chapter, there is evidence that the male hormone, testosterone, has a differentiating effect on the mammalian brain similar to that which it has on the genital system. Presence of the hormone early in life during a critical period, which varies for each species, establishes in the brain a permanent control of the pituitary gland such that its secretions take on a masculine pattern. It has been clearly established that it is the brain and not the pituitary gland which has been altered by the hormone (Levine, 1966). Also the evidence that prenatal exposure to androgenic agents increases the aggressiveness and masculinity of female monkeys and human females (Ehrhardt, Epstein, and Money, 1968; Hamburg and Lunde, 1966; Money, 1968) suggests an innately determined slanting of psychological potential. Life experience is extremely important in sexual development, but the evidence does not permit the exclusion of genetic, anatomic, and hormonal determinants (Stoller, 1968; Young, Goy, and Phoenix, 1964). Diamond (1968, p. 418) concludes that sexual behavior in the human is ". . . more dependent upon prenatal and postnatal genetic-endocrine influences than upon postnatal environment."

Freud assumed that for both sexes, libido, or sex drive, is masculine, though he later decided that it is unwise to label libido either masculine or feminine (1962, 1965). Money (1965b) concluded that there is strong clinical and presumptive evidence that androgenic hormones regulate libido in both males and females. Androgens are, of course, the typical male hormones. In the female, they may be derived from the ovary's progestins and/or secreted by the adrenal cortex. Thus Freud's assumption is borne out in the sense that sex drive appears to depend on hormones found in greater quantity in the male. The evidence is not sufficient, however, to rule out completely the role of estrogen (Kane, Lipton, and Ewing, 1969).

Freud maintained that the sexuality of the little girl is masculine (Freud, 1938a, 1950a, 1950b) and that girls do not feel vaginal sensations, only clitoral ones. These Freud considered masculine. In fact, Freud averred that the vagina long remains undiscovered. This is certainly not invariably the case since there are very well documented cases of vaginal masturbation and exploration at early ages. The vagina might remain undiscovered until a late date in the case of a girl who was very closely supervised in a prudish environment. These conditions, in fact, existed for many girls of Freud's milieu. Under current American practices of child rearing, it would be a dull girl indeed who did not discover her vagina. This is not to say, however, that its sexual significance would be accurately appreciated. Vaginal repression in little girls is still a topic of concern to psychoanalysts (Barnett, 1966). Freud's view was that in order to achieve maturity, the girl must change the focus of her sexuality from the clitoris to the vagina.

The research of Masters and Johnson (1966) suggests that it makes no sense to wonder whether the clitoris or the vagina is the dominant locus of sexuality of young girls. Observation of sexual response shows that other nearby anatomic areas are also important to female sexuality and that orgasm cannot rightly be considered as vaginal or clitoral, since it involves both the vagina and clitoris, and the entire body as well. Furthermore, the lower third of the vagina and the clitoris are derived from the same "masculine" embryonic tissue, so that the frequently invoked parallel oppositions of vaginal-clitoral, feminine-masculine are clearly incorrect.

THE FIRST THREE YEARS

Freud supposed that the sexuality of children is centered in different zones of the body at different ages. This is called Freud's psychosexual theory of development. During the first, oral stage erotogenous responses are centered about the mouth. During the second year, the anal stage becomes ascendant and sensuality is focused on bowel functioning. Freud supposed that psychosexual development of boys and girls is much the same during these first two stages (Freud, 1965). While the broader question of the validity of Freud's theory of psychosexual development will not be discussed here, it is clear that there are sex differences in development before age three (Lewis, 1969; Moss, 1967; Stoller, 1968; Watson, 1969; also see Chapter 2). Even at a very early age, the same treatment can have different effects, depending on the sex of the infant. Specifically for Freud's theory, sex differences have been found in orality. For example, the length of time girls were allowed to secure nourishment by sucking did not make any significant difference in their later adjustment. Boys who were weaned from the breast and/or bottle late, defined as after fourteen or fifteen months, subsequently showed poor adjustment if their mothers were judged to be cold and impersonal but better than average adjustment if their mothers were judged to be warm (Heinstein, 1963). Sears (1963) also found differences between the sexes in the effects of their early feeding experiences.

A CAPSULE VIEW OF THE PHALLIC, OEDIPAL, AND LATENCY STAGES

According to Freud, the sexes diverge in their psychological development during the third stage, which he called the phallic stage (1950a, 1950b, 1956, 1965). During this stage, the little girl discovers her clitoris and gains sensual pleasure by masturbating in a clitoral fashion; she is now a "little man" (Freud, 1965). Then, noticing the male phallus, she becomes envious and blames her mother for not equipping her better. She turns from her mother to her father, ushering in the Oedipal phase of development. She is hoping that her father will give her a penis as a gift; later she changes this to a wish for a child. In the case of the girl, castration anxiety is thought to begin the Oedipal stage. In the case of the boy, this phase is ended by his fear of castration from the father. The giving up of the Oedipus complex marks a major step to maturity and is accomplished by identification with the parent of the same sex. In the course of this identification, the superego is formed. Since girls already perceive themselves as castrated, they have less motive for giving up their possessive love for the father. For this reason, Freud thought that women do not develop so strong a superego as men (Freud, 1950b). After resolving the Oedipus complex, children are supposed to move into the latency period, a time of relative desexualization, until the sexual reactivation brought on by puberty. The last stage is that of full maturity, called the genital stage. Later Freud gave more importance to the early mother-daughter relationship and considered normal female development more difficult than male, since the female must not only change the prime object of her affections from her mother to her father, but she must also make a change from clitoral eroticism to vaginal eroticism. So far as an overall evaluation of this theory is concerned, the opinion of McCandless is perhaps typical of academic psychologists. He said, "Such a theory strains credulity and has no direct support." (McCandless, 1961). Nonetheless the theory continues to be promulgated. For an example, see the book, *Adolescence,* authored by the prestigious Group for the Advancement of Psychiatry (1968).

VIEWS ON FREUD'S THEORIES

Alfred Adler

Other analysts were among the first to attack Freud's ideas. Alfred Adler (1927) thought that a sense of inferiority was created in women not because they felt less well endowed physically than men but because an unnatural relationship of male dominance exists between the sexes. This sense of inferiority stimulated what he termed a masculine protest, a neurotic effort to obtain power and prestige. He thought that Freud was absurdly literal and biological in his emphasis on penis envy. According to Adler, the way Freud pictured the situation, when the normal girl married, she accepted the man as an appendage of the penis (Adler, 1927).

Karen Horney

Karen Horney (1967) originally accepted Freud's ideas, but later rejected them. After coming to the United States, she was unable to find verification for Freud's theories in her own patients. In an early paper (Horney, 1924) she elaborated on the reasons why girls might develop penis envy and a castration complex. She pointed out that urination is an event of great interest to children and that the greater visibility of the male organ and the permission to handle it during urination made little girls feel at an erotic disadvantage during the pregenital period. Girls might have trouble overcoming masturbation since they felt they were unjustly forbidden something boys were allowed, namely permission to touch their genitals. However, she concluded that it was wounded womanhood, not thwarted maleness, that gives rise to the castration complex and exaggerated masculinity in women. She observed that the women who showed such characteristics had had a strong attachment to their father which had met with disappointment. They had given up this attachment with resulting identification with the father.

Two years later (1926), she pointed out quite convincingly that Freudian notions of female development parallel the typical childish ideas boys have of girls; she concluded that female psychology had been falsely viewed from an androcentric position. She focused instead on male envy of the female formulating the hypothesis that the femininity complex of men leads to male overcompensation in achievement. In her opinion, the masculinity complex in women is usually less severe than the femininity complex in men. Bettelheim (1962) has developed this point in an astute reconsideration of aborigine puberty rites. He has concluded that penis envy has been exaggerated and womb envy underestimated.

Later (1932) Horney presented the view that little girls might abandon the Oedipus complex, not from gradually growing awareness that the father is not going to give them either a child or a penis but from fear of vaginal injury by the large adult penis. Such fears, combined with fears arising from menstruation, childbirth, and injuries to the hymen during masturbation, could eventually result in a denial of the vagina and sexual frigidity (Horney, 1933).

Soon Horney (1939) was to repudiate completely the anatomical-physiological-emphasis characteristic of Freud's thinking. Insofar as female psychological development was concerned, this revision meant a total rejection of the anatomical basis of penis envy. Further, she did not see penis envy and the castration complex as a part of normal female development. She pointed out that the so-called castrating female is hostile to everyone, not just males, and that her cries of mistreatment frequently function as a dodge to escape responsibility for her own shortcomings. So far as the Oedipus complex is concerned, Horney pointed out that sexual stimulation from the parents themselves plays a role in creating this difficulty. The vast majority of excessive infantile attachment to one parent, however, she attributed to clinging because of need for reassurance.

Clara Thompson

Clara Thompson's writings (1942, 1943, 1949) are in general agreement with Horney in objecting to the androcentric view of Freud and in pointing out the disadvantage of women in our culture. Thompson conceived of penis envy as only a symbolic expression of female envy of the perquisites of the male role. In dreams, phallic symbols are used to express this conflict simply because dreams are pictorial thinking, and phallic symbols are pictures of maleness. She believed that the heavy emphasis on dream data had resulted in too narrow and concrete an interpretation of penis envy. Thompson also indicated yet another route to a masculinity complex in an adult woman. In some of her patients, she was able to trace this end result to a traumatic early dependency relationship with the mother. The child learned that it was unsafe to be dependent, but in adopting an independent attitude, she would, of course, be adopting behavior more typical of the male role.

Sandor Rado

Sandor Rado (1933) provided one of the more ingenious elaborations of the masculinity complex. He set himself the task of explaining castration anxiety in women when, in fact, they do not have a phallus to be castrated. He surmised that perception of anatomical differences between the sexes only has serious consequences when the girl is in a phase of masturbation at the time of the discovery. The psychic shock becomes sexualized and results in masochism, a distinctly abnormal development in his view. The ego, in order to protect itself from this masochism, restores the penis in a dream. The girl then gives up masturbation since it reminds her of her lack. Later the girl is likely to shift the illusory penis from its proper place to somewhere else on the body, frequently to the nose or eyes. The new site, then, becomes the locus of a conversion reaction (bodily expression of psychic conflict). Sometimes the illusory penis is shifted to the entire body or to the intellect. Female castration fear was characterized as fear of the return of the internal genital masochistic instinct. Abraham (1942) also gives an insightful account of the vagaries of the castration complex in women.

Erik Erikson

Most people find Erik Erikson's (1963, 1959) restatement of Freud's theory considerably more palatable than the original. While it is not always clear in exactly what ways Erikson agrees and disagrees with Freud, he has stated (1968) that while he thinks that psychosexual stages occur as Freud outlined them, he does not think they dominate the normal picture. He denies the importance of penis envy; instead, he suggests that women envy the greater importance of men (Evans, 1967). He considers the Oedipus complex to be less common in women. He denies the importance of masochism but grants the importance of acceptance of pain (1968).

Erikson's own special interest has been identity. By this he means not, "Who I am," but, "What do I want to make of myself and what do I have to work with?" (Erikson, 1968). As he has applied it to women, the identity question centers about the inner space. His conclusion (1951) that females have a special affinity for inner space has sometimes been discussed as though it were some kind of innate psychological characteristic. No explicit claim of that kind has been made, nor should it be. The study from which he concluded that inner space has special importance in female psychology was not well controlled and used subjects much too old to allow any such conclusion. However, regardless of whether or not the phenomenon is innate, findings of other investigators (Franck and Rosen, 1949) suggest that the observation is a valid one. Erikson considers that identity for a woman is formed and expresses itself in the selective nature of her search for the kind of man by whom she wishes to be sought (Erikson, 1968). Erikson's theoretical framework has the advantage of extending through the life cycle rather than ending with the achievement of adulthood. His emphasis on identity finds some reflection in research studies reviewed later in the book, especially in connection with motherhood.

Summary of Other Views

It is apparent from this survey of psychoanalytic theory that Freud's theory of feminine development has evoked considerable dissent from other psychoanalysts. His emphasis on the importance of sexuality, particularly infantile sexuality, and his assumption of constitutional psychological bisexuality have been seriously challenged. Freud's notion of the lack of psychological sex differences before age three is unverified. His hypothesis of a masculine clitoral fixation in girls is a misleading formulation which should be abandoned. In the next sections, we will examine more closely the empirical evidence for other hypotheses of Freud.

PENIS ENVY AND/OR SEX-ROLE ENVY: REVIEW OF EVIDENCE

Methodological Problems

Before launching more deeply into a review of studies relevant to Freud's hypotheses about female development, it might be well to consider some special methodological problems. Mention has been made of some methodological problems in earlier chapters and some will be discussed in the context of the studies being reviewed. One important general problem, however, is what has come to be known as the Rosenthal effect (Rosenthal, Mulry, Persinger, Vikan-Kline, and Grothe, 1964). This study demonstrated that how experimenters believe a study should come out can unintentionally influence the results. The folly of depending on a single research finding is immediately evident. Barber's (1969) recent failure to demonstrate the Rosenthal effect hopefully indicates that it may not be too prevalent (Barber, Calvenley, Forgione, McPeake, Chaves, Bowen, 1969).

A methodological problem more specific to the evaluation of Freudian theory has to do with what is appropriate evidence to test the theory. Psychoanalysts have typically objected that the evidence cited regarding Freud's theory is irrelevant because it does not tap unconscious feelings. This criticism is not entirely cogent in terms of this review for several reasons. Some of the studies to be cited use dreams or projective test techniques* which are considered to tap unconscious feelings. Other studies use child subjects too young, by Freud's theory, to have developed major repressive defenses. Without the development of repressive forces, attitudes unconscious in adults would be expected to express themselves directly. In addition, the whole thrust of Freud's findings is that unconscious motivation is expressed in behavior. Thus there appears to be no reason to rule out arbitrarily studies measuring ordinary behavior in ordinary ways, so long as there is logical reason to suppose that the data bears on the theory. Supporting evidence for Freud's theory from psychoanalysts or from any source is surprisingly scanty. Said Scriven of psychoanalysis, "As a set of hypotheses, it was a great achievement fifty years ago; as no more than a set of hypotheses it is a great disgrace today" (1959, p. 226).

Also of interest is Freud's beguiling statement about his penis envy hypothesis, "If you reject this idea as fantastic and regard my belief in the influence of a lack of a penis on the configuration of femininity as an 'ideé fixe,' I am of course defenceless" (Freud, 1965, p. 132). In this section, evidence* regarding Freud's idea of

*Projective tests, e.g. Rorschach Ink Blot Test and Thematic Apperception Test, consist basically of ambiguous stimuli which the subject is required to interpret. His interpretation is believed to reflect his unconscious motivations.

*John Wisdom (1953) took Sears to task for his 1943 review of Freudian theory and would surely object to the forthcoming material on some of the same grounds. Wisdom believes that it is wrong to limit truth to that verified by observation or by calculation. Even though one may accept this view, surely empirical evidence is not irrelevant to the validity of Freudian theory.

penis envy will be examined. The slight amount of support for this hypothesis found in observations of children and studies using projective techniques leads to an examination of the evidence for sex-role envy. The evidence will show that among adult women, envy of the male role is widespread and that the wish to be a male is not so abnormal as Freud's theory would lead one to expect. The reality basis of the female attitude of envy toward the male role becomes apparent from the evidence that male children, males, and the male role generally are preferred and more highly valued. Finally the relationship between status and sex role is considered.

Review of Evidence Regarding Penis Envy

Freud supposed that before puberty, little girls are masculine and clitoral in their sexuality (Freud, 1938a, 1950b, 1965). Noting the larger, more prominent male genitals, they feel cheated and envy the penis. Some idea of the attitude of young children regarding anatomical sex differences can be obtained from an excellent early study by Hattendorf (1932). She reported data from home interviews of Minneapolis mothers. About 1800 children were reported to have asked sex questions. About 49 per cent of the questions came from the two-to-five age group. The finding supports Freud's observation of a lively early curiosity. This age group did show more relative interest in sex differences and the function of sex organs than older children. The origin of babies, however, was the topic that elicited the most questions from this and all age groups combined. The tone of the 865 questions asked by the preschool children reflected simple curiosity for the most part. Only three questions suggested anxiety about the phallic sex difference, and these came from boys. As much concern was shown about breasts and lactation. There was no evidence that the girls envied the penis. While special techniques to tap unconscious feelings should not be necessary with most of the children in a preschool group, the data would have provided stronger evidence were it based on direct observation rather than on the mothers' reports.

Using play techniques which are considered sensitive to revealing unconscious attitudes, Conn (1940) studied 128 boys and 72 girls ranging in age from four to twelve. About three-fourths of the children had seen the genitalia of the opposite sex and about a third of these (about fifty) were willing to discuss their reactions to this experience in the doll play. The majority indicated a lack of emotional reaction, but five girls and eleven boys of the fifty were shocked by it and worried over the cause. Conn concluded that viewing the genitals of the opposite sex does not disturb the average child.

Levy (1940) criticized Conn's research on several grounds. He felt that the children were being seen by professional personnel because of problems and thus in no sense constituted a random sample of normal children; many of the children were so old that it was doubtful that their doll-play reactions would be a reflection of the feelings they first had when noting the genital differences between the sexes, and only a small minority of the entire sample was willing to discuss their feelings. Levy reported that his own semicontrolled observations of young children (also mostly children with problems) led him to conclude that perception of genital differences does arouse in boys castration anxiety and in girls feelings of envy and destructive impulses toward the penis. While he concludes that such reactions are common, he points out that the key question is under what conditions they create neurotic symptoms.

Kreitler and Kreitler (1966) failed to find evidence of castration concern in either boys or girls, ages four and five, of extremely diverse national backgrounds. Only 17 of 202 child subjects could not be interviewed either because of anxiety or lack of cooperation, so that the subjects were much more representative than those of the Conn or Levy studies. This study must count as a very strong negative finding against the theory, since it is a carefully controlled study of a representative group of young children.

Landy (1967) concluded that he had demonstrated the presence of penis envy in women and castration anxiety in men by the everyday psychopathology technique of how the two sexes open a pack of cigarettes and remove the first cigarette. This study illustrates a particular methodological problem in testing theory—that of establishing a valid relationship between the theory and the method used to test it. In this case, it seems doubtful that a high percentage of experts would agree with the sorts of responses that Landy classifies as indicating penis envy.

"It was predicted that for women, having penis envy and the desire to possess a penis would constitute reaction formation; they would reject phallic images in everyday life and recreate by repetition compulsion the cavity (vaginal fenestra. . .) to have within them a child. Freud explains this as the sublimation of penis envy. Thus, female smokers should tend to open an unopened pack of cigarettes and obtain a cigarette by lifting open the folded part of the cigarette pack, lifting the flap up to make a form similar to a cavity, and pushing the bottom of the pack to expel the cigarette from the top. In this manner the female creates a cavity in the bottom of the pack and expels the cigarette (the penis object) which may be considered a passive expression. . ." (Landy 1967, p. 576) . While significantly more women than men opened a pack of cigarettes in the prescribed manner, nonsmokers (among whom women were more numerous) also significantly more often opened the package in this way. The author was undeterred by this indication that being a smoker or a nonsmoker regardless of sex may be the determining factor. He concluded that "The observed behaviors are consistent with the Freudian hypothesis that castration complex in males and penis envy in females is expressed in everyday living" (Landy, 1967, p. 579) .

Friedman (1952) studied 305 normal children, half males and half females, ages five to sixteen, randomly selected from several Cleveland schools. Only his results having to do with castration anxiety are discussed in this section; other results are considered in later sections. Believing that most studies of psychoanalytic concepts have failed to confirm them because of techniques inadequate for study of unconscious feelings, Friedman attempted to tap unconscious material by asking children to make up stories in response to certain pictures. This method is a variant of standard projective-test technique. Friedman's instructions, however, violated a basic tenet of projective testing–neutrality in the examiner. The subjects were asked to tell a story about a monkey who was "very fond of his tail," and then "something different happened." The tail is considered a phallic symbol. Seventy-five per cent of the children ended the story with comments about loss of the tail or some important quality of it; these findings were interpreted as evidence of castration anxiety. Friedman's instructions would seem biased, however, in the direction of promoting a story ending that contrasted with the monkey's happy state of being fond of his tail. A better technique would have been the simple request to finish the story.

The girls' data were not presented separately, but Friedman says that castration anxiety was less among them than among boys. The author concluded that it seems likely that most children have fears relating to castration. The total balance of the evidence, however, suggests that while such reactions do occur, they are not universal in boys and are even less common in girls. If such reactions were strong, typical, and important in development, one would have expected to find more supporting evidence in the data cited.

Hall and Van deCastle (1966, 1965) analyzed the dreams of sixty male and sixty female college students. They found that the dreams of females showed significantly more castration wish and penis envy than castration anxiety. The opposite was true for males. This finding supports clinical reports regarding the existence of the phenomenon of penis envy and its greater prevalence in females than in males. Perhaps an accurate perspective of the problem of penis envy in women can be gained from the fact that evidence of penis envy occurred thirty-two times in 956 dreams of the women while it occurred sixteen times in the 953 male dreams. About three per cent of the unconscious mental life of this sample of females showed evidence of penis envy. Furthermore even this estimate may be high, as the girls were attending psychology lectures where Freudian theory may well have been taught.

Similarly Rabe (1963) found that wish for a penis was significantly more often present in the 500 dreams of twenty-five female, compared to twenty-five male, college students. Again this problem manifested itself in about 3 per cent of their dreams. Females were also significantly more fearful of the penis and more rejecting of the vagina. Male dreams showed more evidence of penis symbols than female dreams (66 to 36). Females dreamed equally of male and female sex symbols, while males dreamed of penis symbols at a ratio of over four to one. This would suggest that the penis is more a problem for males than for females.

The lack of supporting evidence for the importance of penis envy is not surprising when one reconsiders some of the evidence Freud used to formulate the notion of castration anxiety. Part of the evidence was drawn from a father's report of his analysis of his own son (Freud, 1953a). The father was a doctor and friend of Freud, who supervised the analysis. The fact that the boy, Little Hans, had some help in developing his confusions and worries was little noted for many years. Hans asked his mother, who had been a patient of Freud's (Jones, 1953), if she had a penis. Rather than dealing in any appropriate manner with the question, she told him that she did. It does not seem surprising that the child was confused. Others have also suggested that this case needs reinterpretation (Edel, 1968; Fromm *et al.,* 1968; Fromm and Narváez, 1966; Strean, 1967; Wolpe and Rachman, 1963).

Some tangential support for Freud's theory of penis envy may be found in the study of Blum (1949). He used the Blacky Test, a specially devised projective technique, to study psychoanalytic theory of psychosexual development in 119 male and 90 female Stanford undergraduates. Freud (1965) had stated that the lack of a penis was experienced by women as a narcissistic blow resulting in an intensification of self love and vanity. This narcissism tended to find expression in the choice of a love object who represents what they would have liked to become. Freud labeled this a narcissistic object choice. (Another person might have given it a label with more favorable connotations, such as altruistic object choice.) Freud thought that males more frequently made an anaclitic object choice, that is, picked a mate like someone they had loved in the past, commonly like their mothers. Blum concluded from Freud's statements that the greater the amount of penis envy, the greater should be the tendency to narcissistic object choice, and he found modest confirmation for this in his data with a correlation of .34. Unfortunately Blum provided no direct evidence about the prevalence or intensity of penis envy in women. He did report that narcissistic object choice was significantly more frequent in the women.

Greenson (1967) reported that to his surprise two thirds of his sample of individuals applying for surgical changes of sex were men. While this is certainly a graphic illustration of the fact that male envy of the female has been underestimated, doubtless the ratio of applicants has been affected by the obviously greater ease of changing from male to a facsimile female than the reverse.

Sex-role Preference Among Adults

While the evidence fails to support the importance of widespread anatomical envy of the male, there are many studies indicating that both males and females generally think it is preferable to be male. A Fortune Survey (Roper, 1946) found that while 91 per cent of the men would remain males if they could be born again, 25 percent of the females would rather change sex. These women did not feel men were superior but that they got the breaks and had more fun. Some mutual envy is suggested by the fact that each sex tended to think the other had an easier time of it. There were sharp differences among the women, depending on their social class. Only 25 per cent of the women of the lowest class felt that women had an easier time of it while 47 per cent of the women of the upper class thought so. Among the reasons for men having an easier time, the most prominent were fewer family responsibilities, shorter hours, "It's a man's world," and fewer social and moral restrictions. Less than three per cent of both men and women mentioned childbearing.

In Puerto Rico, when asked what sex they would choose to be if they came to life after death, 67 per cent of the women would choose to be male, while only 7 per cent of the men would prefer to change sex (Sanchez-Hidalgo, 1952). In an English sample, Chesser (1956) found 21 per cent of the most happily married women and 40 per cent of the least happily married had at some time wanted to be a male. Terman (1938) found that 31 per cent of the wives of 792 couples wanted to be a male at some time in her life, while only 2.5 per cent of the husbands had wished to be a female. Landis, Landis, and Bolles (1940) found that 61 per cent of 294 women, about half of whom were normals and half psychiatric patients, wished to be male at some time in their lives. Contrary to psychoanalytic prediction, significantly more of the normal females had wanted to be male.

Sex Role and Mental Health

Wishing to be a male and/or to be masculine is simply not so related to psychological abnormality as has been assumed. Heilbrun (1965a, 1968) from a review of the literature and from his own studies, has concluded that femininity in females may even be associated with poorer adjustment. As already discussed in Chapter 2, stereotyped femininity contains an element of built-in incompetence (Broverman, Broverman, Clarkson, Rosenkrantz, and Vogel, 1970). It is therefore not very surprising that femininity does not necessarily indicate adjustment. It is something of a mystery, however, just how and why unadaptive characteristics would become part of a cultural ideal. One would suppose that the answer must lie in the balance of the relations between the sexes. Some hint as to what investigations in this area might reveal can be found in the study of McCandless and Ali (1966). Athletic competence was found to be related to girls' popularity in sex-segregated schools, but not in coed schools. Data reviewed in this chapter make it clear that wishing to be a male is not at all uncommon. While at most, only 9 per cent of men would rather be female, the percentage of women who might like to be male ranges from 21 per cent to 67 per cent, depending on the sample. Not only is it much more normal for a woman to wish to be male than vice versa, but the evidence suggests that it may be beneficial to adjustment to have some characteristics that have been stereotyped as masculine (see Chapters 2 and 5). It may well be that the crucial point is "for woman to know where to apply her masculinity appropriately," as Marie Bonaparte (1965, p. 162) quoted Freud as saying.

Preference for Male Children

Pohlman (1969) concluded that a mass of evidence attests that parents in the United States tend to have preferences (a) for boys, and (b) for at least one child of each sex (Freedman, Freedman, and Whelpton, 1960; Landis and Landis, 1963; Rainwater, 1965; Weiler, 1959; Westoff, Potter, and Sagi, 1963; Westoff, Potter, Sagi, and Mishler, 1961; Whelpton, Campbell, and Patterson, 1966; Winston, 1932). An interesting behavioral datum is the fact that when the first child was a boy, the interval before a second child was conceived averaged three months longer than when the first was a girl (Westoff, Potter, Sagi, and Mishler, 1961). There was no support for the hypothesis that this might be because first boys created more problems for the mother, but instead the result seemed to be caused by sex preferences (Westoff, Potter, and Sagi, 1963). Another such item is the fact that having a female rather than a male child was significantly associated with postpartum emotional disturbance (Gordon and Gordon, 1960). In the dreams of women pregnant for the first time, twice as many male as female babies appeared (Gillman, 1968).

Dinitz, Dynes, and Clarke (1954) were surprised to find traditional male bias among college students. If they were only going to have one child, 91 per cent of the males preferred a boy, while 66 per cent of the women preferred a boy. If not forced to choose one sex or the other, many who voted for a male took the no-preference option. The authors interpreted this as lip service to equalitarian principles, and noted that covert discrimination might be even more emotionally damaging than overt discrimination.

Among unmarried college students, Hammer (1970) found that if they were going to have only one child, 90 per cent of the males and 78 per cent of the females preferred a son. Among married students, 83 per cent of the males and 73 per cent of the females preferred a boy. Among noncollege adults, 90 per cent of the males, compared to 30 per cent of the females, preferred a son. Hammer comments that the less-educated woman is more likely to see future kinship, companionship, and help in a daughter than in a son. The greater preference for girls shown in the following study may also be due to the presence of fewer upper-middle-class and upper-class individuals in the sample.

Among 1444 Indianapolis couples who already had children, the husband preferred a boy and the wife a girl if they were to have had only one child. In general, the couples seemed satisfied with the sex of their children, and the authors concluded that there is no reason to hold the assumption that sons are more important in American culture (Clare and Kiser, 1951). However, the weight of the evidence is against their conclusion, and it is important to realize that parents may well be reluctant to admit dissatisfaction with the sex of an already existing child.

Opinions about the Sexes

Kitay (1940) found both sexes shared a low estimate of the female sex. McKee and Sheriffs (1957) reported that both male and female college students tend to regard the male more favorably. They also found results suggesting a veneer of equalitarianism. In a study of seventy-four male and eighty female college students, both sexes more frequently accorded high valuation to stereotypically masculine characteristics (Rosenkrantz, Vogel, Bee, Broverman, and Broverman, 1968). MacBrayer (1960) found that unmarried female students have a more favorable opinion of males than the unmarried male students have of females. Content analysis of the data suggested that this was partially a function of the fact that the girls felt more need for a marriage partner than did the boys. Fernberger (1948) tried to convince his college classes that there are no established psychological sex differences. To his chagrin, he found that his lectures had little apparent effect. About 90 per cent of the males and 75 per cent of the females strongly believed in the all-around superiority of males, and espoused belief in many other items of sex difference that the professor had tried to establish as nonexistent. Wylie (1961) concluded that while women's self concepts are not clearly more unfavorable than are men's self concepts, stereotypes of "women in general" seemed less favorable than "men in general."

Sex-role Preferences of Children

Generally among children also, various measures of sex-role preference indicate that boys prefer the male role more than girls prefer the female role (Hartup and Zook, 1960; Mussen, 1969;

Oetzel, 1966;* Ward, 1968). Some of these studies used the standard administration of the It Scale as a measure of sex-role preference. This version of the test utilized a gingerbread-type figure and the child was to choose which activities "It" preferred. It, however, looks more like a boy than a girl, so that the test is not valid as a measure of female sex-role preference (Brown, 1962; Hartup and Zook, 1960; Sher and Lansky, 1968). A few studies (Lansky, 1968; Lefkowitz, 1962; Sher and Lansky, 1968) have concluded that girls have about as much preference for the female sex role as boys have for the male sex role. Lansky and McKay (1963) found kindergarten boys of the upper middle class preferred the female role more than the girls preferred the male role. The girls made mostly feminine choices, while the boys were more variable. Among black persons of the deprived lower class, the female role has significantly greater prestige than among a nondeprived white group (Thomas, 1966). This is consistent with the greater power of the mother in lower-class black families (Blood and Wolfe, 1960). However, even excluding data based on the standard It Scale, among American white children, the balance of the evidence leans in the direction of more male preference for the male role. Future research may clarify these relationships. There is a need to control for class and subculture, and there may also be a need to control for philosophy of the nursery school. Some settings stress traditional sex typing, and others stress freedom to choose activities sex-typed for the opposite sex.

From Norway (Brun-Gulbrandsen, 1967) comes an interesting study of mothers who believe they are rearing their boys and girls as similarly as possible. However, only 77 per cent of them thought boys and girls should assist equally with work in the house and 60 per cent thought it was fine to give girls fewer theoretical subjects in school than boys. The conflict of reality and ideology is obvious. Fifty-seven per cent of the eight- and eleven-year-old chil-

---

Oetzel's (1966) classified summary of research in sex differences lists boys and men showing greater preference for sex-appropriate activities in all seven studies: Borstelmann, 1961; Rabban, 1950; DeLucia, 1963; Hetherington, 1965;* Brown, 1957;* Sutton-Smith, Rosenberg and Morgan, 1963; Maccoby, Wilson and Burton, 1958. Starred studies used the It Scale. Data regarding sexual identification rather than sex-role preference will be considered in the next chapters.

dren of these mothers thought that *girls* are better off. Of their mothers, however, 46 per cent thought boys had a better time of it; only 13 per cent thought girls were better off. Among their eight to eleven-year-old children, 88 per cent of the girls and 85 per cent of the boys would choose to be their own sex. At ages fourteen to fifteen, only 71 per cent of the girls wished to be girls compared to 84 per cent of the boys who wished to be boys. One certainly gains the impression of dwindling enthusiasm for the female role.

Judgments of the comparative desirability rating of the two sexes give other indications of their relative status positions among children. Smith's (1939) study is a classic in this area. One hundred boys and one hundred girls, ages eight to fifteen, voted as to whether boys or girls possessed the greater degree of each of nineteen desirable traits and fourteen undesirable ones. The traits seem quite representative of personality characteristics. With increasing age, the boys increased their relatively poor opinion of girls, while the girls' relative opinion of the boys improved. Similarly, Rudy (1966) found that early adolescent boys view masculine attributes more favorably than girls view feminine attributes. It should be noted, however, that in Smith's study, each sex thought better of itself than of the other sex, a finding also reported by Harris and Teng (1957).

Hartley, Hardesty, and Gorfein (1962) concluded that their results call into question the validity of the assumption that culturally enforced adult partiality for the male is generally operant in children's sex-role identification and development. Their subjects, however, would generally be considered past the decisive ages of the formation of sex-role identification (Hampson and Hampson, 1961). The subjects were 132 eight- and eleven-year-old children. While the children thought that the adult male prefers boys, they felt that the women prefer girls, a finding congruent with that of Clare and Kiser (1951). For their own children, the girls wanted girls and the boys wanted boys. Girls of employed mothers thought fathers less likely to prefer boys to girls, and girls of the upper-middle class were not so sure that mothers prefer girls as were girls of the lower middle class. The uncertainty of the upper-middle-class girls is more in line with the overall results and with the study of Hammer (1970) points up the importance of class in determining sex-role attitudes.

Social Class and Sex Role

In the lower classes, the sexes are more separated psychologically and socially (Kagan, 1964; Newson and Newson, 1963; Seward, 1956). Rabban (1950) found that working-class children, especially girls, showed awareness of sex-role differences at an earlier age than upper-middle-class children. Girls of higher class were said to be not entirely clear in their sex-role choice even at age eight. Rather than to say they were unclear, it might be more accurate to say that a narrower sex role is characteristic of the working class, while the role of the upper-middle-class female is expanded to include elements often considered masculine. This could explain the fact that girls of a working-class sample show more sex solidarity and earlier role clarity or feminine homogeneity of role.

Historically, women of the upper classes have tended to enjoy an expanded sex role (Beard, 1946). However, among the lower classes, the right to work has been an onerous part of the female tradition, especially in agrarian societies. Even today, the women of the upper classes in Europe and in other parts of the world hold a more privileged position in relation to their counterparts in the United States because of the greater class distance and stratification. These women have a tradition of high status which is part of their lives and which is acknowledged by others. They are used to relegating most nurturant activities to servants, and it has not been uncommon for an upper-middle-class French woman to board out her newly born infant. Ironically, because of class inequality, it has thus sometimes been easier for these privileged European and Asian women to reduce sexual inequality than it has for American women.

Status Discontinuity and Arrogation of the Male Role

The relationship between masculine values in women and the status variable has also been noted in a primitive tribe (Lewis,

1941). "Manly hearted women" as Lewis called them, were characterized by (a) efficient management of property, (b) conspicuous behavior in public, (c) dominant and attractive sexual play regarding their husbands, and (d) willingness to perform public ceremonial roles and a reputation for sorcery. They were ambivalently regarded by others. Six of the fourteen (out of a total of 109 adult women in the tribe) had been favored children in the family. Lewis conjectured that upon growing up, they experienced a marked discontinuity between their favored status as a child and the sacrifices expected of an adult woman. He inferred that the unusual adult masculine behavior represented a solution to a problem of status discontinuity; they arrogated aspects of the male role in order to continue a high-status position.

A Comparison of Penis Envy Versus Sex-role Envy

The emphasis on contrasting sex-role status as a source of the masculinity complex was of course characteristic of many of Freud's critics such as Adler, Horney, and Thompson. A study by Rachael Levin (1963, 1966) provides evidence relevant to a comparison of the anatomical versus cultural source of masculine protest. She compared a group of twenty-six unmarried women with careers in masculine occupations with a group of twenty-five homemakers. All the women were college graduates, and there were no significant differences in intelligence or general psychological adjustment between the two groups. She devised a Female-Castration-Complex Measure based on the Rorschach Test, a test considered capable of assessing unconscious attitudes. Of the four indices meant to tap reaction to anatomical sex differences, only one significantly differentiated the two groups, and the combined indices did not differentiate them. Four other combined indices meant to tap nonanatomical components of the castration complex did significantly differentiate the groups. Of these, the individual indices of greater activity and need for achievement were significant discriminators. Although the author did not consider this study a critical test of psychoanalytic theory, her conclusion that it provides more support for the cultural position seems justified. Kohlberg (1966) has concluded that perception of sex-role differences is more influential in shaping personality than perception of genital differences. He based his conclusion on the fact that "children are still confused about genital differences at an age (four-five) when they clearly stereotype sex-roles in terms of size, strength, aggression, and power. . ." (Kohlberg, 1966, p. 104).

SUMMARY

Taken as a whole, there is little evidence of castration anxiety in women or of widespread anatomical envy, though of course this does not mean to deny that cases of penis envy exist. The girl's lack of a penis, however, may well be more upsetting to boys than to girls. Moreover, boys also show biological envy of the female sex. The evidence suggests that it is extremely unlikely that penis envy plays the crucial role in the psychology of normal women that Freud assigned to it. In finally accepting her sex, Freud comments that the female accepts a baby as a substitute for the penis. While it seems likely that one can find instances of such an unconscious equation as evidently Freud did, Freud's view is a distortion of the attitudes of the normal girl. The doll is a ubiquitous intercultural item and there even exists a sort of imperative that every little girl has a right to a doll even more than to a pair of shoes. It seems likely that girls are given a doll so that they may have a tangible, manipulatable sign and symbol of their sex and of the fact that they are "fancier on the inside." For the normal girl and woman, a baby is a first-choice item, not a consolation prize.

While the importance of anatomical envy in normal female development is very doubtful, there is pervasive evidence of differential sex status positions and preference for the higher male sex-role status. There are some suggestions that the sex-segregated women of the lower classes feel more solidarity with a traditional female sex role while at the same time they are more envious of the greater privileges of the male role. Upper-middle-class women tend to be less envious, probably partly because they are less strictly held to a narrow concept of the female role.

Chapter 4

THE FEMALE OEDIPUS COMPLEX AND ITS RESOLUTION

FREUD HYPOTHESIZED that between the ages of three to five, a girl turns from her mother as an object of affection to her father (1950a, 1956, 1965). She feels hostile toward her mother, and desiring to usurp her mother's position, she fears her mother's jealous rage. This situation is called the female Oedipus complex. From six until puberty, the complex is supposed to be quiescent, only to be roused again by the physiological changes of adolescence. The hypothesis of the Oedipus complex was first subjected to criticism on the basis of cross-cultural evidence that the complex is not so biologically inherent and universal as Freud indicated. Roheim (1950) has ably defended the proposition that while the Oedipus complex takes different forms in different cultures, these are but variations on a single theme. His defense, however, as with most discussions of the Oedipus complex, centered on the male version. The Oedipus complex has been used to explain the nearly universal incest taboo. However, this explanation is not necessary since it is now clear that inbreeding seriously depresses the quality of stock allowing recessive gene errors to reach expression (Aberle *et al.,* 1963; Lindzey, 1967; Spuhler, 1967). This explanation is probably sufficient to account for the prevalence of the incest taboo.

So far as the female Oedipus complex is concerned, it is certainly clear from case-study documentation that some such phenomenon exists, but is it usual? Does it arise from within the child at a particular stage of development? How important is it among women in our culture? In this chapter, the evidence of a female Oedipus complex will be reviewed. Following this, evidence will be considered regarding the consequences of sex differences in the resolution of the Oedipus complex. This has to do with sex differences in superego functioning. Finally, evidence regarding the latency period will be discussed.

REVIEW OF THE EVIDENCE

That the Oedipus complex is not frequent is suggested by Benjamin's (1942) review of 5,000 cases of children with psychological disturbance. It is not clear, however, how adequate the case records were for judging the presence of an Oedipus complex. Benjamin found only two girls and seventeen boys who showed evidence of an Oedipus complex. Even in these instances, he noted that the parents played a definite role in creating the complex. Benjamin's conclusion was that psychoanalytic views resemble snapshots taken from strange points of view. The pictures seem distorted and look like caricatures, some parts being exaggerated while other parts are microscopic in size or even invisible.

Anderson (1936) presented data on the mother's report of the family preferences of 1,626 normal children ages one to twelve. About half of the children were reported to have no preference; about 20 per cent preferred the mother, and about 15 per cent the father. There was little difference between the sexes. Siblings, especially sisters, became important preference figures for the girls ten to twelve.

Simpson (1935) studied the parental preferences of 250 boys and 250 girls, 50 at each age from five to nine. Only white children, mostly middle class, living with both parents were included in the study. The examiner began and ended her individual session with the child by directly inquiring about parental preference. Interspersed were more indirect methods of measuring preference. In the final preference choice, both sexes chose mother nearly three to one, with about one tenth declining to give a preference. Among the five-year-old girls, however, there was a significantly greater number who chose father, rather than mother. On the first questioning, no such difference appeared, but since many of the children would not make a choice the first time asked, these results are rarely noted. Use of the indirect measure of preference indicated that both sexes prefer the mother, girls significantly more so than boys. Overall, this study, which is sometimes cited in support of the female Oedipus complex, provides only slight support.

In another study by Ammons and Ammons (1949), twenty-four girls ages three to five preferred mother when directly asked. When their preferences were discerned by an indirect doll-play interview, the girls were either neutral or preferred mother. Kohlberg and Zigler (1967) studied sixty-four children ages four to eight. They found that four-year-old girls were clearly mother oriented. They became less mother oriented with age but not to the point of being father oriented. Piskin (1960) found no significant difference between boys and girls ages three to five in the parent they liked best; they both preferred mother. This evidence is particularly negative, since ages three to five is supposed to be the period of most marked Oedipal reaction. In later years, the girls of the Piskin study made more father choices and no preference choices while boys made more no preference choices.

The study of Liccione (1955) does not deal with children too young to have mobilized major repressive forces, but it does attempt to get at unconscious material by using a projective device, the Thematic Apperception Test. This test consists of having the children make up stories to fit a set of pictures. The stories are later analyzed by the examiner. Liccione gave the test to 250 girls ages nine to seventeen. He found that the girls imagined more disharmony with mothers than with fathers but that they also imagined greater interaction with mother. The greater disharmony seemed to be a simple function of the greater mother-daughter interaction. He did not find statistically significant increases in mother-daughter conflict from the latency period to adolescence, as Freud's hypothesis would predict, nor did the amount of conflict decline in the later years. Much of the conflict seemed to be about independence. Another study (Smith and Powell, 1956), which is discussed in greater detail in the chapter on adolescence, also does not support the hypothesis of the female Oedipus complex.

Stagner and Drought (1935) found no sex difference in the attitudes of 400 college students toward their parents. Miller (1969) found that seventeen of thirty-two college girls chose as lover a photograph most like the physique of father (of eight possible physique choices). Winch (1950, 1951) attempted to test the validity of the Oedipus hypothesis by measuring the relationships between courtship progress and attitudes to parents. He reasoned that marked attachment to the opposite-sex parent should retard courtship progress. While persistently finding verification for the hypothesis among the males of his sample of 1000 college students, he was just as persistently unable to find verification of it for females. In fact, he found that the women most attached to father were most advanced in courtship. He did not, however, conclude that there is no sexualized relation to the father. i.e., no Oedipus complex, nor did he conclude that father attachment served to emancipate from the more binding mother attachment. Instead, Winch concluded that Freud was correct that an unresolved Oedipus complex does little harm in a woman.

Hamilton (1929) gathered a great deal of interesting material from a select sample of 200 New York men and women. As is so often the case with the early studies, however, tests of statistical significance were not applied. Some of his data have been quoted as supporting the Oedipus hypothesis, though Terman (1938) reported that subsequent statistical analysis showed that none of these findings is significant. Eight women admitted having had some degree of incestuous feeling toward the father, and seven women admitted being disturbed by evidence of sex feelings of family males (not necessarily their father) toward them. However, when 90 of 100 women say they never had any fear of incestuous relations and 81 say no to a question as to whether they had been tortured by thoughts about persons in the family of the opposite sex having "breeding desires," it is hard to consider this much support for the female Oedipus hypothesis. Two other studies showed trends consistent with Freud's hypothesis, but it is not clear that they are statistically significant (Landis, Landis, and Bolles, 1940; Meltzer, 1941).

In Terman's study (1938) of 792 California married couples, both sexes expressed more attachment to the mother than the father and for women there was little difference in the amount of conflict experienced with each parent. Terman was unable to find any clear trace of the effects of the Oedipus complex on orgasm in women. There was, however, a significant tendency for women to obtain an unfavorable marital happiness score if they were overly attached to either mother or father. Also negative for the Oedipus hypothesis are the findings of Chesser (1956) that 29 per cent of her sample of 1211 English women preferred their father, 40 per cent the mother, and 31 per cent did not indicate a preference. Among adults, such data does not count as very strong negative evidence. On the other hand, had father been preferred, the same evidence would doubtless be cited as evidence in favor of the female Oedipus hypothesis.

Friedman, whose study (1952) provided some positive data about the castration anxiety and penis-envy hypothesis, also investigated Oedipal feelings. Friedman predicted that there should be a drop in castration anxiety from the Oedipal age of five to the older ages of the latency period. This he did not find and he suggested that the girls may have been too old for a measure at the height of their anxiety since the Oedipal period has been thought to begin at age three. The comparison of the girls in the latency period with those in adolescence, however, did show a significant difference. The difference is all the more convincing, since a comparison of the male and female curves showed that anxiety rose earlier in females consistent with their earlier puberty. It should be pointed out, however, that Friedman's measure of castration anxiety was an index of reaction to phallic symbolic material. The anxiety shown may not have been due to fear of castration but to general sexual shock. A rise in general sexual anxiety at puberty does not provide specific support for the Oedipus complex.

Friedman also asked the children to make up stories in response to standard pictures. He then asked them which parent the child in the story loved best and which loved the child best. He obtained no significant sex differences using this technique, which was similar to the indirect method of the Simpson study (1935). Friedman cited these negative findings as an example that the failure of previous investigators to find support for Freudian hypotheses was caused by inadequate technique. After correcting for the greater male number of aggressive story themes, Friedman found that, as Freud would have predicted, there were significantly more instances of father-son conflict than father-daughter conflict, and significantly more mother-daughter conflict than mother-son conflict. There was no evidence of developmental changes in parental conflict in the boys, but among the older girls, there were significantly fewer conflict stories to the father picture and significantly more conflict stories to the mother picture than among the younger girls. Friedman concluded that for girls, there is apparently greater persistence and development of the Oedipal relationship in the teenage years.

Liccione (1955) did not find a significant increase in mother-daughter conflict from latency to adolescence, but he found a trend in this direction. He interpreted the greater mother-daughter conflict not as evidence of the Oedipus complex, but simply as a function of greater mother-daughter interaction. Friedman, however, has some specific evidence of the Oedipal character of the father-daughter relationship. A child-father picture had a toy in it. Friedman predicted and found that significantly more girls than boys fantasied the father taking some positive action in regard to the toy. At a symbolic level, this was interpreted to mean giving the girl a penis. There was also a staircase in the picture. Mounting stairs is a stock symbol of sexual relations (Freud, 1938b). It was therefore predicted and found that significantly more girls than boys imagined the father mounting the stairs and going into the house, the house being a female symbol. This evidence is certainly consistent with the Oedipus hypothesis insofar as it indicates greater evidence of a sexualized relation between fathers and daughters than between fathers and sons. One still cannot assume, however, that the motivation for the relationship arises entirely from the daughter without the father's participation.

Hall and Domhoff (1963b) analyzed dreams from 1399 men and 1418 women ages two to eighty. They found that men dream more about other men than about women, while women dream of both sexes equally. Reasoning that dreams are more about those feared than those loved, they interpreted this finding as supporting the Oedipus complex. While it might fairly be supposed to support the male Oedipus complex, the support in the female case appears to be weaker and more ambiguous.

The importance of mother rather than father was demonstrated in the projective test study of Blum (1949). Significantly more of the female subjects than male showed evidence of pre-Oedipal attachment (attachment to mother), and they showed significantly less intensity of the Oedipal relationship compared to the males. Blum concluded that the development of women is more complicated than that of men and that the Oedipal involvement is less complete in females, since the fear of losing the mother continues as a dominant motif. Cohen (1966) found that women's relationships with their husbands seemed more closely patterned after their relations with their mothers than with their fathers. This again does not support the hypothesis of the female Oedipus complex.

THE ROLE OF THE FATHER

It may be that one of the important positive aspects of the father's role for both sexes is to provide a way of resolving the dependency relationship with the mother. This view has been presented by Parsons (1964) and Forrest (1966). Data consistent with this hypothesis are found in the results of the study of Lynn and Sawrey (1959). Daughters of absent Norwegian fishermen were more dependent on their mothers than those whose fathers remained home. Winch (1951) pointed out that while boys are close to their mothers as children, they are actually emancipated earlier as a cultural expectation. An undue part of the girl's struggle for independence may be postponed until adolescence or even later. Certainly an hypothesis of late dependency conflicts in girls would be consistent with studies cited in this chapter and with the evidence about sex differences in dependency already considered in Chapter Two.

In those instances in which the father does have an important role as a sexualized love object, does this come about as a function of the daughter's sexual impulses? This concept is being increasingly questioned (Friedman, 1966; Rangell, 1955). Noting that Freud's theory of psychosexuality has passed into conventional wisdom, Gagnon (1965, 1967) nonetheless finds that a major difficulty with Freud's scheme is, ". . . the location of the instinctual energy within the child; the child is invested with initiatory capacities that would seem to be better allocated to the parent. This theory projects upon the child . . . the sexual desires of the parents . . ." (Gagnon, 1967, p. 22). An interesting finding is that fathers' care of daughters when they were *babies* significantly correlated with daughters' emotional health and ego strength (Westley and Epstein, 1969). The authors offer the explanation that fathers with a solid care relationship before their daughters make Oedipal advances can accept the girls without accepting or rejecting the advances. Obviously they assume that Freud's theory of the female Oedipus complex is correct. An alternative explanation might be that these fathers have a beneficial and more deeply nurturant attitude toward their daughters.

Before he formulated the Oedipus complex, Freud (1953b) had placed great weight on seduction before age eight as a causal factor in emotional disturbances. Later he discounted the seduction hypothesis (1938a; 1953c) and transferred etiological significance from the event itself to the fantasies it evoked in the child and the child's need for defensive reaction. The shift is basically from an emphasis on a traumatic incestuous event in which the child is passive to an emphasis on incestuous fantasies in which the child is active.

Glueck (1963) suggests that a change in the kind of case Freud was observing may have contributed to his decision to make this revision. Freud's earlier patients tended to be more disturbed and from a lower socioeconomic level than later cases. The more disturbed schizophrenic patients (then often called cases of hysteria) might be expected to have had more actual sexually traumatic experiences, rather than fantasies about them, as in the case of neurotic patients. This would be consistent with the fact that both schizophrenia and incest are more prevalent in the lower classes. In keeping with Freud's first formulation, Glueck has found that actual incestuous experiences are an important element in the developmental background of some schizophrenics.

Others have advanced the opinion that the crucial factor in Freud's change of mind was the discovery of his own incestuous motivations toward his mother, a result of his self analysis (Jones, 1953; Sadow, Gedo, Miller, Pollock, and Sabshin, 1968). This would certainly account for why Freud's theories of women seem androcentric. Among other reasons he gave for his change of mind, Freud cited the fact that it was difficult to believe that so many fathers could be perverse (Jones, 1953). Freud was loath to attribute incestuous motivation to his own father (Jones, 1953) and for many years he also concealed the incestuous attempts of the fathers in the cases of Katharina and Fräulein Elisabeth von R. (Breuer and Freud, 1957). In 1924, he added footnotes apologizing for having originally disguised these facts. Freud was sexually motivated toward his mother, but are little girls usually sexually motivated toward their fathers? There is little evidence of the female Oedipus complex, and even less that its motivational source lies in the child.

IDENTIFICATION

Freud believed that the female Oedipus complex was not smashed by fear of castration as in the case of the male but that it dwindled away from a variety of disappointments and realizations (1950b, 1965). According to Freud, a consequence of this sex difference in the manner of resolving the Oedipus complex is a difference in the strength of the superego in the two sexes. Freud stated that the female superego is never so inexorable, so impersonal, so independent of its emotional origins as in men. Moreover, he stated that women have less sense of justice and that their judgments are more influenced by feelings of affection and hostility (Freud, 1965). In his later writings, he hypothesized that in the case of women, fear of loss of love rather than fear of castration is the main motivating factor resulting in identification with the parent of the same sex and superego formation.* In Freud's formulation, sexual and moral identification occur together, presumably about age five or six. Freud placed a very heavy explanatory burden on the concept of the resolution of the Oedipus complex. Fearing to lose her mother's love, the little girl identifies

*There is a very large literature concerning sex identification and moral learning, some of it inspired by Freudian theory, and much of it deriving from other theoretical orientations. Rather than attempting to put new wine in old skins, it seems preferable to discuss this literature in the next chapter.

with her mother and takes on her values. Sex-role identification and morality are apparently thus acquired. From this time until puberty, the child falls into a period of relative sexual disinterest known as the latency period.

It is not easy to specify exactly what evidence would be sufficient to infer identification with another person even without supposing it is an unconscious process. It is easier to say what does not show identification. Similarity does not necessarily demonstrate identification, since the similarity might have been acquired by exposure to the same milieu or the similarity could have been acquired by direct instruction. However, lack of similarity, especially in the areas of sex-role behavior and value orientation, would count very heavily against identification. Similarity of behavior is more impressive evidence of identification than perceived similarity (Lynn, 1969b). In order to demonstrate convincingly any similarity supportive of Freud's concept of resolution of the Oedipus complex by identification, one should at least show that similarity to the same-sex parent is greater than to the opposite-sexed parent and/or to random adults of the same sex and social grouping.

Fitzgerald and Roberts (1966) found that girls in grades one through four perceived themselves as more similar to their mothers than to "my friends' mothers." In the fifth grade, perceived similarity to mother was not significantly greater than to the measure of generalized feminine role. Helper (1955) did not find girls were more similar to their mothers than to other women. Lazowick (1955) also did not find that girls were any more similar in test behavior to their mothers than to randomly matched women. This data does not convincingly show girls to be uniquely similar to their mothers.

Adams and Sarason (1963) compared anxiety scale scores of parents and children. The scores of both boys and girls were related much more to mothers' anxiety scores than to fathers'. Byrne (1965) studied the relationship between scores on the authoritarian scale (F scale) of college students and their parents. Again there was significant similarity between F-scale scores of mothers and children of both sexes. Gray and Klaus (1956) found the mother-daughter relationship on the Allport-Vernon-Lindzey Study of Values was closer than the mother-son relationship, and the correlation of mother-daughter test scores was higher than the father-daughter correlation. Fisher (1948) found that the mother-daughter relationship on the Watson Survey of religious and political preferences and Allport Vernon Study of Values was greater than that of mother-son, father-daughter, or father-son relationships. Reviewing the evidence of family similarities in values, however, she concluded that both sons and daughters appear to be more influenced by mothers than by fathers. While only part of the data from one of three studies shows girls to be more similar to their mothers than to women in general, the data do show them to be more similar to their mothers than to their fathers. However, the fact that sons also tended to be more similar to their mothers than to their fathers weakens the support that this data provides for Freud's theory of same-sex identification.

EVIDENCE OF SEX DIFFERENCES IN SUPEREGO

If one considers Freud's opinion that the female superego is less "inexorable" to mean that women fail to conform to societal requirements as well as men, his contention is difficult to support. At the turn of the century, Ellis (1908) commented on the greater "criminal tendency" in males. Scheinfeld (1944) supported this conclusion with data that there were twenty-five men behind bars for every woman. There are obvious social factors that favor the jailing of males, but the difference is so great that it is probable that a true difference exists. Wallerstein (1947) obtained data from 1700 middle-class adults about "off the record" offenses which they had committed. Sixty-four per cent of the males compared to 29 per cent of the females admitted offenses amounting to felonies under state law. It might be argued that males will admit offenses more readily than females, just as females may more readily admit anxiety. Nonetheless, the data are so clear-cut that any broad generalization of superior superego in males appears entirely untenable.

There are numerous other studies, moreover, relevant to this topic. Oetzel's bibliography of sex differences (1966) listed comparisons from sixteen studies under the heading of moral development. There was no difference between the sexes in six instances; females showed superior moral development in thirteen comparisons; males were significantly superior in three. Under the heading of conformity and suggestibility, Oetzel listed six other studies which had to do with conformity to socially sanctioned values. Again, females were significantly superior in four, boys in one, and no difference was found in two studies.* Contrary to Freudian prediction, the evidence warrants the conclusion that girls and women show less lawless behavior, more conformity, more upset after deviation, and a stronger moral code. There was little or no difference between the sexes in cheating or in Piaget-type judgments of the maturity of moral code.† It should be noted that more conformity is expected of females, especially in the area of sexual behavior (Schoeppe, 1953).

Several studies not included in the Oetzel (1966) bibliography show that females judge social violations more severely than do males. Crissman (1942) found that females rated forty of fifty

*No difference was found in the following studies: Boehm and Nass (1960), two comparisons from Grinder (1964), Luria, Goldwasser, and Goldwasser (1963), Sears, Rau, and Alpert (1965), and Whiteman and Kosier (1964). Girls were significantly superior in at least one comparison from the following studies: Bennett and Cohen (1959), Douvan (1957), McDonald (1963), Rempel and Signoi (1964), Sears, Maccoby, and Levin (1957), and Walters and Demkow (1963); and in two comparisons each from Porteus and Johnson (1965), Rebelsky, Alinsmith, and Grinder (1963), and Sears, Rau, and Alpert (1965). Men and boys were found to be superior in these comparisons: Hartshorne and May (1928), Lansky, Crandall, Kagan, and Baker (1961), and Terman and Miles (1936). Of the studies of conformity to socially sanctioned values, boys were significantly less accepting of the answers of others to test questions in the study of Patel and Gordon (1960). Significantly greater conformity to rules and socially accepted values were found in girls in the following studies: Douvan (1957), Getzels and Walsh (1958), Gill and Spilka (1962), and McGuire (1961). No differences were found in the studies of Crandall and Orleans (1958) and Tuma and Livson (1960). Since Oetzel (1966) girls showed significantly more guilt in the cross-cultural study of Biaggio (1969), and were significantly superior in resisting temptation in the study of Ward and Furchak (1968). Three other studies (Barbu, 1951; Ganley, 1968; and Krebs, 1968) also failed to show male moral superiority, though college girls with high self esteem cheated more in one study (Jacobson, Berger, and Millham, 1969).

†Piaget, and Kohlberg following him, have postulated a series of universal stages in moral development. Level of moral maturity is ascertained by verbal moral reasoning responses.

items more severely than males. Skaggs (1940) found an 80 per cent similarity in the way some 400 male and female college students ranked moral behavior, though women considered sexual relations outside of marriage as more serious than did the men. Eisenman (1967) found that of the extreme scorers on moral judgment, there were significantly more lenient males and significantly more condemning females. In Scotland, Opum (1967) had sixty-seven individuals rate the seven deadly sins. Men were more lenient than women in their ratings of envy and lust. Two studies found no overall sex difference in harshness of moral judgment but that sex of offender is a factor (Richey and Fichter, 1969; Klinger, Albaum, and Hetherington, 1964). Overall, however, this material might be quoted to show that women have a stronger sense of morality.

In this context, a second look at the Terman and Miles study of 1936 appears to be in order. This study has been cited by Kohlberg (1963) and Oetzel (1966) as indicating that males have more sense of justice. The data are based on 554 grade school and high school students and 100 college students. On the basis of an overall survey of the results, it was concluded that the male has more "objective" moral judgment than the female who tends to exaggerate minor offenses. The girls had rated many items as more "wicked" than the boys. It was not concluded that girls are more morally sensitive since women are "more emotional generally." "Moreover, had females been really sterner moralists than males to the extent of the difference in the scores this would have forced itself upon general notice long ago." (Terman and Miles, 1936, p. 404). Thus in the end it was concluded that women are less just than men.

Blum (1949), reasoning from psychoanalytic writings, predicted and found greater guilt feelings and internalization in women. By his reasoning, guilt is presumed to arise from fear of losing the love of the superego, an internalized parental agent. Blum supposed fear of losing love should be more prominent in the psychology of women, since the little girl fears her Oedipal strivings will bring down upon her the jealous rage of her mother. She is thus never so secure in the affection of her mother as is the little boy. Bradford (1968) found no difference between the sexes in castration anxiety, though she found females significantly higher on a measure of anxiety over loss of love. Joseph Rheingold (1964) is of the opinion that the little girl has good reason for her uneasiness; he has given a chilling account of maternal destructiveness directed especially at female children. That girls do feel more rejected than boys is suggested by the finding of Winch (1951) that 41 per cent of the college girls in his large sample reported having the fantasy of being adopted, compared to only 21 per cent of the males.

Sears, Maccoby, and Levin (1957) interviewed 379 mothers of kindergarten children regarding their child-rearing practices. Significantly more girls than boys were found to be high in conscience; girls developed inner control earlier than boys. They found that a precondition of the formation of guilt and conscience for both sexes was a loving relationship with a warm mother. Withdrawal of this love or threat of withdrawal (a sign of disapproval or disappointment) was most effective in conscience formation. Physical punishment was not so effective, but reasoning was found helpful. It is interesting to note that the background of many criminals and delinquents is characterized by large amounts of physical punishment (Bowlby, 1951). At the other extreme, Levy (1966) reported that conscience failed to develop in certain overprotected children. In these cases, the mother almost never frustrated the child but met his every need as quickly as possible.

Kohlberg (1963) reviewed evidence of sex differences in superego and concluded that there was no quantitative difference between the sexes. However in 1966 he stated that, "Where sex differences are found in measures of resistance to temptation or in measures of guilt under conditions of apparent nonsurveillance, the differences are in the direction of a stronger conscience in boys . . ." (Kohlberg, 1966, p. 123). His review, however, only concerned children. He also did not consider very fully the contrast in law violations between the sexes, and he tended to discount some data (conforming to rules and authority, being upset after deviation) as not necessarily indicative of superego. He also found a qualitative sex difference in superego; thirteen-year-old boys were more justice oriented than girls in verbal moral choices. Kohlberg attributes this finding to cultural factors and not to differences in the resolution of the Oedipus complex.

Douvan (1960, 1957) stated that the boys of her national sample of over 3,000 adolescents showed greater concern with establishing internal standards and personal control than did the girls, suggesting that it was more difficult to do so. Boys were more likely to consider rules as external control than to have internalized them. Internalized in this context means to conform because it is believed right rather than merely to evade punishment. Other investigators have also found the male conscience to be more externalized (Siebert, 1966; Blum, 1949). These findings, of course, are also consistent with a weaker male conscience. Nonetheless, Douvan and Adelson (1966), apparently interpreting the same data, expressed the opinion that girls are less likely to act at the behest of principle or abstract justice. It is less a matter of being "good" for abstract, internalized principles and more a matter of retaining the love of others or a good reputation. These authors interpret their findings to support Freud's theory of superego sex differences. They found that a comparison of externalizing and internalizing boys related to their ego control while the same was not true for girls. This is not surprising in view of the fact that they found that control of hostile feelings and sex was not the problem for girls that it was for boys. The girls showed a placid tone with an absence of preoccupation with drives and their control.

Hoffman (1963) has raised the question of sex bias in investigations of moral behavior, pointing out that moral values are tinged with masculinity and that studies often have a paucity of realistic female items. The development of forgiveness and mercy, prominent in the Christian ethic but more identified with feminine than masculine qualities, does not appear to have been studied or even considered as an attribute of ethical development. Not all moral behaviors are equally appropriate to both sex roles. That this variable does make a difference has been demonstrated by Medinnus (1966). Girls showed less resistance to temptation on tasks socially approved for girls and boys showed less resistance to temptation on tasks socially approved for boys.

The study of Haan, Smith, and Block (1968) concluded that development of autonomous, principled morality may be more difficult for women, as it is counter to their role. Their sample of principled college women were dysphoric; they felt that they were a disappointment to their parents. Kohlberg (1963) points out that the role of authority and law is not given to women and that they therefore do not develop themselves in this direction. It might also be added that women are expected to offer solace, not judgment. In situations of conflict, it seems likely that women, more than men, are expected to side with their own children and family regardless of their merit. Women are also given different training as a function of sex role.

An example of an area in which boys receive more training in rules is in the control of bodily aggression. While girls are simply not expected to aggress in this way, there is a very complex set of expectations for boys. Some factors governing proper fisticuffs are the boy's age (little boys are sometimes encouraged to stick up for themselves with bodily aggression, but older ones are not) ; the age, sex, size, condition, and kinship of the other child; the location of the fight; what part of the body it is permissible to hit and with what, and what constitutes justifiable provocation. Furthermore, these rules vary with other factors such as social class, religion, political views of parent, and region of the United States.

One might interpret Freud's comments about sex differences in superego as referring only to the strength of the internal structure of the superego (Reik, 1960) . Even though in males the conscience fails more often, the absolute size or development of the conscience, at least in some areas, might be greater. There is evidence that males have stronger aggressive and sexual urges (see Chapters 2 and 8) . A more powerful machine may, in effect, require more powerful brakes. Generally speaking, it would be considered laughable to teach women restraint in the use of physical violence. Women rarely punch; therefore they are not taught to pull their punches. Thus, on the unusual occasions when they are moved to violence, there is no prior buildup of restraint. As mentioned before, boys more often are subjected to a whole set of expectations governing bodily aggression. Ellis (1908) commented on the greater physical violence of female mental patients and this observation is still part of the lore of psychiatric hospitals. Perhaps it is attributable to the sex differences in aggression training.

Hall (1964) found that males dream more often that misfortunes befall them and females dream more often that they are victims of aggression. From this, he has concluded that males have a more internalized superego and females have a more externalized, weaker superego as Freud averred. The logic and validity of this conclusion is not entirely apparent.

Brodbeck (1954) utilized a different test of Freud's hypothesis of superego formation. He reasoned that if internalization of values arises solely as a result of resolution of the Oedipus complex by identification with the parent of the same sex, then one should expect to find values mostly sex-typed. The hypothesis was not confirmed. Fisher (1948) reviewed the evidence regarding family similarities in values as was mentioned previously. There was no clear indication that mothers influenced daughters more than sons or that fathers influenced sons more than daughters. Fisher concluded that both sons and daughters are more influenced by their mothers than by their fathers and that certainly there is no support for the notion of greater paternal than maternal influence in superego formation, as some have interpreted Freud's writings to mean. Kohlberg (1969) also concluded that expected relations between measures of identification with same-sex parent and measures of moral and sex-role maturity have not been found. Bennett and Cohen (1959) concluded that their extensive data suggested extreme similarity between masculine and feminine thinking, with the feminine mode basic for both groups. In addition to this large core of shared values, males had some extra ones which served to differentiate them from the females. Blum (1949) also found no evidence of a fatherly superego for either sex. The superego of both sexes showed influence from both parents. However, significantly more males than females attributed fatherly characteristics to the superego, and significantly more females than males attributed motherly characteristics to the superego.

Lampl-de Groot (1933) saw that if girls are first attached to the mother and then to the father, they might be described as having had a double Oedipus complex. In resolving these, they would identify with both parents and thus take on the superego of both parents. Such a superego she thought would ordinarily be lacking in stability and uniformity, and the double identification would be likely to result in internal conflict. This concept is similar to that of Mowrer (1950) in supposing that double identification results in conflict. While double identifications may be a source of conflict, the evidence already reviewed suggests that it is quite frequent for children to share their values with both parents. It is not clear, however, that these shared values represent unique identifications; they may instead represent exposure to a common culture.

EVIDENCE OF A LATENCY PERIOD

Freud supposed that with the resolution of the Oedipus complex and identification with the parent of the same sex, the child enters what he called the latency period. The latency period has been given somewhat different interpretations. The most usual one is of sexual disinterest, but it has also been considered merely a period during which no significant psychosexual modification takes place. Discussions of the latency period frequently emphasize the sex composition of the social groupings. Maintenance of like-sexed groups is taken as evidence of a latency period. The child-development text of Mussen, Conger, and Kagan (1969), for example, points out that children from ages seven to eleven associate primarily with same-sex peers, and that this pattern is common in other cultures, and also found in infra-human primate species.

Freud supposed that the energies freed during the latency period allow the child to acquire knowledge and skills. He believed that it is not accidental that the beginning of the latency period, age six, coincides with the beginning of formal schooling. The latency period has been variously quoted as from age six or seven to eleven or twelve. Just as it was the anthropologists who first challenged the universality of the Oedipus complex, it was also they who objected to the assumption of a universal latency period in the sense of sexual disinterest. Mead (1958) concluded, however, that there is "pretty good evidence" of a latency period for boys in most societies, but that the latency was stronger in boys than in girls in all societies she had observed except the Tchambuli society (the society showing reversal of sex-typical roles).

Observations in our culture indicate that the latency period is a relative matter (Alpert, 1941), and that disruption of latency, evidenced by plentiful sexual activity, is not invariably accompanied by poor scholarship (Bender and Cramer, 1949). Hamilton (1929) reported that 76 of his 100 male subjects and 68 of his 100 female subjects reported love interests between the ages of six and eleven. Thirty-seven of the men and 60 of the women reported data showing evidence of some sort of latency period. Campbell (1939) studied children in the Merrill-Palmer Clubs. She found no sharp break in heterosexual associations in the six- to eight-year-old group or at the beginning of puberty. Instead, for girls there was a gradual development of sex-consciousness between the years of nine and eleven. This development was characterized first by rejection and avoidance of the opposite sex, then shy acceptance, and finally whole-hearted seeking at fifteen. As evidence against a latency period, Kohlberg (1969) cited the findings of Bernick (1965) that latency-age children show pupil dilation to pictures of the opposite sex. Also providing no support for the latency period is the study of Gelford (1952). Sears (1943) concluded that there was no data to indicate whether the relatively smaller amount of sexual behavior in American and European children than in certain primitive groups is a function of the suppression of the Oedipus reaction or whether it is a function of increased effort at nonsexual socialization, partly through formalized schooling and partly through specific control of sex behavior by authority.

The study of Broderick and Fowler (1961) suggests that if there is a latency period, it does not extend past age nine. They found 74 to 86 per cent of a sample of 264 fifth, sixth, and seventh grade children claimed to have a sweetheart. In fifth grade, 45 per cent of boys and 36 per cent of girls had had some dating experience; by seventh grade the percentages were 70 per cent of the boys and 53 per cent of the girls. To some extent, one wonders if there is not now a cultural counterlatency force whereas previously there was cultural enforcement of a latency period. Kinsey (1965) concluded there is no evidence of a biological latency.

Part of Friedman's test (1952) of the castration and Oedipus hypotheses rested on the assumption of a latency period, and once again this study is one of the few supporting Freudian theory. As predicted, he did find significantly less evidence of castration anxiety in males during the latency ages compared to both earlier and later ages. Girls, however, failed to show a significant difference between the early period and latency, though the comparison between latency and the adolescent period was significant. Friedman's data thus supplies some support for the latency period.

While it seems clear that same-sex association is typical during the ages of the latency period, heterosexual activity and interest do not universally cease. It is certainly true that sexual activity is not so great during this period as it is later. Whether this relative quiescence could be the result of renunciation of the Oedipus complex seems unlikely. In the case of females, since an Oedipus complex has never been established as a typical occurrence, and since sexual activity does not increase drastically at puberty (see Chapter 8), one wonders whether the concept of the latency period is even relevant.

SUMMARY

The whole discussion of the Oedipus complex is grossly oversimplified in concentrating on only three individuals. Fortunately, the emotional sphere of most families is considerably broader immediately resulting in an emotional dilution which does not favor such convoluted developments. There is very little evidence of the female Oedipus complex, though the question has not been sufficiently studied. The existing studies point more toward the importance of the mother-daughter attachment. While there is some evidence of a sexualized father-daughter relationship, it seems doubtful that the Oedipus complex, when it exists in girls, arises largely out of the child's sexual motivation. Moreover, the concept of the Oedipus complex condenses several developmental tasks which might better be considered separately. These are as follows: (a) recognition and acceptance of age status, (b) the problem of renouncing sensual gratification (especially snuggling) from the mother, (c) recognition and acceptance of sex status, and (d) adoption of a general moral framework. (See discussion of Parsons in the following chapter.) The prevalence of resentment and refusal to accept age status, i.e. status as a child, has often been mistaken for evidence of the sexualized motivation of the Oedipus complex.

So far as resolution of the Oedipus complex is concerned, since there is so little evidence of a female Oedipus complex, it is not at all clear that there is anything to resolve. While it is widely supposed that girls identify with their mothers, it is not clear that they have any unique, exclusive identification with them. Contrary to Freud's opinion, a review of the evidence indicates that if any generalization is to be made, females, not males, have the stronger superego, though Kohlberg (1963, 1966) has arrived at the opposite conclusion. Females show more superego in the sense of less lawless behavior, more conformity, stronger moral code, more upset after deviation, and anticipating punishment from an internal rather than an external source. Females also tend to judge social violations more severely. Douvan and Adelson (1966) and Kohlberg (1969, 1963) concluded that adolescent boys show greater justice than adolescent girls, though unlike the former, Kohlberg does not interpret his finding to support Freud's view of superego sex differences. The evidence and interpretations reviewed suggest that it will be important to direct more attention to the problem of sex bias and to the relationship between sex role and various moral behaviors.

The evidence pertinent to same sex typing of values fails to show the sex typing expected from Freud's theory. Aside from the Blum (1949) data, the other data including the Fisher (1948) and Kohlberg (1969) reviews do not show same-sex-parent value typing. The evidence is more consistent with greater maternal influence for both sexes, though both parents appear to influence the standards and values of their children of both sexes. It is extremely doubtful that males, much less females, are motivated to adopt standards of behavior because of their fear of castration (Sears, Rau, and Alpert, 1965). Fear of loss of love has more support as a motivation for moral learning. Kohlberg (1969) concluded, however, that only a certain minimal positive relationship is required and that moral development is not a continuous function of this variable. The latency period appears to be much less biological and universal than Freud supposed. The cultural influence on latency is well attested by changed American mores of the last generations.

Chapter 5

MORAL AND SEX-ROLE DEVELOPMENT: OTHER THEORIES

FREUD'S THEORY of how girls acquire their sexual identity and moral values is clearly not very satisfactory. In this chapter, the following viewpoints will be considered: Parsons from sociology, Kohlberg representing the Piaget school, and social learning theory represented by some empirical work on the development of sex role. It is not possible to review all the important literature on sexual and moral identification because that would direct attention from the main theme of the psychology of women per se.*

DEFINITIONS AND DISTINCTIONS

The literature on identification is a maze of terms and theoretical variations. Stoller (1968) in disgust decided to ignore the whole concept. While defining terms has been a time-honored device for resolving these difficulties, it is actually less useful than one might suppose in a review of this kind, since various authors use terms in different ways, not always explicit. However, it would

*Goslin's (1969) *Handbook of Socialization Theory and Research* contains several articles on aspects of identification research with lengthy reviews and bibliographies by Aronfreed, Bandura, Gewirtz, Kohlberg, and Mussen. These would be helpful to the reader looking for more general treatments of the topic. Some of the view points not being considered in detail include the following: (a) Gewirtz (1969); (Gewirtz and Stingle, 1968), who considers identification to be generalized imitation explainable by simple learning concepts. (b) Mowrer (1950, 1960), who postulates that imitation, especially of vocal behavior, occurs because cues from the model's behaviors have acquired reinforcing value through pairing with primary reinforcers. Their imitation has secondary reinforcement value for the copier, thus maintaining the behavior. (c) Bandura (1962, 1965, 1969) who emphasizes observational learning. Matching behaviors are acquired by exposure to the model without necessity of reinforcement. (d) Aronfreed (1968, 1969), who talks of identification based on a cognitive template. Like Bandura he stresses observational learning, and like Kohlberg (1969), he accepts the view of the intrinsic reinforcement of responses. (g) Other important approaches to identification include Bronfenbrenner (1960), Maccoby (1959), Kagan (1958), Sanford (1955), Sears (1957), Sears, Rau, and Alpert (1965), and Whiting (1960).

appear to be beneficial to consider some fundamental distinctions. "Imitation" is to copy the behavior of someone else. Behavior learned by imitation may be modified by experience. It is fairly well agreed that identification is more total than imitation. Identification has been described as generalized imitation (Gewirtz, 1969; Gewirtz and Stingle, 1968). To Parsons (Parsons and Shils, 1959), it involves internalizing a cognitive map, while Aronfreed (1969, 1968) speaks of internalizing a cognitive template, a pattern of behaviors. Kohlberg (1969) contrasts his position on identification with Freud's by saying that Freud views identification as permanent and achieved at a young age, while he (Kohlberg) does not. Kohlberg's description of Freud's view takes into account only his hypothesis of identification as a way of resolving the Oedipus complex. In later writings, Freud indicated that he did not limit identification to a permanent introjection of the same-sex parent at the time of the resolution of the Oedipus complex (Freud, 1951). Freud's later view of identification provides the starting point for Parsons' theory of identification (Parsons, 1958).

There is little agreement about motivation for identification. Freud mentioned the following two sorts of motivation: (a) fear of castration, also called identification with the aggressor and (b) fear of loss of love, also called anaclitic identification or developmental identification (Mowrer, 1950). Kohlberg (1969) emphasizes perceived similarity and competence (White, 1959) as motivation for identification. Parsons (Parsons and Shils, 1959) included the necessity of attachment to the model in his concept of identification. He uses identification to refer to the learning of *both* sides of a role relationship. A boy internalizes what his mother and father are like and also how he is expected to act in relation to his mother and father. Obviously not all these identifications are expressed in behavior at the same time.

"Internalization" is sometimes used by learning theorists merely to mean something was learned. As with the term "identification," the Freudian-derived theorists, including Parsons, intend some idea of acceptance in their use of the term "internalize." It is not merely to know but to take as one's own. The extreme example of lack of internalization is the psychopath who knows very well how people should behave but has no motivation to act in that way. He has not internalized values. Kohlberg uses the term "internalized" with still a different connotation, one implying orientation to a set of universal principles rather than merely acceptance of standards. "Introject" or sometimes the word "incorporate" are Freudian terms that mean to take into the personality. Argyle (1964) analyzes introjection as a special form of social learning. These terms (imitation, identification, internalization, introjection) refer to the mechanisms, sometimes with implied motives, for acquiring important behaviors. In Freud's theory, both sexual and moral orientation are acquired in this way. In Parsons' theory, the cognitive frame of reference for interpersonal relations and the common system of expressive symbolism are also acquired in this way.

Parsons (1964) does not see the need for the distinction between the ego (executive self) and the superego, and in general, theoretical and research interest has shifted from the superego to ego control functions (Grim, Kohlberg, and White, 1968). Bandura and Walters (1963) also concluded that the term "superego" is superfluous. Aronfreed (1968) hardly used the term in his entire monograph, *Conduct and Conscience*. Like Bandura and Walters (1963), Kohlberg has not been impressed with the generality and longitudinal stability of moral character (Kohlberg, 1964, 1969). While the cohesion and unity suggested by Freud's conceptualization of the superego is no longer accepted, the evidence does appear to support a modest degree of consistency (Barbu, 1951; Nelson, Grinder, and Mutterer, 1969). Superego refers to a group of behaviors internalized together at a particular period of time and as a result of identification with the same sex parent. Freud used the concept because he observed that this part of the personality tended to split off from the rest in certain abnormal mental reactions. He saw the personality as getting into conflict with itself, for example, in superego-id battles (conflicts between moral values and impulse strivings). Because later theorists have not been so interested in abnormal behavior or have denied that data from abnormal reactions are relevant to formation of normal personality, they have not been inclined to retain the term. Furthermore, it has been shown that moral behavior can be learned in other ways than by identification. In fact, as seen from the last chapter, the evidence is not at all clear that same-sex parents are most influential in value formation. For these and other reasons, theoretical focus has now shifted to behaviors such as resistance to temptation, postponement of immediate reward, regulation of self-administered rewarding resources, confession and upset after deviation, and maturity of moral code.

Like the term "superego," "sexual identification" has proven to be too global a term to be useful for research purposes or for any precise purpose. This facet of psychological research has been much influenced by sociological theory (Linton, 1942). The concept of sex role and sex-role learning has become of more importance in research than sexual identification. A role refers to a prescribed set of behaviors and attitudes expected of a group of people in a given culture. It is necessary to distinguish between sex-role preference, sex-role adoption, and sex-role performance (Brown and Lynn, 1966). Sex-role preference refers to which sex role is preferred and is independent of which sex role is adopted and/or performed. For example, in Chapter 3, studies were reviewed showing that the male sex role tends to be preferred by males and females alike. However, while many females prefer the male role, they do not adopt it nor do they perform it. "Sexual identity" is usually employed to mean what sex an individual considers himself to be; Stoller (1968) uses the term "nuclear identity" for this concept.

Talcott Parsons

Parsons is a sociologist, but perhaps above all else, he is a theorist. He aspires to no less than a unifying theory of the social sciences. It is therefore not surprising that his work in the area of psychology is not highly specific and detailed. He has the reputation of being a difficult writer, but his work is stimulating and evocative. His theory shows definite signs of psychoanalytic influence. Perhaps the most original aspect of his psychological theorizing resulted from his attempt to apply what had been learned about the functioning of small groups to an analysis of the family (Parsons and Bales, 1955). The nuclear family is viewed as a small group. One individual is the "idea" man with greater "instrumental" specialization (the husband-father), and one individual has the greater "expressive" specialization of the "best-liked" man (wife-mother).

Johnson (1963) has provided a more detailed description of the instrumental-expressive distinction. The feminine expressive role is characterized by giving rewarding responses in order to receive rewarding responses. A woman is supposed to be oriented to relationships among people, toward the self and others. By being solicitous, appealing, and understanding, a woman seeks to get a pleasurable response by giving pleasure. The instrumental (masculine) role is defined by a behavioral orientation toward goals which transcend the immediate interactional situation. The interaction is viewed as a means to an end; therefore the instrumental role player is not primarily oriented to the immediate emotional responses of others to him. Rather than soliciting positive responses, instrumental role playing requires ability to tolerate the hostility which it will very likely elicit. The instrumental role player deals with relations outside the system. In terms of the family, the father would be expected to take the lead in relations outside the family, while the mother would be more active within the family. Notice that Parsons sees the parental role distinction as a relative one; father is more instrumental and mother is more expressive.

Zelditch (1955) confirmed this general role division in a cross-cultural comparative study. Strodtbeck and Mann (1956) studied the spontaneous behavior of twelve mixed-sex juries. The men were found to initiate long bursts of activity aimed at solution of the task problem; the women tended more to react to the contributions of others. The women showed a social-emotional emphasis while the men showed a task emphasis. The authors concluded that sex role constitutes a slight but persistent continuity, and that sex-typed differentiation in interaction role can be reliably demonstrated.

Levinger (1964) found that recently married couples divided

the instrumental tasks of marriage involving the manipulation of objects (repairing things around the house, doing evening dishes, and paying the bills), but contrary to Parsons' views, they shared the social-emotional tasks in the marriage more or less equally. Levinger attributed these findings to the fact that between two people, social-emotional behavior is ultimately reciprocal. If the husband does not participate, the system breaks down. As mother in the large family subsystem of parents and children, she can play the role of the expressive leader, but as wife she cannot. Objections have also been raised that the comparative abilities of a couple influence their instrumental and expressive functions (Dahlström and Liljeström, 1967). Two American studies report failure to confirm the instrumental-expressive sex distinction (Machotka and Ferber, 1967; Staus, 1967). The former authors observed thirty-three families and concluded that the expressive and instrumental terms characterize different activities each parent performs at different times of the day and week rather than separate spheres of activity divided between them.

It might well be that Parsons himself would not disagree with these conclusions since (a) he stated that the distinction was a relative matter, (b) he has stated that the mother has the primary internal instrumental responsibility in the family (Parsons, 1953), and (c) while the mother is more expressive in the overall family situation, she is more instrumental than expressive in relation to the child (Parsons and Bales, 1955). Obviously Parsons intends only the most general and overlapping distinction between the sexes. After struggling to apply these concepts in research, Weaver (1969) wryly concluded that instrumentalness is probably not accurately interpreted as a factor of personality but will prove to be more valid for role theory than for personality theory. Parsons, however, does use the distinction in describing the development of personality. He sees boys as giving more importance to the instrumental need dispositions of adequacy and conformity compared to the expressive need dispositions of security and nurturance which he considers to be dominant for females.

Parsons sees two important axes in the structure of the nuclear family. These are as follows: (a) the instrumental-expressive continuum expressed in sex-role differentiation and (b) power expressed in the age-generational dimension. Thus during the Oedipus phase, Parsons sees the child as not only learning his sex category but also learning his age category, i.e. that he is a child and not an adult. Parsons, much more than Freud, stresses the importance of overcoming infantile dependency. In fact, he thought that the incest taboo is basically made necessary by the fact that eroticism is tied to infantile dependency and the two are repressed together. Thus, eroticism may not safely be aroused until much later in life and then only with a different object. Because of the father's greater involvement with the outside world and the less infantile, dependent quality of the child's relation to him, he plays a pivotal role for both sexes in providing transition from dependency to the outside world (Parsons, 1964). (In Skinnerian terms, he provides a way of fading out infantile dependency responses. Regardless of the mother's personal qualities, her role as infant nurturer makes it inevitable that it will be easier for father than for her to perform this task.)

Parsons' concept of identification is not of a single event but of repeated events. Not only is the role of the other internalized, but the reciprocal role is internalized as well.* The individual may express either the role or its reciprocal in behavior at different times during the life cycle. At any given stage in the child's development, he identifies not with the parent as a total person, but with the reciprocal role-relationship functional for the child at that particular time. A very simple personality structure is first established through internalization of a single social object, the mother. While both sexes first identify with the mother, this identification is not sex-typed. Identification must involve a cognitive map and an attitude of attachment to the model. As development proceeds, identifications and differentiations occur through a series of stages. The "ego's personality" is a complex system of patterned action subsystems which relate to "n alters" (the various significant other persons in the individual's life) and not only alters as individuals but as categories (e.g. mother-figure, teacher,

*Reciprocal role identification may be a normal equivalent of the kind of behavior Freud classed as transference and Sullivan called parataxic distortion.

old man, etc.) (Bronfenbrenner, 1961; Parsons, 1958; Parsons and Bales, 1955; and Parsons and Shils, 1959.) Unlike Freud, Parsons stresses that during identification, the cognitive frame of reference for interpersonal relations and the common system of expressive symbolism are also internalized. Sex role is an example of a cognitive reference system. It is important to note that Parsons does not see the mother as inculcating a feminine system in the daughter and the father inculcating a masculine system in the sons. He believes the husband and wife, while sharing common values, participate differently in the implementation of subcategories of the overall shared value system (Parsons and Bales, 1955).

Johnson (1963) has proposed that the crucial factor in learning the masculine sex role for males *and* the feminine sex role for females is identification (in Parsons's meaning of the term) with the father. She presumes that while the father is capable of both instrumental and expressive behavior, the mother is capable of only expressive behavior. The latter statement appears to be in contradiction with Parsons' statements about the instrumental role mothers play vis à vis their children (Parsons and Bales, 1955). Johnson's idea is that by behaving in an instrumental way with his boys and an expressive way with his girls, the father sets the course of sex-role development for both sexes. She found no difference in the way 105 female students and 131 male students viewed their mothers, but the females saw their fathers as more expressive than did the males. Heilbrun (1965a) found that identification (in the sense of similarity) with the instrumental father produced the most appropriate sex typing in terms of both sexes. It did not appear, however, that girls who identified with an expressive mother were any less well sex typed than those identified with an instrumental father. Daughters identified with (similar to) expressive mothers had more passive qualities and were described as more extremely expressive.

It is interesting, and certainly contrary to Freudian theory, that father-identified (father-similar) girls were appropriately sex typed, but as Heilbrun pointed out, it is identification with the *reciprocal* role of the father that Johnson considers crucial to sex-role development. A more direct test of the hypothesis that reciprocal role identification with the father is crucial to the sex-role development of the girls might use data from father-daughter interactions. Daughters of fathers who related to them in instrumental fashion would be expected to be the most masculine, or only masculine, group of girls, while daughters of fathers who related to them expressively would be expected to be the most feminine, or only feminine, group of girls. In fact, though, there is evidence that a warm (expressive) relationship with the father tends to masculinize girls (Lynn, 1962; Sears, 1965; Wright and Taska, 1966). In general, Johnson would appear to be overstating her case if she supposes that the father is as crucial to appropriate sex-role behavior for the girl as for the boy or that the father is *more* crucial for the girl than the mother (see Chapter 4). Several studies show greater father influence on sex typing in boys than in girls (Hetherington, 1965; Mitchell, 1966; Santrock, 1970; Sears, Pintler, and Sears, 1946).

On the other hand, sex-typing in girls was found related to the amount of encouragement the father gave to feminine activities (Mussen and Rutherford, 1963). Furthermore, Johnson (1963) and Heilbrun (1965a, 1968) point out that several studies show that normal females, as well as normal males, identify in important respects with their fathers, that female identification with (similarity to) the father does not necessarily mean masculinity, and that a feminine identification is not necessarily adjustive (Cosentino and Heilbrun, 1964; Emmerich, 1959; Gray, 1959; Heilbrun, 1960, 1962; Helper, 1955; Johnson, 1955; Osgood, Suci, and Tannenbaum, 1957; Sopchak, 1952). Douvan and Adelson (1966) reported that adolescent boys chose their fathers as models *less* than girls. Father was chosen as a model by 31 per cent of boys at age fourteen, dropping to 18 per cent at age sixteen, while 35 per cent of girls chose father as a model at age fourteen, dropping to 30 per cent at age sixteen and to 24 per cent at age eighteen. Heilbrun and Fromme (1965) found that adjusted girls were identified with low-feminine mothers, while maladjusted girls (in counseling) were identified with highly feminine mothers. These findings indicate the possible significance of the father as an identification figure for girls. They are also consistent with the positive relationship found between stereotyped masculinity and competence and stereotyped femininity and incompetence (Broverman, Broverman, Clarkson, Rosencrantz, and Vogel, 1970).

However, Heilbrun (1968) points out that while feminine females showed somewhat poorer adjustment, being masculine did not signify mental health either. He found about the same proportion of masculine to feminine girls in a maladjusted group as in a nonclient group. There was very little difference between the feminine girls who had sought counseling and those who had not. Compared to the nonclients, however, the maladjusted masculine girls were significantly less need-achieving, dominant, enduring, and exhibitionistic. They were more succorant and abasing. Apparently they were less instrumental than the better-adjusted masculine girls, and more socially alienated, while at the same time needing succorance and support from others. Their masculinity appeared in the guise of social independence. Heilbrun points out that of the 14 normal, feminine girls, 9 were identified with feminine mothers, 2 with feminine fathers, and 3 with masculine fathers. "The predominant identification pattern for mediating a feminine sex-role identity in better-adjusted girls was with the feminine mother." (Heilbrun, 1968, p. 135). Presumably these mothers were not stereotypically highly feminine women (cf. Heilbrun and Fromme, 1965). Klein and Gould (1969) found that alienated college women who scored high in acquiescence, social introversion, and admission of psychopathology, did not identify with either parent. Identification was measured by response similarity on an attitude questionnaire. The unalienated girls identified more with their mothers than with their fathers, and in contrast to the alienated girls, they reported a positive perception of their mother and appropriate sex-role differentiation in the way their parents had treated them. They saw their mothers as less ignoring and less dominating. This study again suggests that in studying the contribution of the father to the girl's sex-role development, it will be well not to overstate the case to exclude the mother's role.

Parsons' best known and perhaps most widely misinterpreted contribution to the understanding of the psychology of women is his generalization that women tend to take the expressive role, while men tend to take the instrumental role, especially in dealings outside the family. Too often, Parsons' interpreters have placed the emphasis on the expressive-instrumental distinction as an inherent quality of an individual rather than of a role. Such an emphasis does not do justice to the subtlety and complexity of Parsons' theory. The expressive-instrumental distinction used in this global way adds only a handy, stereotypic term to what is already known about sex differences in personality (see Chapter 2). A more fruitful result for psychology of Parsons' theorizing has been to focus on the father-daughter relationship as it affects sex-role development.

Cognitive-Developmental Psychology

Psychology is not Parsons' primary interest, nor is it Piaget's. For Piaget, the study of how children think, play, and imitate serves primarily to shed light on problems of genetic epistemology. This erudite Swiss has a large bibliography (1970); Flavell (1963) has provided a useful and reliable introduction to this work. Like Freud, Piaget aims for a universal delineation of development, and like Freud, he uses the concept of stages of development. Stages of development imply hierarchical, invariant sequences of qualitative change. Unlike Freud, Piaget's emphasis is decidedly on normal development especially of cognition. He views development as a continuing series of organismic structural changes wrought by the interaction of an innate unfolding with the intrusive demands of the environment. Unlike American psychologists, Piaget has been almost totally disinterested in the problems of individual differences. As a result, he has not focused on sex differences or on problems particular to female development. An American, Kohlberg, working within Piaget's framework, has considered some matters of interest including the question of sex differences in moral functioning discussed in the last chapter. In this section, Kohlberg's other ideas will be presented in the context of his theoretical orientation.

In contrast to most learning-theory accounts of development, Kohlberg (1969) assumes that development cannot be explained by associationistic learning but by transformations of cognitive structure involving parameters of organizational wholes or systems of internal relations. His assumption of innate cognitive structures allows some rapprochement with Chomsky's (1968) assumption of innate language structure. His contention that imitation is motivated by a desire to create interesting consequences articulates with White's notion of competence (White, 1959). Use of role concepts is consistent with Parsons' theory. Cognitive-developmental theory is thus enjoying a favorable confluence of ideas.

In regard to moral development, neither Piaget nor Kohlberg has been much concerned regarding the relationship between judgments regarding moral issues and behavior. Guilt and conformity do not show regular age progression as do cognitive judgments on moral issues; as a result, guilt and conformity hold much less interest for Kohlberg (1969). This characteristic stance partially accounts for the difference between the present author and Kohlberg in conclusions regarding sex differences in moral development (see Chapter 4). Kohlberg (1969) divides moral development into six stages; not everyone is expected to arrive at the last stages. The first stage is one of orientation to obedience and punishment, an egocentric deference to superior power or prestige, or a trouble-avoiding set. The second stage includes an element of naive egalitarianism and orientation to exchange and reciprocity. Piaget, unlike Kohlberg, stresses the importance of peer relationships in developing reciprocity. The third stage is characterized as the "good-boy" orientation. Emphasis is on conformity, though judgment of intention is taken into account. The fourth stage is one of maintaining authority and social order for its own sake. The fifth stage involves a contractual legalistic orientation. There is a recognition of an arbitrary element or starting point in rules or expectations for the sake of agreement. There is a general avoidance of violation of the will or rights of others and majority will and welfare. The sixth stage is that of conscience or principle orientation. Orientation is not merely to rules but to chosen principles involving appeal to logical universality and consistency. Mutual respect and trust are seen as important, and orientation is to the conscience as a directing agent. Kohlberg (1969) states that girls reach good-girl (Stage 3) morality earlier than boys and persist in it longer so that as adults, most Stage-3 persons are female. He believes that this happens because girls are forced to differentiate the prestige of goodness from the prestige of power in defining their own sex roles. According to Kohlberg, this good-girl morality is associated with an idealized love relationship to the father, first found in girls at age seven to eight, rather than in the Oedipal (three to five) period.*

Sex-role development, as Kohlberg views it, is turned topsy turvy. Girls do not become girls because they identify with or model after their mothers; they model after their mothers because they have realized that they are girls. Like Johnson (1963), however, Kohlberg (1966) stresses identification with the reciprocal or complementary role of the father in the sex-role development of the girl. He believes that identification with the (father) complementary role is more important in the girl's development than is identification with the (mother) complementary role for the boy. In Kohlberg's view, both sexes define themselves in terms of the father's acceptance and approval.

Kohlberg (1966) argues that the stability of sexual identity depends upon the cognitive ability to understand the sex-role category and the principle of conservation. Understanding that one is a girl and will always be a girl is merely one part of a general stabilization of constancies of physical objects that takes place between the ages of three and seven. Kohlberg (1966) points out that the ability to label oneself boy or girl at age two or three does not mean that the child understands sex categories; this requires a more abstract cognitive capacity. Kohlberg reports substantial correlations ($r = .52$ to $.73$) between tasks measuring gender identity and other conservation tasks. Kohlberg considers intelligence, as opposed to physiological development or age-graded socialization pressure, as the single most important general de-

*Unfortunately, Kohlberg's ideas on female development are not elaborated in readily available published form as yet.

terminant of regular age developmental trends. Holding chronological age constant, Kohlberg and Zigler (1967) found that mental age correlated with sex-role development. The validity of this interpretation rests on the assumption that physiologic maturity and mental maturity are virtually uncorrelated. Not everyone would agree with this assumption (Ljung, 1965; Tanner, 1962).

Kohlberg emphasizes the active, valuing character of children; he believes that because they preferentially value their own sex, they are motivated to appropriate sex-role behavior. Kohlberg questions whether sex-role behavior can be influenced by reinforcement. He supposes that children comprehend their proper sexual identity and sex-role behavior as an adaptation to social reality. Kohlberg found that four- to five-year-old children were aware that only males play the extrafamilial roles (policeman, soldier, fireman, robber, etc.) involving violence and danger, and by ages six to seven, nearly all of a small sample of American children were aware that high-power roles (President, policemen, general) are male roles. He concludes there is basic clarity about sex-role differences before there is clarity about genital differences. Sex-role concepts he believes are cross-cultural universals which children are able to perceive; he does not believe sex-role concepts differ substantially from culture to culture. While the general proposition that males are cross-culturally perceived to be more active, powerful, and aggressive can be supported (see Chapter 2), there are differences in sex-role behavior between cultures, even between social classes in the United States. Some of this material is discussed later in this chapter and in Chapters 2, 3, and 8.

It seems clear that Kohlberg has established the point that constancy in gender identity is related to cognitive development. Since more specific details of his theory of female development should soon be published, it seems premature to make any further critical evaluation of Kohlberg's theories at this time. He is a nimble, energetic, and provocative theorist. His viewpoints tend to be fresh and original on the American scene though his views and assumptions are sure to evoke vigorous dissent.

EMPIRICAL STUDIES OF SEX ROLE

The problems of women, their satisfactions, and particularly their role problems have been ably discussed by Beauvoir (1949), Benedict (1938), Epstein (1970), Friedan (1963), Komarovsky (1953), Mead (1935, 1955), and Myrdal and Klein (1968), to mention only a few of the books on the topic. The concept of sex role has also been the subject of considerable psychological research, and there is now a large body of studies devoted to the development of acceptance and mastery of the sex role. Most of these studies are guided by the idea that sex role is learned. They have been reviewed by Kagan (1964), Spencer (1967), and Tyler (1965). Some material relevant to the sex-role concept has already been considered in Chapter 3.

Less Role Acceptance Among Girls

It would appear that women and girls do not accept their role as readily as males, i.e. they show less preference for their role. Oetzel's bibliography (1966) listed twenty studies of sex-role acceptance; the boys and men showed significantly greater sex-role acceptance as defined by these various measures and studies in fifteen instances.* Also consistent with this conclusion is the study of Ward (1968) who found that boys preferred boys' toys significantly more than girls preferred girls' toys. These findings are consistent with the material discussed on sex-role envy, and masculine protest.

There are those who believe that females are more certain of their sexual identity, or nuclear sex identity as Stoller (1968) calls it. Sexual identity in the sense of what sex a child considers himself to be has been thought to be established by the age of two or three, and rarely altered afterward without psychological conflict (Hampson and Hampson, 1961). It is at about this time that children begin to discriminate the two sex roles. For example,

---

*If one excludes studies using the Brown It Scale, which does not appear to be a valid measure of sex-role preference for girls (Hartup and Zook, 1960; Sher and Lansky, 1968), there are seventeen studies of sex-role acceptance listed with males showing greater acceptance in twelve. Also see Chapter 3.

children from thirty to forty months of age were able to sort artifacts of sex role with 75 per cent accuracy (Vener, 1966).

Women and girls could be more certain of their nuclear sexual identity without this fact being contradictory to the evidence on sex-role acceptance. To be quite clear in one's nuclear sex identity is very different from happily accepting all aspects of the cultural role prescribed for that sex. A girl may know very well that she is a girl, but she may not like it. Lynn (1962) has suggested that girls may originally be more strongly identified with the female role than boys with the male role but that cultural influences, especially recognition of the greater status of the male role, leads to erosion of role acceptance in girls and strengthening of role acceptance in boys. This may be true and it is an inviting thesis, but the data do not strongly support it, since males seem to prefer the male role more than females prefer the female role as early as ages two to five (Oetzel, 1966). Lynn (1962) cited several studies to support the view that satisfaction with the female role fades as little girls grow older, and results from Norway (Brun-Gulbrandsen, 1967) detailed in Chapter 3 also support it. Kohlberg (1966) found support for this view with the It Scale, but not with another measure. The findings of Ward (1969) do not support it. Kohlberg suggested that the invalidity for girls of the Brown It Test (See footnote) may have distorted research results in the direction of girls appearing to have less female sex role preference as they grow older. In general, however, the data do seem to indicate that adult women are less pleased with their role than are girls.

The argument might be raised that surely it is the males who are more poorly adjusted to their sex role, since sexual deviations are so much more common in males than in females. But again sex-object choice and sex-role choice can be two different things. There are some very "masculine" male homosexuals (Hooker, 1965). Gebhard (1965) pointed out that it is the difference in strength of the sex drive that probably accounts for greater male sexual "perversions" of all kinds. He believes that "perversions" may sometimes be established by one trial learning under strong drive conditions. If he is correct, the mechanisms producing sex-role acceptance and those producing homosexuality are largely unrelated.

Factors Influencing Sex Typing

Sears (1965) concluded that an upbringing restrictive of sensual and aggressive gratifications contributes to the feminization of both sexes and that the affectionate intrusion of the father into the girl's rearing tends to masculinize her. The masculinizing influence of a warm father, especially when accompanied by a cold mother is supported by studies of two very disparate age groups (Lynn, 1962; Wright and Taska, 1966). Of a group of sixty girls, five to seven years old, Lynn studied the forty girls who received the most extreme scores on the Brown It Scale, a test of sex-role preference. She found that the highly feminine group attributed more warmth to parents than the low feminine group. This finding is consistent with that of Gray and Klaus (1956) that girls with more affection for their mothers assumed themselves to be more like her and were so, in fact. Significantly more of Lynn's low feminine subjects attributed hostility to the mother doll than to the father doll, and the low feminine subjects attributed significantly more warmth to the father than the mother doll. Unfortunately the questionable validity of the Brown It Scale casts doubt on the results of this study. Among the extremes of femininity of 2650 female college students, Wright and Taska (1966) found that the feminine women recalled an emotionally satisfying mother and a successful father. The masculine women recalled an emotionally satisfying father but a frustrating, unsympathetic mother. This certainly casts doubt on the idea that an "expressive" relation with the father leads to femininity (Johnson, 1963).

Mitchell (1966) found that the father's discipline and authority were crucial for boys but not for girls. Among these ninth graders, the mother's love and support was the important factor for the girls. Mothers who were more restrictive of their daughters than were their husbands had irresponsible, rebellious, unmotivated, hostile daughters. Mussen and Rutherford (1963) found that sex typing in girls related to the mother's score for nurturance, power, and self-acceptance, and to the father's masculinity score and the amount of encouragement the father gave to feminine activities. Rutherford (1965) found that feminine sex-role preference of girls related to maternal behavior of the mother, indicating dominance and mastery in the home. Mother dominance in the family, however, did not facilitate the ability of third grade girls to make masculine and feminine sex-role discriminations (Rutherford, 1969). This does not appear surprising because girls from mother-dominant homes are having a sex-role discrepant experience. Biller (1969) found that maternal salience is significantly related to the extent to which girls manifested feminine behavior in fantasy. Doherty (1970), however, found that maternal control produced contradictory results in regard to daughters' values and behavior. Hetherington (1965) found that for girls, father dominance in the home led to equal identification with both parents. In these homes, the girls identified more with the father than in mother-dominant homes. Boys were more seriously affected by the reverse situation. These studies indicate the importance of the factors of nurturance and power.

Another factor known to have an effect on sex-role modeling is the sex and age composition of the family (Sutton-Smith and Rosenberg, 1969). Oldest daughters were more highly identified with their mothers than later ones (Heilbrun and Fromme, 1965). Becker (1968) hypothesizes that older siblings have the effect of attenuating sex-role learning since they do not display differential behavior to younger children on the basis of that child's sex. He reported more difference in the dependency behavior of first-born males and females than between later-born children. First-born males were more independent and first-born females more dependent. Girls with older brothers were more masculine than girls with older sisters (Koch, 1956). Santrock (1970) found that father-absent girls with all male older siblings were significantly more aggressive than father-absent girls with older female siblings only. Kammeyer (1967) was disappointed in his expectation that girls with older brothers would have a more traditional orientation to the feminine role; in fact, they had less traditional views about female personality traits. Rosenberg and Sutton-Smith

(1964) found that girls in two-child families with boy siblings were less feminine than girls with girl siblings. The only girl was the least anxious of all the girl groups, but more masculine than average, perhaps, they thought because of more attention from her father. These authors concluded that girls from the ages of nine to puberty had difficulty in establishing appropriate sex-role behavior. Those girls having an older sister were apparently less anxious, since they had a model to follow.

Requirements of the Female Role

Freudian emphasis on the central importance of sexuality in determining psychological development has contributed to the notion that the passive, receptive qualities which they consider appropriate to female sexual behavior, should be generalized to the entire arena of female behavior. In fact, it seems highly unlikely that Freud would have espoused such an idea, and it is especially inappropriate since Masters and Johnson (1966) have shown that passivity is even an inaccurate characterization of sexual response in women.

Another type of narrow definition of sex role is found in segments of the working class. Customs in this group allow women activity and even dominance, but only within the sphere of home and children (see Chapter 3). The more flexible sex roles of the upper-middle class are in keeping with the more complex behavior demanded of individuals in this group. It is more difficult to learn two roles than one. Johnson (1963) has pointed out that one reason the masculine (instrumental) sex role is more valued is because it requires an extra push to master. When women died at forty and spent all their adult years in childbearing, it certainly made no sense to expect more, but different times exact different requirements.

Conformity to stereotyped sex roles, if taken seriously and literally, would incapacitate individuals for tasks in broad areas. How could the completely and solely aggressive male sit through long board meetings listening to his superiors debate alternatives? A concrete clinical example is the case of a first generation Polish-American of the working class. He grew up settling disputes with his fists. As an adult, he was hospitalized in a psychiatric facility because of psychosomatic back pain. The cause? Promotion to foreman, requiring him to mediate and not to battle with his fists. Conversely, how can a completely passive and unmechanical female cope with a dishonest washing-machine repairman? How does the completely passive woman cope with an alcoholic husband or no husband and a house full of children. Obviously anyone that masculine or that feminine, regardless of class, is going to be in trouble except in the most protected of circumstances. As a generalization, it does seem that the more complex the role the child is being socialized for, the less likely that narrow stereotypes of sex role will be observed. No personality of any complexity can be developed with only half the possible traits.

Sex-role prescription is ordinarily defined by what people believe *should* be the behavior of each sex. Another approach to the problem is provided by Kagan (1964). He reviewed studies of differences actually found between the sexes as a basis of defining sex role in our culture. According to his summary, females are supposed to inhibit aggression and open display of sexual urges, to be passive with men, be nurturant to others, cultivate attractiveness, and maintain an affective, socially poised, friendly posture with others. Males were to be aggressive in the face of attack, independent in problem situations, sexually aggressive, in control of regressive urges, and suppressive of strong emotions, especially anxiety.

Overconcern about Sex-role Congruence

A study of McKee and Sherrifs (1960) suggests that the need for conformity to sex role has been overinterpreted. These authors found that women believed that men want to restrict them to feminine qualities, but that this was not actually true. The men, on the other hand, were quite correct in their belief that women would prefer them to be more feminine. The one masculine characteristic men were intent on retaining had to do with strength and personal force. Steinman (1963) also found that a sample of college girls greatly exaggerated the extent to which their fathers wanted them to be other-oriented, a characteristic usually associated with the feminine role. They imagined that their fathers expected significantly more of this quality than their mothers. Steinman concluded, however, that the fact that the fathers perceived the ideal woman as significantly more other-oriented than the average woman may explain why women feel under pressure from men to be more feminine in this way.

SUMMARY

Theorizing about moral and sex-role development has become considerably more complex than Freud's view that both are accomplished by identification with the parent of the same sex. While there is consensual agreement that Freud's formulation is inadequate, there is certainly not consensual agreement on any one viewpoint. The theoretical contributions of both Parsons and Kohlberg emphasize the importance of the father in the girl's sex-role development. Johnson's view, however, that identification with the father's reciprocal expressive role behavior is crucial to feminine sex-role development is not supported. The very interesting question raised by Parsons of whether the father does indeed help wean the daughter from a potentially infantilizing mother relationship has not been sufficiently investigated. Identification (similarity) with the father is not clearly maladjustive for girls nor is feminine identification clearly adjustive, perhaps because the feminine cultural ideal contains built in nonadaptive qualities. In general, however, girls identify more with their mothers than with their fathers. Parsons' concept of instrumental and expressive roles would seem to have its greatest usefulness applied to roles and not to people.

From the review of the material on sex-role development, it seems clear that girls and especially women accept their sex role with less enthusiasm than boys and men. The factors which produce this appear to be largely unrelated to those influencing nuclear sex identity and homosexuality. Factors influencing the girls' adoption of behavior congruent with sex role include level of cognitive development, the relative power and nurturance of the parents, ordinal position, and the age, sex, and status of siblings.

Chapter 6

ADOLESCENCE

Adolescence has been considered a period of particular psychological importance because of the concomitance of decisive events in biological maturation, emancipation from parental ties, and often mate choice and career choice as well. Furthermore, an unforeseen side effect of the rigid age segregation of our system of education and work has been to create a heightened sense of class consciousness in this group. As a result, adolescence has come to have a more distinct psychology of its own than might otherwise be the case. In this chapter, the general problems of adolescent girls will be considered as well as some more recent psychoanalytic thinking on this life phase. The physical changes of adolescence will be outlined and the effect of menarche evaluated. Finally social and peer influences will be examined.

STORM AND STRESS

Adolescence has been popularly known as a period of terrible stress and upheaval, yet 84 per cent of a sample of American girls, 82 per cent of a sample of English girls, and 92 per cent of a group of Swiss girls described their childhood and adolescence as happy (Barschak, 1951). In another study, the majority of a sample of over one hundred girls were happy in both childhood and adolescence. Twice as many happy as unhappy experiences, however, were remembered for childhood, while memories of adolescence were about equally divided (Wall, 1948). Women's retrospective reports of their adolescence may not be very accurate, however (Rosenthal, 1963).

Typical Problems

While most are happy, it is clear that girls do have their problems. A national survey of nearly 2,000 girls ages eleven to eighteen showed that over 50 per cent worried about their looks (Survey Research Center, 1964). Rokeach (1943) found appearance a very important variable in women. He obtained correlations of .45 between ratings of beauty and dominance, and .55 between beauty and feelings of personal security. Among married graduate women, however, having a sexually attractive figure was associated with greater anxiety and insecurity (Burian, 1969). The realistic importance of beauty among adolescents is also documented in the study of Coleman (1963). In one study, the only important determinant of a boy's liking for his date was her physical attractiveness (Walster, Aronson, Abrahams, and Rottman, 1966).

For nearly half the girls over age fourteen, another serious problem was concern about the loyalty and trustworthiness of their friends (Survey Research Center, 1954). This becomes more understandable when one realizes that for more than half of the girls, friends, not the family, were the major focus of confidence and emotional support. It is interesting to note that only 3 per cent of these girls wanted to be housewives. There were indications of strong ambition to move from working-class status to the middle class. The prevalence of this desire led the investigators to speculate that many will be disappointed and frustrated.

Harris (1959) found the four main problems of adolescent girls were study habits, money, personal attractiveness, and mental hygiene. Girls tend to be more concerned about interpersonal and family problems than boys, and recently they have begun to show less concern about school problems than boys (Adams, 1964). In a study of 2,000 southern California high school girls, Hertzler (1950) found that 25 per cent said their mother would not understand their problems. Thirty per cent reported trouble making friends, and 25 per cent worried how to break off with the wrong crowd. Eighteen per cent debated the question of career versus marriage, and 17 per cent were concerned about religion with 14 per cent indicating conflict about the teaching of evolution. Twenty-two per cent reported trouble with colds and menstrual difficulties, 19 per cent with diet, 18 per cent with skin. Fourteen per cent said they felt nervously exhausted. Twenty-one per cent said they did not have enough clothes and 11 per cent felt inferior on this account. Twelve per cent were not financially able to attend school functions. Conduct questions of how to get along with the crowd and not drink, smoke, and engage in sexual activities troubled 21 per cent. Parental quarreling was reported by 13 per cent, and 24 per cent worried about the financial problems of their parents.

This material from southern California is interesting to contrast with the findings of a projective study of 300 girls in the New York City area (Frank, Harrison, Hellersberg, Machover, and Steiner, 1951). The sample contained a wide economic range and a large percentage of ethnic and national minorities, especially Jewish girls. About half of the parents were born in the United States. Adjustment showed a drop with puberty. The major trends were emotional constriction, introversion, and inner tension. One third of the girls, mostly from the lower class, showed antisocial trends, while the girls from higher classes showed feelings of inadequacy in the face of ambition. Part of the lower-class girls showed evidence of an early sex shock. Lower-class girls were generally less ambitious, and those not traumatized seemed more relaxed than girls of higher socioeconomic status. The latter showed pressure from ambitious, intellectual parents. These girls were bright, with a wide range of knowledge but anxious and tense, with little desire to mature as feminine personalities. This finding is in marked contrast to the pressure for social rather than intellectual achievement, which Coleman (1963) recently found exerted on a similar group of girls from a later generation. In the New York City study, role problems were greatest among the upper-middle-class girls and least among the nontraumatized lower-class girls. A popular way of attempting to master the feminine role was adoption of the glamour-girl image. This was characterized by the prestige of increased dates and exhibition of sophisticated, precocious conduct. Girls otherwise too immature used the stylized speech, gesture, aids, and appurtenances of the glamour cult as a device to help master the female role.

Douvan (1957) studied nearly 2,000 adolescent girls and about 1000 boys. She concluded that the problem of identity for a boy means, "What is my work?" while for a girl it is, "Who is my husband?" While the boy chooses his occupation, the girl is chosen.

The areas of achievement, autonomy, authority, and control focus and express boys' major concerns. For girls, friendship, dating, popularity and the understanding and management of interpersonal crises hold the key to adolescent growth and integration (Douvan and Adelson, 1966). The conclusion was that for girls, the issue of identity in the sense of completing all role choices, tends to be postponed until marriage and often the issue of independence is postponed as well.

A MORE RECENT PSYCHOANALYTIC VIEW

Most of the psychoanalytic literature on adolescence reiterates Freud's ideas, usually in an even more speculative and less defensible manner. The work of Blos (1962), however, is an exception. After an initial bow to orthodox Freudian theory, he presents his own observations. In keeping with the evidence reviewed, he places much stronger emphasis on the role of the girl's relation to her mother. He indicates that it is as frequently the negative Oedipus complex (love of mother), rather than the positive Oedipus complex, which is revived at adolescence. Blos believes that one of the great differences between the sexes is caused by the girl's need to repress pregenitality, since this is equated with her mother. To protect herself against the pull of an infantile relation with mother, she may develop exaggerated heterosexual desires and attach herself to boys in frantic succession. This, not the positive Oedipus complex, is seen as the cause of sexual acting out. This pull toward the mother may also be reacted against by excessive independence, hyperactivity, and an excessive show of unreasonable hostility. Blos states that girls are usually aware only of their negative feelings toward their mothers. Thus, those hoping to show the importance of the positive Oedipus complex in adolescent girls are on much stronger grounds in showing an increase in sexual interest toward the father than in documenting an increased hostility to the mother. There is little evidence of the Oedipus complex and in reviewing the evidence, one gains the impression that the struggle for independence—especially from the mother—is much more important.

Blos stresses the importance of girl friends during early adolescence. He characterizes early adolescence as a bisexual period, with crushes on older women being very common. Reality is vaguely perceived. In this stage, the girl shows remarkable facility for living by proxy, that is to effect a temporary identification as a trial action. He believes that premature sexual relations usually have a traumatic effect and result in regression. Friendships, crushes, fantasy life, intellectual interests, athletic activities, and preoccupation with grooming help to protect the girl from premature sexuality, but in Blos' view, the best protection is the emotional availability of the mother or a mother substitute.

According to Blos, a decline of the bisexual tendency marks entrance into adolescence proper. He views the notorious narcissism of adolescents as partly a result of emotional withdrawal from the parents who are likely to be undervalued. Loss of the parental cathexis results in object hunger (a need to find someone or something to become attached to). This need may result in excessive eating, or rather than actually looking for a boy to love, girls may spend much time daydreaming about boys. Their fantasy serves the useful purpose of trial acting out and protects them from premature action. Girls especially like diaries which aid in developing their sense of reality and identity. The two broad affective states of adolescence are those of mourning and being in love —mourning for the loss of childhood and childish affections and love expressed in the sudden and shifting enthusiasms of new affections. Blos points out that uniformity is a characteristic adolescent defense uniquely American. The herd-like conformity gives a feeling of security.

During late adolescence, Blos believes there are individual gains in purposeful action, social integration, predictability, constancy of emotions, and stability of self esteem. During the post-adolescent period, the main task in order to reach maturity is to make peace with the same-sex parent image.

In Blos' opinion, pseudomodernity in sexual standards accounts for many complications in the development of femininity. The single standard ignores the fact that the female sex drive is far more intimately attached to her ego interest and personality attributes than is the male's. In his opinion, the double standard will never be relinquished, at least not by men. Blos thinks that the masculine qualities of women today make it hard for them to be passive and dependent and that their masculinity makes them feel guilty about the biological regression of motherhood. While Blos's opinions coincide better than most analysts with the data, these last statements and his notion of a bisexual phase in early adolescence are especially open to question. Gelford (1952), for example, found no evidence of a bisexual phase, though 29 per cent of a small, random sample of college girls reported that especially during the ages of twelve to fourteen, they had had crushes on older girls. None of these college girls were homosexual (Freedman, 1965). The notion of the regressive tendencies of motherhood has little empirical support, and the advisability of passivity and dependence in women is questionable.

PHYSICAL CHANGES OF ADOLESCENCE

Having taken a general view of the character, personality, and problems of the adolescent girl, it might be well to examine the physical changes of adolescence. It is during adolescence that most of the adult sex differences in height and strength occur (Tanner, 1962). After the age of eleven, increasing sex divergence in the production of hormones is noted. Blood pressure and pulse rate diverge, with females having the higher pulse rate. After menarche, pulse rate and basal metabolism decline. For many adolescents, physiological adjustments are rapid and abrupt (Shock, 1953). The growth spurt begins about two years earlier in girls than in boys, with girls attaining their peak velocity of growth between twelve and thirteen. It is during these ages that Ljung (1965) also found a mental growth spurt in girls. The sequence of change is quite regular, but there is wide variation as to when the sequence begins. In girls, the first signs of puberty are likely to be pubic hair growth, occurring between the ages 8 to 14; next breast budding, ages 8 to 13; then height spurt 9½ to 14½.

Menarche occurs later, from ages 10 to 16½. The average age of menarche now in the United States is 13½, lowest in the world (Tanner, 1962). Though nutrition is known to be a factor, it is not entirely clear why menarche should occur earlier in the United States. It does not occur earlier in tropical countries as is popularly believed. After menarche, axillary (underarm) hair appears, the hips broaden, and fat increases. Menarche almost invariably occurs after the apex of the height spurt has passed (Tanner, 1962, 1963). Menstruation may be irregular at first. The cycle varies from 23 to 43 days, with bleeding from 3 to 7 days; the average blood loss is 25 cc with a range of 10 to 55 cc. The average loss of iron is 12 mg, but blood loss can range to 312 cc and up to 150 mg of iron (Brewer, 1961).

Other changes of adolescence are deepened skin pigmentation, especially in brunettes; more luxuriant hair growth, larger thyroid gland, and voice fuller and lower in scale. Full reproductive function is not attained for a year or two after menarche. Tanner estimates the period of adolescent infertility as 12 to 18 months in most but not all girls. Maximum fertility is not reached till the early or middle twenties (Tanner, 1962, 1963). Ovulation, when it begins, may range from the eighth to nineteenth day. A transitory gland, the corpus luteum, is formed from the ovarian follicle which had just ovulated. Its secretions (progesterone) build up for a couple of days and continue until one or two days before menses (Brewer, 1961). While estrogens have been present earlier in adolescence, progesterone secretions do not begin until ovulation.

MENARCHE

Information about Menarche

Girls today are better informed as to what to expect at menarche and consequently are spared the experience of trying to interpret an unknown bloody discharge. Larsen (1961) gathered data from 732 women ages fourteen to eighty-one, mostly of the middle class. She found that the mother still tends to be the main source of information about menstruation. Ninety-four per cent of the teenagers learned about menstruation from the family, compared to 87 per cent of the women in their mothers' generation and 88 per cent of those in the generation of their grandmothers. Of course more of today's mothers are alive to teach their daughters. Four per cent of today's teenagers had been unprepared for menarche compared to 9 per cent of those in the twenty- to thirty-nine-year-old group and 12 per cent in the over-forty age group. The author suggests that mothers should be made more aware of the early signs of puberty—pubic hair, breast budding, and growth spurt—so they will be alert to educate the girls who mature early. Henton (1961) found that 76 per cent of 133 white and 63 per cent of 801 black girls ages eleven to eighteen had been prepared for menstruation. Very few of the black girls were given information by their mothers.

The information that girls pick up from their family and friends is likely to be influenced by the folklore of their ethnic background. An interesting study of this has been presented by Abel and Joffe (1950). Among the Italians, menstruating women are regarded as easily excited sexually, and therefore they are expected to stay away from men. They are protected from shock, since it is believed harmful if the blood flow should stop. They are to avoid heavy work, cold, baths, and washing the hair. It is believed to be better not to change the sanitary napkin, as retaining a partially saturated napkin helps increase the flow. This is considered desirable. The notion also exists that others should be protected from the menstruating woman.

By contrast, the German emphasis is on keeping clean, though they also advise not to bathe for two days. Menstruation is to be concealed and there is an attitude that women should take this in stride and not be pampered. The Poles tend to regard menstruation as disgusting and men avoid menstruating women. The Irish are described as more secretive and silent than the Poles about menstruation. Irish mothers are dismayed when their girls pick up the notion of not bathing from their Italian neighbors.

Among the orthodox Jews, a menstruating woman is regarded as dangerous, but also weak and vulnerable. Intercourse during the period is taboo, and it is thought that children conceived during menstruation will be deformed. Girls tend to be protected from sex until the day they are married, but after marriage they are regaled with stories of sex, childbearing, and the like. In the United States, Abel and Joffe believe that the first date tends to be a more important event than menarche, and the menstruating woman as a threat is a less common belief than that women are vulnerable.

Psychological Effects of Menarche

What effect does menarche have on girls? Kestenberg (1965) suggests that prepubertal girls are confused and poorly organized, prone to attacks of giggles. She feels that the pain from the menstruating organ reduces fear in helping to organize and define an organ heretofore vague and unknown. She also observes that among girls of "progressive" families menarche is not regarded as traumatic. Kroth (1968) found that a group of twelve premenarchial girls were more anxious than a matched group of twelve postmenarchial girls.

The findings of empirical studies of premenarchial and postmenarchial girls are not very consistent. The classic study of Stone and Barker (1939) contained data on about 400 middle-class, junior high school girls. The investigators found that compared to other girls the same age, girls of the postmenarche period were significantly more interested in heterosexual activities, and personal adornment, and significantly less interested in games requiring vigorous gross motor activity. They daydreamed more, but there was no significant difference in family friction or revolt against family discipline. Compared to premenarchial girls, the interests of postmenarchial girls were more similar to girls of an older chronological age. The authors believe that their finding of a significantly higher IQ in the already pubescent girls was not an effect of menarche but attributable to selection factors.

Smith and Powell (1956) tested 138 junior high school girls with four pictures from the Blacky, an apperceptive test devised to study psychoanalytic concepts. Stories made up in response to the picture designed to measure Oedipal intensity showed results opposite of that expected. The premenarchial subjects significantly more often imagined the parents in love while the postmenarchial subjects significantly more often felt deprived of attention, a pre-Oedipal response. Similarly, premenarche subjects were interpreted to prefer the opposite-sexed parents, while postmenarche subjects seemed to prefer the same sex parent. After menarche, the girls appeared to feel less secure in attaining their ego ideal. This data once again supports the impression of the greater importance of the mother relationship and provides no evidence of the revival of the positive Oedipus complex. From this data, the overall effect of menarche appears to be one of regression rather than movement toward maturity, as Stone and Barker found. About the only point of consistency is the finding of Stone and Barker of increased daydreaming, which could be considered regressive.

Gelford (1952) gathered stories from twenty-seven premenarche and postmenarche pairs of girls matched in age. The Symond Pictures, a collection of pictures especially selected to elicit stories from adolescents, was used. He concluded that junior high school girls are ambivalent to other girls, mercurial, more consistently friendly to boys, and more oriented to peers than to adults. He could see no sign of a latency period or a homosexual phase. He found evidence of heterosexual interest before menarche and concluded that this created awkwardness for early-maturing girls. He reported no significant premenarche and postmenarche differences and concluded that the social field within which the child operates is the primary force creating adolescent personality traits. Davidson and Gottleib (1955), using very few subjects, also found essentially no premenarche and postmenarche differences, nor did Landis, Landis, and Bolles (1940).

These discrepant findings make it difficult to draw any conclusions at this time regarding whether or not menarche is associated with personality change. It may be that the event of menstruation is simply not that momentous for girls in our present culture. It should also be noted that menstruation is not a very good index of physiological change, since it occurs about halfway in the sequence of adolescent changes. The physiological states of some samples of premenarchial postmenarchial girls might not be too different.

Menarche, Status, and Adjustment

Menarche, or more likely the physical changes accompanying it, clearly have their social consequences, however. Faust (1960) examined the prestige of 731 girls in the grades six through nine. In the sixth grade, being postmenarchial appears to be a social disadvantage, but these early-maturing girls are later at a social advantage in high school. By the seventh grade and from then on, the girls who had already reached menarche were rated higher in social prestige than late-maturing girls of the same age. The latter tended to be quieter, to avoid fights, and to receive less attention.

The earlier literature on adjustment and maturation rate reviewed by Eichorn (1963) was quite confusing, but these conflicting results now appear to be resolved. In a study of older girls (Jones and Mussen, 1963), those who matured early were found to be better adjusted. The hormones of maturity retard linear growth, with the result that girls who mature early are less slender than the late maturers, but there is some evidence that they have been less slender since childhood (McNeill and Livson, 1963). Tanner (1962) points out that the true relationship may not be between adjustment and early or late maturation, but between adjustment and body build. Early maturers may be better adjusted because they are mesomorphs (a build with muscle predominating) and not ectomorphs (a build with bone and skin predominating).

Since the hypothalamus appears to be in control of the initiating mechanisms of adolescence, Rheingold (1964) raises the question as to whether the physical changes of adolescence can be inhibited by psychogenic factors. Girls afraid of growing up, for example, might influence the body to delay puberty changes. In this regard, it is interesting to note the finding of physical sexual immaturity among a group of psychiatric patients (Landis, Landis, and Bolles, 1940). Cases of anorexia nervosa (deliberate self starvation) certainly illustrate the possibility of psychic factors retarding sexual development. Starvation results not only in loss of bodily curves but in elimination or delay of menses as well. Frequently the girls are fearful of growing up. It is unclear, however, whether maturational delay could be accomplished in some less drastic and dramatic a manner than near starvation.

While it appears that early maturers are better adjusted in later adolescence, it is difficult to know what the causal factors are.

Do they mature early because they are better adjusted? Are they better adjusted because they have more peer status? Or are both the early maturation and good adjustment attributable to a third factor, mesomorphic body build? Or is more than one factor involved?

PEER GROUP INFLUENCES

Social and peer effects in adolescence are very considerable. Several studies already mentioned have stressed the importance of friends and peer groups. The nature of peer influences and perhaps also their strength have greatly changed in the last decades. Dating and heterosexual activity of all sorts now begin earlier. After World War I, the median age to begin dating was sixteen; now it is fourteen (Hurlock, 1967). A study of over 2000 adolescents in grades six, nine, and twelve showed a significant increase in the cross-sex preference choices made on sociometrics given in 1963 compared to 1942 (Kuhlen and Houlihan, 1965). Because of these social changes, it is somewhat difficult to know if data from earlier studies is still appropriate.

One of the earlier studies of social influence is that of Tryon (1944). She found that in a group of California girls, the peer standards for conduct changed from early to later adolescence. At first, emphasis was on being quiet, demure, and having a rather ladylike demeanor. At fifteen, however, there was a change, and the most popular girls were active, talkative, and characterized by aggressive good fellowship. In order to keep her status in a group, a girl would have to change considerably.

A more recent study (Coleman, 1963) found that getting into the leading crowd depended upon a girl having a "good personality," "good looks," "nice clothes," and a "good reputation." Being smart helped, but being from the right family helped even more. Moral reputation was found to be consistently important for girls but not necessarily for boys. In the upper-middle-class high school, the major way of gaining prestige for girls was to be important as an activities leader, the prototype of the future clubwoman. Almost none of the elite girls wanted to be remembered as brilliant. The brainy girl was partly looked down upon as overly conforming to parental expectations. Intellectual achievement was not valued much for girls in any social class but particularly not in the upper-middle class. It is ironic that this group is the source of most girls able to get higher education. The middle-class environment tended to be a little more serious about intellectual achievement for girls, while the lower class considered good grades a *female* province. Intellectual activity actually reversed sex-role assignment from the lower to the higher classes.

Coleman concluded that the social system of the high school has powerful effects on the individual's self evaluation. He considers this especially unfortunate since the peer culture tends to promote false values and values opposed to the educational intent of the institution. For girls, these values are good looks, clothes, enticing manner, and popularity with the opposite sex. Girls actually moved away from the scholar image during high school. Beauty was found to be much more important than brains. Girls were faced with a difficult problem, since their status depended greatly on their popularity with boys. The boys attempted to gain sexual favors, but a girl who failed to withhold them lost status. A definite double standard was found. Coleman noted that girls, more often than boys, wanted to go to another town, especially a bigger one. He wondered if this was a reaction to community constraints that are more oppressive on them than on boys. Pressure for conformity has been found to be greater on girls (Milner, 1949; Schoeppe, 1953).

CONTEMPORARY DATING CULTURE

Like Blos and Coleman, Hurlock (1967) is extremely critical of current dating culture. She feels that dating is not a good preparation for marriage, since it is dominated by a quest for thrills and excitement and an effort to deceive others by pretense of love and devotion. She believes that the exploitative element of dating is likely to be harmful and that the capacity to love may be permanently injured. She notes that many girls are forced into early dating, early going steady, and early marriage by mothers who regard their daughter's heterosexual prowess as a prestige symbol.

SUMMARY

Adolescence is apparently not a time of storm and stress for most girls, though it tends to be unhappier than childhood. Sources of unhappiness tend to center about the vagaries of the all-important peer group acceptance rather than biological sources such as menarche. Not only are false and artificial values promoted by contemporary peer groups, but an adolescent girl may find herself a pawn in a cruel game of scoring coup. Parents often unwittingly tighten the knot of conflicting demands of morality, reputation, and the importuning of status-conferring suitors. Some consequences and correlates of premarital sexuality will be discussed in Chapter 8.

There was no evidence of a revival of the female Oedipus complex; there was some evidence of a bisexual phase, although the topic has not been sufficiently investigated. The picture is rather one of struggle to manage conflicting feelings toward the mother, engendered largely from dependence-independence conflicts. Sisters and girl friends are probably more important than fathers at this point in providing substitutive relationships which help wean the girl away from the mother. The intense same-sex peer friendships may be a way of working through the mother relationship. (Working through is psychotherapy jargon which means to reexperience in multiple and slightly varying ways a conflictual situation so that eventually a calmer, more realistic, and more mature response can be made.) For most girls identity issues tend to be postponed and to center about the question, Who will be my husband?

Chapter 7

CYCLIC CHANGES

MENSTRUATION has long been a subject of mystery and fear. Briffault (1927) recounts the history of European menstrual taboos. Pliny, the Roman savant, believed in a frightening list of the ill effects of menstruating women. Rural populations in Italy, Spain, Germany, and Holland have believed that flowers and fruit trees are withered by contact with a menstruating woman. In France, menstruating women have been kept from the wine for fear they might turn it to vinegar. In Holstein, they were prohibited from making butter, and in France, mayonnaise. In England, bacon was not to be cured by a menstruating woman. Mirrors and bright objects were thought to be rendered dim by her reflection. Ford (1945) lends some credence to these beliefs by reporting that there is a substance, menotoxin, in the perspiration, saliva, and blood of menstruating women which is harmful to plant life. The existence of such a toxin, however, is not a settled matter (Lloyd and Leathem, 1964).

CROSS-CULTURAL DATA

In his study of the reproductive customs of primitive tribes, Ford (1945) found that menstrual taboos tend to be less severe among those tribes which have developed efficient methods of sanitary collection of the menstrual flow. Stephens (1961), however, was unable to confirm this finding. Ford found that most tribes directly or indirectly taboo intercourse during menses as well as during the last part of pregnancy and the first postpartum weeks. Ford also claims that modern medicine provides some support for these taboos, since contact with menstrual fluid during intercourse can cause inflammation of the male urinary tract. Ford states that intercourse during menses may also be harmful to the woman by altering her menstrual functions and by increasing the chance of pelvic infection. However, numerous marriage manuals emphasize that refraining from sexual relations during the menses is a groundless myth. Menstrual symptoms and discomforts are not confined to modern civilized women; Ford found that about one third of the tribes he reviewed had charms to protect women, or medicine to alleviate discomfort, or other practices designed to protect her from illness or sickness during the menses.

THE WITCH AND THE MENSTRUATING WOMAN

Many primitive tribes and also the ancient Hebrews completely isolated menstruating women. Chadwick (1932) emphasized the importance of unpleasant psychological symptoms as the basis for these taboos. She also pointed out the similarities between the disturbed menstruating woman and the witch. Like the menstruating women, witches show signs of hormone imbalance, such as long chins, noses and fingers, and masculine characteristics. They are mean to children, as mothers tend to be at the time of their period.* Witches are frequently pictured as older women; women with premenstrual symptoms are thought to become worse as they grow older. Witches wander at night as do prostitutes, while increased sexual urgency has been described as characteristic of the premenstrual period. Weiss and English (1957) in their text on psychosomatic medicine state the opinion that menstrual taboos stem from a desire to protect community stability from the danger of sexual excitement.

BIOLOGY OF THE MENSTRUAL CYCLE

An outline of the simple biology of the cycle may prove helpful to the understanding of later discussions. The menstrual cycle is an intricate hormone-feedback system. It begins with the pituitary's secretion of follicle-stimulating hormone (FSH). This causes the Graafian follicles in the ovary to grow and secrete estrogen. Estrogen has a pronounced effect on the endometrium, the lining of the uterus, causing a proliferative growth of its cells. The estrogen cuts back the pituitary's production of FSH and

*Dalton (1966) found that children with apyrenic colds and coughs were significantly more often brought to the doctor during the paramenstrum (last four days of the old cycle and first four days of the new cycle). The children were frequently normal; mothers appeared to have lapsed in judgment.

initiates the making of luteinizing hormone (LH). This, in turn, triggers the follicle to release its ovum and evolve into the corpus luteum, which secretes progesterone and a little estrogen. The ripe follicle may secrete progesterone two to three days prior to ovulation (Woolever, 1963). Progesterone helps prepare the uterus to receive the egg if it is fertilized and it also cuts back LH production. After ovulation, there is about a sevenfold increase in progesterone secretion and a twofold to threefold increase in blood levels of progesterone (Dorfmann and Ungar, 1965). If fertilization does not occur, the level of both estrogen and progesterone drops. This causes the uterine lining to slough away and permits FSH production to start, beginning the cycle once more. If the egg is fertilized, a fifth hormone, chorionic gonadotrophin (from the embryo) is produced. It causes the corpus luteum to produce more estrogen and progesterone. If the egg is not fertilized, however, the corpus luteum shrinks up. This, of course, describes an ovulatory cycle; not all cycles are ovulatory, especially in the first months after menarche and before menopause. A more complete account of the myriads of cyclic bodily changes may be found in the article of Southam and Gonzaga (1965).

OVERVIEW

When one thinks of psychological factors associated with menstruation, the following three general problems come to mind: (a) dysmenorrhea (painful menstruation), (b) amenorrhea (no menstrual period), and (c) psychological changes associated with the cycle, the most well known being premenstrual tension. Each of these problems will be considered in turn. It should be obvious that all sorts of physical factors, inflammations, and structural abnormalities may cause pain and disturbances of menstrual functioning, but these effects are outside the range of this study. Of interest here are the more subtle psychosomatic and biobehavioral effects.

In general, the evidence will show that (a) primary dysmenorrhea has been wrongly considered (by some) to be a psychosomatic complaint, (b) psychological factors have been demonstrated as a cause of amenorrhea and (c) both psychosomatic and biobehavioral effects have been associated with menstrual cycle distress. The sort of etiology which is most likely to be stressed will depend on the specialty of the physician. Psychiatrists tended to think that emotional factors are more important in causing painful menstruation, while the reactions of gynecologists were more diverse. Some gynecologists stressed psychological factors and others stressed organic factors (Paulson and Wood, 1966).

In general, studies of psychosomatic factors have been of four sorts. These are as follows: (a) those relating stress and symptoms; (b) those relating anxiety, neuroticism, or attitudes toward femininity to bodily symptoms, (c) those attempting to find a relationship between general personality types, e.g. immature, dependent personality, and bodily symptoms, and (d) those which relate a very specific emotional attitude or feeling to bodily reactions which if continually recurring could plausibly be expected to result in a particular psychosomatic syndrome (Graham and Stevenson, 1963; Stevenson and Graham, 1963). Most of the studies considered in this book are of the first three types. The latter approach, of course, is much more specific and much more effective in treatment, especially since the experimental interview permits the physician to establish the psychological cause for a specific patient with reasonable certainty. No pertinent studies utilizing this technique were found, however.

DYSMENORRHEA

Herzberg (1952) concluded that he had demonstrated the psychosomatic nature of dysmenorrhea. Instead, he may well have illustrated the ubiquitous role of secondary gain. He obtained his dysmenorrhea subjects from among those clerks who came for medication to a department store dispensary during work hours, while some of his subjects in the no-pain group were those recommended by supervisors as rarely impaired in their work. No medical examinations of the subjects were conducted. The forty-nine in the dysmenorrhea group obtained significantly higher scores on the hypochondriasis, depression, psychopathic deviate, and psychasthenia scales of the Minnesota Multiphasic Personality Inventory. The highest average score, however, and the only one outside the normal range was obtained by the dysmenorrhea group on the psychopathic deviate scale. This scale measures self-centered, irresponsible characteristics, suggesting that the "dysmenorrhea" group probably had an excessive number of goldbrickers simply ducking out of work. Irresponsibility, not neurosis, would seem to be of more importance in motivating the behavior of this particular sample. The findings of Mann (1963) strongly indicate that primary dysmenorrhea is caused by hypertonicity of the uterine isthmus. The puzzling variability of the symptoms is due to inconsistency in ovulation. Ovulation has the effect of increasing tonicity and hence increasing the symptoms. Childbirth usually cures the syndrome.

PSYCHIC AMENORRHEA

One psychological effect is very clear. It has long been known that menstruation may stop entirely in response to stress. Osofsky and Fisher (1967) studied the effect of stress, in this case entering nursing school, on a group of student nurses. An advantage of this study is that it is a prospective one; that is, the whole population was studied prior to the onset of the amenorrhea. The girls who responded to the stress with amenorrhea were those with a history of menstrual irregularity and who had a weak body-image test score.

Another prospective study (Shanan, Brzezinski, Sulman, and Sharon, 1965) investigated the factors producing amenorrhea in 64 American girls training in Israel. Girls with a history of gynecological disorder were excluded from the study. Twenty-five per cent of the girls studied developed amenorrhea of three-months' duration. The authors believe that amenorrhea should not be considered a symptom but a technique used more by some than by others to cope with social stress. Girls developing the amenorrhea showed a more active orientation. On the projective Draw A Person test, for example, they envisioned themselves as standing firmly on the ground. Those developing amenorrhea were not significantly more anxious than the others. They showed significantly more excretion of adrenal cortical hormones (17-

OH), but not cortical androgens (17-KS). All tests were repeated six months later, and no significant differences were found between the groups. This finding is consistent with many others that suggest that immediate attitudes and reactions are more useful than more general personality characteristics in demonstrating psychosomatic relations.

DRAMATIC CORRELATES OF THE MENSTRUAL CYCLE

Lest it be supposed that there are no cyclic psychological effects, it may be well to examine first some obvious menstrual correlates. One of the most dramatic of the cyclic effects is that the frequency of epileptic seizures increases before, during, and just after menstruation, when progesterone levels are lowest. The ratio of this hormone to estrogen appears to be the important factor (Hamburg, 1966), though the causal agent may be another hormone, aldosterone, which is normally antagonized by progesterone (Janowsky, Gorney, Mandell, 1967). During the premenstrual phase, review of the evidence shows that there is a significant increase in emergency psychiatric hospital admissions, suicide attempts, assaultive behavior among hospitalized psychiatric patients, crimes of violence, and accidents (Dalton, 1964). Ribeiro (1962), for example, found that 19 of 22 Hindu women who had committed suicide by burning themselves alive in kerosene were menstruating. Two others were pregnant. Mackinnon and Mackinnon (1956) wanted to relate cause of death to phase of the menstrual cycle. They began doing autopsies, but were unable to fulfill the aim of the study, since 46 of the first 47 cases were all in one phase, the luteal or premenstrual phase of the cycle. So impressed were they by their findings that they recommend that physicians warn women who are "highly strung" or chronically diseased to take more care during this time, get additional rest, avoid operations, or other severe stress. While studying premenstrual tension in a group of prison women, Morton and his colleagues (Morton, Addition, Addison, Hunt, and Sullivan, 1953) found that of the crimes of violence that these women had committed, 62 per cent occurred in the premenstrual week. Of 200 instances of assault and violent behavior among psychotic women,

Torghele (1957) reported that 184 came in the premenstrual period. He found that cyclic changes persisted in the absence of menstruation. Of his 273 subjects, 21 were amenorrheic, a not-uncommon feature of psychotic illnesses.

There are three monthly peaks of disturbance. The maximum psychological disturbance is early in menstruation; the second greatest peak is premenstrually, and the smallest rise is at midcycle (Dalton, 1964; Mandell and Mandell, 1967). This latter study used calls to a suicide prevention center as its index of psychological disturbance. Until recently, it had been thought that the premenstrual period was the one of greatest disturbance and the midcycle upset was rarely recognized at all. Among the 95 women studied, increased suicide attempts were found premenstrually and at midcycle; suicide attempts were significantly greater among those women living with a man (Tonks, Rack, and Rose, 1968). Seward (1946) complained that cyclic effects were mostly of a subjective nature, but these facts appear objective enough.

MORE SUBTLE CYCLIC CHANGES

More subtle cyclic changes were investigated in the classic biobehavioral study of Benedek and Rubenstein (1942, Benedek, 1952a). Benedek's work has often been misrepresented as overemphasizing the effects of hormone cycles on feminine behavior. She has clearly stated (1952, 1959) that she believes that these effects are not so great in normal women as in the neurotic, sexually frustrated women that she studied. Even with her patients, she considered the hormonal influence as a shadowy background, present, but easily obscured by other factors.

Benedek studied 152 cycles of 15 neurotic patients who were in psychoanalytic therapy with her. From a record of temperatures and vaginal smears, Rubenstein determined the phases of the cycle and dated ovulation. Benedek successfully predicted these findings (correct in 2128 of 2261 instances) by reference to the psychoanalytic material alone. A rather large amount of the raw data has been published. For someone familiar with the language of the unconscious and the symbols and terms of psychoanalysis, her deductions of cycle phase appear quite reasonable.

Benedek characterizes the first or estrogenic phase of the cycle as an active one with heterosexual libido. It should be noted, however, that it is erroneous to interpret Benedek's findings to mean that estrogen determines female sex drive (Waxenberg, 1969). As discussed in the next chapter, androgen, not estrogen, apparently underlies sex drive. General feelings of well being, however, relate to estrogen. More on estrogen effects may be found in Chapter 11.

Just prior to ovulation, Benedek described a preovulatory tension caused by conflicting psychodynamic tendencies which appear in correlation with the increase in estrogen and the incipient progesterone activity. A midcycle tension increase has been confirmed (Dalton, 1964; Mandell and Mandell, 1967). Ovulation itself was marked by a sudden decrease of active object-directed sexual tendencies. There was an inward turning and relaxation. Benedek noted that the incorporative, receptive mood of ovulation is really a sexual orientation, but that it may not be recognized as such, since it lacks an active quality. During the progesterone phase, dominant only a few days, the libido turns from the outer world and the individual appears more passive. Hamburg (1966) has reported a quieting, sedative effect of progesterone which is consistent with Benedek's observation.

During the latter part of the postovulatory phase, progesterone begins to drop. If estrogen is maintained at a fairly high level, a high degree of emotional tension is created, which may express itself in heterosexuality, though in this phase, Benedek states that what appears as sexuality may only be a general nervous irritation and restlessness. Money (1965b) aptly observes that the ovulatory phase might better have been described as sexual willingness and surrender and the premenstrual phase as one of increased initiative.

When estrogen also drops, as it does just prior to menses and in the first days of menstruation, the mood is mainly that of depression. Decreased psychophysiological arousal and slowed internal clock have been found in women during this time (Kopell, Lunde, Clayton, Moos, and Hamburg, 1969; Moos, Kopell, Melges, Yalom, Lunde, Clayton, and Hamburg, 1969). According to

Benedek, the low-hormone phase is characterized by eliminative, pregenital destructive tendencies. A study of cyclic variations in the dreams of four normal women over an eleven-week period showed significantly greater overt hostility during menses, which is consistent with Benedek's observation, but also significantly more manifest sexuality (Swanson and Foulkes, 1967). The latter finding, though consistent with the ideas of Weiss and English, is an unusual one and it remains to be seen whether it will be replicated. Ivey and Bardwick (1968) found significantly higher anxiety and increased hostility and depression during the premenstrual period. Reynolds (1969) found depression before and during menstruation. Low hormone phases are present not only during menses but also after childbirth and abortion. Benedek characterizes the low-hormone phase as one of depression, slowed intellectual function, fearfulness, crankiness, and sensitivity. The menstrual flow, once it starts, is accepted with relief, but depression may continue until estrogen increases (Benedek, 1952a, 1959).

A later study (Altman, Knowles, and Bull, 1941) also provides some support for these findings. These investigators studied fifty-five cycles in ten college women. The ovulative phase, especially the day of ovulation, was characterized by a mood of elation in 68 per cent of the cases. Physical and mental activities were also at a peak at this time in 85 per cent. Tenseness was found in 31 per cent. In the premenstrual phase, depression was found in 61 per cent; activity in 72 per cent, and tension in 80 per cent. One or two days before menses, activity was particularly likely to be cleaning, putting in order, and being critical. The subjects reported being very tired in the premenstrual phase, but this did not seem possible to the investigators, since they observed unusual amounts of activity. It seems likely that they have missed the point. The girls may have felt very tired indeed but nonetheless also felt impelled to activity. This is part of the uniqueness of this mood state. Bursts of activity have also been reported just prior to parturition, another occasion of hormone drop. Restless activity is also common in animals prior to giving birth.

OPINION ABOUT CYCLIC CHANGES

Menstrual psychological changes have been most often called premenstrual tension. However, as has been pointed out, symptoms may occur in the middle of the month at the time of ovulation or during the menstrual period, as well as immediately before the period. They have also been reported in the absence of menses just prior to menarche and just after menopause (Sutherland and Stewart, 1965). In recent years, a common sophisticated opinion has been that such symptoms are of psychogenic origin. Seward (1944, 1946) has minimized the evidence of any direct effect of menstruation on psychological function, attributing any observed effect to cultural expectation of invalidism. Psychoanalytic writers have emphasized the role of various neurotic attitudes in creating menstrual symptoms. These are feelings of masculine protest, fear of pregnancy, frustration of pregnancy wishes, and a revival of original castration anxiety. Weiss and English (1957) concluded that women hate menstruation as a symbol of their femininity. Much ignored have been such positive notions of menstruation as cleansing, revitalizing, and a part of an expected rhythm of life (Drellich and Bieber, 1958).

While the extreme psychogenic viewpoint is by no means absent at this time, opinion has changed to some extent. Recent advice recommends a psychotherapy consisting of educating women to the normality of these symptoms in order to relieve them of the additional burden of guilt brought on by their feelings of failure in being unable to control their emotions more effectively (Dalton, 1964; Melody, 1961). Morton (1962) concluded that ample evidence exists that premenstrual tension is generally not primarily psychogenic in origin. It is doubtful, however, that anyone is of the opinion that psychogenic factors are completely absent in all cases. If nothing else, one must deal with the problem of secondary gain.

INCIDENCE OF PREMENSTRUAL SYMPTOMS

Depending on the definition of the premenstrual syndrome, estimates of its incidence have ranged from 25 per cent to nearly

100 per cent. Pennington (1957) found that only 5 per cent of a group of 1000 presumably normal American women were entirely free of symptoms. The percentages of symptoms he found were as follows: dysmenorrhea, 62 per cent; irritability, 47 per cent; nervousness, 38 per cent; back pain and headache, 30 per cent each; nausea, 27 per cent; general ache, 19 per cent; painful breast, 18 per cent; insomina, 11 per cent; acne, 10 per cent; abdominal enlargement, 2 per cent; anorexia, 2 per cent; difficulty concentrating, dizziness, weakness, edema, frequent urination, water retention, each 1 per cent. It seems probable that many more women had swelling who were unaware of it or simply did not consider it a problem. Eight per cent of the group had only psychological symptoms; 19 per cent had entirely somatic symptoms, while 72 per cent had both bodily and mental symptoms.

Similarly, a study of 150 nulliparous (never pregnant) British students ages fifteen to twenty-five (Sutherland and Stewart, 1965) showed that 15 per cent lost at least one day of work each period; only 3 per cent were entirely free of symptoms. During the premenstruum the following symptoms were reported: acne, 70 per cent; irritability, 69 per cent; some swelling, 63 per cent; depression, 63 per cent; increased periocular pigmentation (circles around the eyes), 40 per cent; greasy scalp or hair, 35 per cent; headache, 32 per cent; constipation, 27 per cent; diarrhea, 20 per cent; dizziness, 16 per cent; and spots before the eyes, 2 per cent. The triad of irritability, depression, and swelling occurred together in 39 per cent, which the authors take as the incidence of cyclic tension state. This group was younger than Pennington's, which may account for some differences in symptoms, acne for example.

The sample that Kessel and Coppen (1963) studied was an unusually good one—500 women ages eighteen to forty-five randomly selected from medical practices of various doctors in Great Britain. Because of the program of national medical care in Britain, this population is quite representative. Seventy-two per cent of these women reported swelling, 45 per cent moderate or severe pain, 32 per cent irritability, 23 per cent depression, 22 per cent headache. Irritability, depression, tension, headache, and body swelling tended to cluster together as a syndrome occurring maximally one to two days before the period.

Hamburg, Moos, and Yalom (1968) point out the need to look for subgroups of menstrual distress reaction types. They reported the responses of 1100 wives of graduate students to a questionnaire of forty-seven symptoms. The responses appeared to form the following eight symptom groups: (a) pain, (b) concentration, (c) behavioral change, (d) dizziness, (e) water retention, (f) negative affect, (g) positive arousal, and (h) control symptoms. While the authors recommend these symptom groupings for use in systematic studies, for example of the effects of drugs, it seems questionable that all important symptoms are represented. Notable omissions are acne, diarrhea, and ease of bruising or capillary fragility. The latter factor seems particularly important, since it may underlie breakage of blood vessels as in cerebral stroke. Unfortunately, it is not possible to get out of a factor analysis any more than is put into it; in this case, it seems doubtful that a large enough pool of relevant symptoms was used.

ETIOLOGY OF PREMENSTRUAL SYMPTOMS

There is evidence in support of a psychogenic view of premenstrual tension, but it mostly consists of correlations which do not convincingly demonstrate causality. Shainess (1961) studied 103 middle-class women, part of whom were her psychotherapy patients. Twenty-one per cent had no preparation for menarche, a high figure compared to the 9 to 12 per cent found in a more normal sample (Larsen, 1961). Only 15 per cent of the mothers of these women reacted with pleasure to the news of their daughter's menarche, and these daughters were mostly free of the premenstrual tension found in the rest (87%) of the group. This sample was obviously not a representative one, and the association of mothers' attitudes and premenstrual tension need not necessarily be a causal one, as implied.

One study frequently quoted to support an extreme psychogenic view of premenstrual tension surveyed over a hundred student nurses, but its negative physical findings appear to be based on an intensive study of only ten subjects (Lamb, Ulett, Masters, and Robinson, 1953). Because the hormone values of the ten subjects were in the normal range, the investigators discounted any connection between hormone changes and emotional changes. This finding, however, does not rule out the possibility of a covariance of normal hormone changes and emotional changes, nor does it rule out the possibility of more extreme hormone and emotional changes occurring in some individuals.

The study of Paulson (1961) of 255 young women found significant correlations between degree of premenstrual tension and attitudes toward menstruation and toward self. The fact, however, that the attitudes related best to the more psychological symptoms and not to the physical ones (such as edema) weakens the author's argument that attitudes are generally a causal factor in the development of premenstrual symptoms. Fifty-eight per cent of the mothers of girls with the most severe premenstrual tension also suffered from the syndrome, compared to only 27 per cent of the mothers of girls in the most symptom-free group. Although the author feels that this supports the notion that the mother's attitude is a predisposing factor, other interpretations are also possible. Fifty-six per cent of the high-symptom group had had experiences or sex shock, compared to only 35 per cent of the low group. Seventy-eight per cent of the high-symptom group said their sex drive increased at various times while only 37 per cent of the low-symptom group reported this. The differences were apparently not tested for statistical significance.

Levitt and Lubin (1967) concluded that it is reasonable to suppose that attitude and personality are a factor in the etiology of menstrual symptomatology. Among 221 subjects, they found correlations suggesting menstrual complaints are related to unwholesome menstrual attitudes and to neurotic and paranoid tendencies. The correlation between menstrual attitudes and menstrual complaints was .32. Psychosomatic complaints generally were related to menstrual problems.

Spera (1969) found significant differences between 130 women ages seventeen to thirty-five with functional menstrual disorders and 105 control subjects in their scores on the hypochondriasis scale of the Minnesota Multiphasic Personality Inventory and in their responses to the Thematic Apperception Test. She concluded that women with functional menstrual disorders are characterized by anger, distrust, dependence, and submission. They see themselves as responsible and nurturant but publicly communicate in a dominant, power-oriented manner.

Coppen and Kessel (1963) came to the conclusion that premenstrual symptoms cannot be dismissed as simply the hysterical or hypochondriacal complaints of neurotic women, even though they found a correlation between premenstrual symptoms (though not dysmenorrhea) and neuroticism. They believe as does Dalton (1964) that these women have been wrongly classified as neurotic. They attribute the association between premenstrual symptoms and neuroticism to physiological changes causing emotional reactions. Of the physiological changes, they have particularly stressed the importance of edema. This interpretation has seemed particularly plausible to them since they found an increase in intracellular sodium in a study of depressed individuals. Sodium, such as is found in common table salt, increases retention of water, resulting in swelling.

The cause or causes of cyclic changes, however, are by no means clear, though some factors are known. Adrenocortical hormones, such as aldosterone which increases water retention, have been suggested as the cause (Janowsky, Gorney, Mandell, 1967), but this is probably too narrow a concept of the etiology. Dalton (1964) summarizes the causal factors of premenstrual tension as (a) water and sodium retention, (b) allergic phenomena, and (c) hypoglycemia (low blood sugar). She points out that the importance of water and sodium retention cannot be judged by overall weight gain, since the swelling may be local or general. One pound of water retained in the head area may cause much more trouble than five pounds generally distributed or collected in the ankles. She believes the swelling is probably the result of an excess of aldosterone, a hormone whose action is normally opposed by progesterone. Aldosterone is an inflammatory steroid that may be discharged in response to what the body perceives as a foreign agent. It increases with exposure to allergens, germs, or other invaders (Selye, 1956). But what could trigger such a reaction in the premenstrual period? Rogers (1962) suggests that some women are allergic to metabolites of progesterone. He points out that many of the symptoms of the premenstrual phase are like those of allergy, and he successfully treated about fifty patients by desensitizing them with hyposensitive doses of pregnandial. He also recommends antihistamine treatment during the last half of the menstrual cycle. Lacking controls of various kinds, his study can only be regarded as suggestive.

The hypoglycemia is the result of altered carbohydrate metabolism, but how and why this happens is not clear. Hypoglycemia can cause trembling, weakness, faintness, irritability, and may be mistaken for an anxiety attack. Another premenstrual symptom that Dalton (1964) mentions is capillary fragility, which may manifest itself in ease of bruising. The condition can rarely result in cerebral hemorrhage. Some symptoms, such as nosebleeding and possibly menstruation itself, may be traced to this factor. A fuller study of this aspect of the menstrual cycle (Clemetson, Blair, and Brown, 1962) reports that not only is there a premenstrual drop in capillary strength but also sometimes a drop in mid-cycle. This drop is nearly as great but of shorter duration than the premenstrual drop. There is also a seasonal variation in capillary fragility. Vitamin C and the bioflavonoids are essential in the diet to maintain the integrity of the capillary wall. The cyclic variation in capillary strength is apparently dependent on estrogen. In experimental tests, the estrogens eliminated hot flushes and raised capillary strength. Estrogen is to some degree a bioflavonoid, and thus it is related to the substances that give color and scent to flowers. It is postulated that estrogens and possibly other steroids enter into competition with bioflavonoids for a substrate in the capillary wall. There they maintain the integrity of the capillary wall until such time as they are metabolized or withdrawn.

TREATMENT

An effective treatment for the premenstrual syndrome was demonstrated in a well-controlled study of prison women (Morton, Addition, Addison, Hunt, and Sullivan, 1953). Treatment groups consisted of various combinations of treatments, such as placebo (phony pill), diet supplement of high protein, and medicine containing the diuretic ammonium chloride. The high-protein diet was meant to counteract the hypoglycemia. It might be thought that frequent carbohydrate meals would be as effective as a high-protein diet in stopping the hypoglycemic reaction, but the carbohydrate tends to stimulate increased insulin production and ultimately makes the problem worse. These investigators found an average premenstrual gain of three pounds in the untreated and placebo groups with only a one-pound gain in the group on medication. There were significant differences between the treatment groups. The greatest improvement, 79 per cent of the group, was with both diet and medicine; 61 per cent of the medicine only group improved; 39 per cent of the diet only group, and 15 per cent of the placebo group improved.

So far as treatment is concerned, Dalton (1964) advocated injections of progesterone. Birth control pills, which contain both estrogens and progestins, have been used to relieve the symptoms, presumably partially by establishing more hormonal constancy (Hamburg, Moos, and Yalom, 1968). Dalton (1964) believes that education of women about premenstrual tension is important, as otherwise they may fear they have some dire disease; many benefited from knowing that the emotional changes had a physical basis. Without this knowledge, the anxious, obsessive-compulsive type of woman may make her symptoms worse by forcing herself to keep up her usual work tempo. It would also seem that the depression, sensitivity, and irritability can be more easily borne if it is clear that the cause will disappear with the menses. Women on guard for these symptoms might also avoid some interpersonal difficulties by realizing that it is not so much the fault of others that they are so easily upset. There actually is some data supporting the value of such education. Women admitting premenstrual tension showed significantly fewer suicidal attempts than those unaware of their premenstrual symptoms (Tonks, Rack, and Rose, 1968). The authors believe that knowledge of the symptoms helped prevent drastic behavior.

CYCLIC EFFECTS ON PERFORMANCE

Considering the prevalence of symptoms, it is surprising how little effect has been found on performance measures. Women apparently are motivated to carry on as usual. Seward (1946) concluded that although her studies did not show any consistent decrement in intellectual performance attributable to menstruation, the women may have had to expend more effort. The often-quoted conclusion of Dalton (1960) that the grades of school girls declined as a function of menstruation is not supported by statistical tests of her data, so that it is impossible to be sure that the results are reliable. Smith (1950a, 1950b) found no consistent effect of menstruation either on absenteeism or industrial efficiency. Treatment at the factory was available to these women, and they had received special instructions on menstrual hygiene. Wickham (1958), in a well-controlled study of 4,000 service women, found a slight depression of test scores with the menstrual period, but the finding was not statistically significant. The effect was described as no greater than that of other common minor ailments such as a cold.

SUMMARY

It is now clear that primary dysmenorrhea is physically, not psychologically, caused. It is equally clear that psychic factors can affect menstruation. This is particularly plain in the case of amenorrhea. There is definite evidence of cyclic mental and physical changes. There is some evidence for a psychogenic etiology of cyclic symptoms, and it seems probable that there are cases of disturbed menstrual functioning caused by faulty attitudes. However, the prevalence of the premenstrual symptoms make it clear that this cannot be solely a neurotic phenomenon. Furthermore, information about physiological effects, such as swelling, hypoglycemia, capillary fragility, and allergy, add to the probability that cyclic emotional changes are physiologically based. Despite cyclic mental and physical changes, women rarely allow them to interfere unduly with their functioning. Nonetheless, many women, together with their families and associates, would no doubt be much happier if the symptoms were alleviated. It is also possible that more careful attention to adverse monthly changes might prevent the development of more serious mental disturbances. For example, hypoglycemia, a prominent aspect of premenstrual tension, has been related to neurotic and schizophrenic reactions (Jarosz, 1967; Meiers, 1967; Tintera, 1967). In any case, much more attention to research and to education in these matters is indicated.

Material such as that cited in this chapter has been used by some to justify the unequal treatment of women. Such arguments frequently rest on uncertain factual and logical grounds since they ignore the following points: (a) the fact that only some women are seriously affected and these are unlikely to present themselves for employment especially at high levels, (b) emotional changes accompanying physical changes can be successfully treated, (c) clear evidence of detrimental effects on performance is lacking, and (d) while women show emotional changes accompanying significant biological changes, they are not generally more emotionally unstable than men (see Chapter 2).

Chapter 8

FEMALE SEXUALITY

FEMALE SEXUALITY has been a matter of perennial interest, but despite this, the answers to many questions remain unsettled (Shuttleworth, 1959). What is the nature of the female sexual drive and capacity? How does it compare to the male's? Is greater sexual freedom for women advantageous to later marital adjustment? Is orgasm for women really so important after all? And is there more than one kind of orgasm? The literature on these questions is surprisingly extensive and suggests that sexuality has not been nearly so taboo in recent times as has sometimes been supposed.

THE KINSEY REPORT

The Kinsey study (Kinsey, Pomeroy, Martin, and Gebhard, 1965), despite its controversial nature, remains an indispensable source of information concerning this topic. It contains data gathered from about 6,000 nonprison, white women. The sample contains a larger number of women from the higher, educated classes than is representative of the United States population. The subjects consisted of individuals from groups that had agreed to participate in the study, but they remain, to some degree, volunteers. Maslow (1963) has severely criticized the study because of the bias introduced by the element of volunteering. He has found that volunteers tend to be high in dominance, promiscuous, and nonvirgin, while nonvolunteers tend to the opposite. The Kinsey data do not adequately represent this low-dominance type of female. In addition, while all major religions and levels of devoutness are represented in the data, devout women and those from more conservative religions tend to be underrepresented. The effects of these sampling biases would, of course, increase the incidence of unconventional behavior.

There is also some question as to the degree to which the stated sex differences merely represent differential sampling biases in the male and female sets of data (Hyman and Sheatsley, 1954). For example, about 30 per cent of the female sample is Jewish compared to 15 per cent of the male sample, and there is a much higher percentage of males with only grade-school education. The way in which sex differences have been distorted can be illustrated by the often-quoted comparison of the fact that 90 per cent of the males had premarital coitus in contrast to 50 per cent of the females. When only college-educated persons are compared, the figures were 68 per cent of the males compared to 60 per cent of the females. Matching for obvious, relevant variables generally decreases differences attributable to sex per se. The manner in which the data are set out makes comparisons matching or controlling relevant variables difficult or impossible.

A surprising feature of the book is the extent to which value judgments are interjected into a scientific report. The philosophical position of naturalism and its logical fruit, hedonism, permeates the book with an enthusiasm suggestive of the true believer. There are also ambiguities and inconsistencies in the book which have contributed to dispute and misunderstanding.

Sexual Development

The Kinsey book describes the sexes as beginning quite similarly in their sexual behavior and gradually diverging. Infantile sexuality is accepted as a fact, though most of the data is based on males (Kinsey, 1965; Sears, 1943). This view is now being challenged (Chodoff, 1966; Simon and Gagnon, 1969). Summarizing their own observations and those of others, the Kinsey group conclude that there is no question that the capacity for orgasm is present in at least some females at a very early age; three was the youngest example. In surveying the literature, reports of female genital preadolescent sexual arousal were found ranging from 5 per cent before eleven to 77 per cent by age ten; the Kinsey data showed an accumulative incidence (per cent of the sample who had ever engaged in the behavior) of 27 per cent before about thirteen. In males, an early adolescence signalled an increase in sexual activity, but early adolescence seemed to have little effect on female sexual activity. Male sexual behavior showed a sharp increase at adolescence and a continuity with previous activity; female behavior did not. Douvan and Adelson (1966) found very little reference to sexuality in their interviews with adolescent girls. The girls showed a placid tone with an absence of the kind of preoccupation with drives and their control such as they had found with boys and had expected to find with girls. Sexuality more often than not was secondary to other motives. The authors were puzzled by this and asked, "Are the girl's sexual impulses veiled and ambiguous because of the operation of massive defenses? Or is the nature of the impulses such that they lend themselves to repression?" (Douvan and Adelson, 1966, p. 110). Both questions assume that sexual impulses have been repressed. The more obvious interpretation that adolescent girls are simply not very sexually motivated was not even mentioned.

The Kinsey investigators found that the male and female curves of cumulative incidence of petting coincided very well, while those for cumulative incidence of orgasm did not. Males had many more orgasms than females. These results were interpreted as indicating that female participation in petting came more from social than sexual motivations. The female orgasm curve rose slowly, not peaking till the thirties and declining little thereafter. The male curve reached its peak at sixteen to eighteen, and reaching a greater height, showed greater relative decline with age. The sex difference in aging is supported by the finding of Terman (1938) that between ages forty-five to fifty-four, women in his sample for the first time preferred more intercourse than they received. Only about a quarter of the Kinsey female sample had masturbated before marriage in contrast to the nearly universal masturbation found among males. The fact that female primates of infrahuman species masturbate less than males (Ford and Beach, 1951), makes less convincing the argument that women do not show more sexual motivation because cultural factors discourage it.

The orgasm curves for both males and females in the Kinsey data nicely paralleled the curves for each sex of urinary excretion of 17-ketosteroids, a measure of androgens from both the gonads and the adrenal cortex. Evidence has accumulated that these hormones underlie pressure to sexual activity (Money, 1965a; Waxenberg, 1963, 1969), though there is not total consensus on this point (Kane, Lipton, and Ewing, 1969). Since the level of androgens is higher in males, they presumably have more sex drive. (Sex drive refers to motivation for sex and not capacity for orgasm.)

Simon and Gagnon (1969) have concluded that the strength of the sex drive has generally been exaggerated, especially by Freud, and that sex drive does not really operate until adolescence. They suggest that a major reason for sex divergence in sexual development is that males move from a privatized personal sexuality to sociosexuality. Females do the reverse and at a later stage of life. Women may . . . "create or invent a capacity for sexual behavior, learning how to be aroused and learning how to be responsive." (p. 746).

Beach (1958) points out that decortication creates less damage to the sexual response in nonprimate and probably primate females than in males. The cerebral cortex seems to contribute less to female sexuality. Male infrahuman primates show sexual behavior before puberty, but females do not. Prepubertal sexual activity does not appear before the primate level. Male primate sexual behavior does not appear to be entirely hormone dependent. Sexual behavior among female primates is less dependent on hormones than is the case for lower species, but this difference is even more marked for male primates. The facts that infantile sexuality in human females has been mostly assumed from observations of males and there is little evidence for the female Oedipus complex suggest that human females may also differ from males in showing less prepubertal sexuality.

Women Less Responsive to Psychological Factors

Kinsey and his colleagues found that women were less sexually stimulated than men by a whole host of factors, such as observing the opposite sex, observing one's own sex, observing portrayals of nude figures, erotic fine art, observing genitalia, observing own genitalia, exhibitionism, interest in genital techniques, observing burlesque and floor shows, observing sexual action, observing portrayals of sexual action, observing animals in coitus, peeping, and voyeurism, sexual activity in the light, fantasies concerning opposite sex, fantasies concerning own sex, fantasies during masturbation, noctural sex dreams, erotic stories, erotic writing and drawing, wall inscriptions, discussions of sex, sadomasochistic stories, fetishism, and transvestism. Women further showed their lower level of response to sexual stimuli in their discontinuity of sexual activity, distractibility during coitus, lesser promiscuity, and in attaching less significance to the sexual element in marriage. Women were stimulated equally or slightly more by observing commercial motion pictures, literary materials, and being bitten.

From these findings, the conclusion was drawn that women are less stimulated by psychological factors than men and that they are thus less easily conditioned to sexual stimuli. The point was made that women are not more moral than men, just less tempted. That the sex difference was not considered categorical is demonstrated by the fact that two to three per cent of women were regarded as more responsive to psychological stimuli than men, one third equal, and the rest less responsive. The fact that women do indeed react to sexual stimuli has been demonstrated experimentally. Loisell and Mollenauer (1965) found that women showed significantly greater GSR response to nude males than to nude female figures. Mosher and Greenberg (1969) found that college girls were sexually aroused by reading erotic material.

The phrasing "less responsive to psychological factors" was undoubtedly chosen to avoid any misunderstanding of their view that, given effective, continuous physical stimulation, women are as capable of sexual response as men, and just as rapidly (Kinsey, Pomeroy, Martin, and Gebhard, 1965). Women have even greater capacity than men in terms of rapid repetition of orgastic response. Some sort of cerebral difference was postulated to account for this sex difference in what was called responsiveness to psychological stimuli.

While an appropriate interpretation of this data would appear to be that men have greater sex drive than women, this formulation is rejected by the Kinsey group (1965) as explaining nothing. Apparently a drive explanation did not seem to do sufficient justice to the qualitative differences found. Beach (1956) objects to the notion of sex drive, since it is a species and not an individual need. He prefers the term "appetite." Gebhard (1965), one of the Kinsey group, apparently accepts the view that males have greater sex drive. Hull (1943) included sex among the primary drives, and the study of Von Felsinger (1948) generally supported his view, at least for rats. A drive is said to exist when there is a need which motivates the organism to action. Probably the greater male sex drive is based on greater androgenic secretions (Money, 1965a) and is culturally augmented and buttressed. Certainly if this is the case, there very likely are differences in the brain, possibly even in the cerebrum, in the concentration of androgenic substances and their metabolites.

Consideration of hunger drive in humans may provide a more neutral example of the appropriateness of the interpretation of greater male sex drive. It is known that people who have not eaten for some time begin to think about food, sometimes even fantasy about it (Keys, Brozěk, Henschel, 1950). Under conditions of prolonged deprivation, they might be expected to look at tantalizing pictures of food, be fascinated to watch other people eat food, read about food, etc. In another individual with sufficient food (lower drive state), there is no fantasy of food, or time spent looking at pictures of food or people eating. Dinner is served to the two individuals, and the second eats and digests the meal just as well as the first. The suggested analogy is, of course, that when presented with a sexual opportunity, a woman though of lower sex drive state might enjoy it perfectly well even though her drive state was not so high that she would have made much of an effort to seek out such an opportunity nor attempted to gain vicarious satisfaction by engaging in various forms of fantasy. *The analogy of sex drive to hunger drive is not meant to be a complete one,* but it has been used to illustrate that responsiveness to psychological stimuli may be modified by physiological state. It seems likely that the greater adult male sexual response to psychological stimuli might be adequately accounted for by an hypothesis of greater male sex drive.

MALE SEX DRIVE STRONGER

Many investigators have considered male sex drive to exceed the female. Burgess and Wallin (1953) concluded that the male sex drive is greater and occurs earlier. They attribute this to both culture and biology. They found that husbands desire significantly more coitus than do their wives. Terman's (1938) sample of husbands preferred to have intercourse twice more per month. Burgess and Wallin pointed out that since Terman's sample involved another generation, the finding appears to be a relatively stable one. Bell (1966), however, interpreted the data as indicating an increase in sexual interest and appreciation compared to earlier periods. While two thirds of the Davis (1929) subjects reported a desire for less frequent coitus, Burgess and Wallin reported 16 per cent compared to 6 per cent reported by Bell (1966). Twenty-five per cent of the women, in contrast to 20 per cent in the Burgess and Wallin data, desired more frequent coitus. Viewing these trends, Bell (1966) wonders if women will end up with greater sexual desire than men. However, the slowed rate of change in more recent years suggests that there is no cause for alarm.

Like Douvan and Adelson (1966), Ehrmann (1959) found sex interest stronger and earlier in males. Eroticism did not become important to girls until their late teens, early twenties, or not until during marriage. The males had more sex experience, initiated more sex, talked much more about sex, and showed a consuming interest in sexual techniques. Girls definitely showed greater aversion to sex than boys. For girls, going steady, an affectional tie, was the most important determinant of sexual activity. The importance of the affectional tie for women was confirmed by Reiss (1967), and with an English population by Schofield (1965), but not for American Negro women (Reiss, 1967). Sex is so secondary for some women that they have been found to use sex in order to attain satisfaction of needs for simple body contact such as holding (Hollender, Luborsky, and Scaramella, 1969). Kirkpatrick (1959), in a commentary on Ehrmann's book, also concluded that Ehrmann's data as well as Kinsey's were more consistent with the interpretation that the male sex drive is stronger.

Reiss (1960), evidently basing his conclusion on the observation of Ford and Beach that there are some cultures in which women initiate sexual activity, concluded that there is no innate difference in sex drive between the sexes. This evidence does not seem sufficient for the conclusion, and it is not necessary to go to other cultures to find examples of female initiative in sexual activity (Hirsch, 1967). Kirdendall (1961a) also thinks there is no innate difference between the sexes in sex drive. Sherfey (1966) supposes that the sex drive of women has been innately much greater than that of men. Masters and Johnson (1970) suggest that because of the greater female sexual-response capacity, cultural restraints on women arose in order to provide a better balance between the sexes. It would seem important to differentiate between sex drive and sex response. Men seem to have more of the former and women more of the latter.

VANITY, MODESTY, AND FASHION

Given the more promiscuous desires of the male and his visual responsiveness, it seems reasonable to attribute female vanity, addiction to fashion changes and a large and varied wardrobe partly to this source. In a new dress, she is a new woman, and that is precisely the point. Female modesty may be another consequence of the higher male sex drive. Some have cited nudity in primitive tribes to indicate the unnaturalness of modesty, but Ford (1945) made the point that in all tribes, the genitals were either covered or there was a code of etiquette accomplishing the same purpose. MacLean (1965) has speculated that modesty is the result of a desire not to arouse hostile and sexual impulses continually. It seems probable that modesty serves the social purpose of channeling sexual drive. These explanations seem much more parsimonious than those offered by psychoanalytic writers, e.g. that women wish to hide the "wound" of castration (Devereux, 1960).

CYCLIC VARIATION IN FEMALE SEX DRIVE

Cyclic variation of female sex drive has been repeatedly reported (Kane, Lipton, and Ewing, 1969). Studies in this area are complicated by the fact that there are two major influences. The first is hormonal and psychophysical variations; the second is the pressure of the psychosocial situation (Masters and Johnson, 1970). Masters and Johnson suggest that the vasocongestion of the genitals during menstruation may result in sexual arousal. A study of dreams found significantly more manifest sexuality during the menses (Swanson and Foulker, 1967). The data, however, were based on only eleven weeks of observation of four girls. The Kinsey study (1965) had concluded that their own data and that of investigators generally were in agreement that desire is greatest just before and just after the menstrual period. Thomason (1955) and Hart (1960) provide somewhat more recent support for that view. Shader (1968) found a premenstrual increase in women who were anxious or upper class.

The Kinsey report (1965) cited the research of Benedek and Rubenstein (1942; Benedek, 1952a) already described in the last chapter as the major exception. It is very doubtful that their findings are, in fact, at variance; the Kinsey interpretation seems to be a case of misunderstanding. Kinsey and the others are talking about active heterosexual desire which Benedek also found increased just before and after menstruation. She characterized the ovulatory period as one of unusual sexual receptivity, a subtle mood distinction involving passivity, not a mood of increased initiative. It seems unlikely that Kinsey gathered any data bearing on the existence of this mood. Benedek's more recent statement (1959b) makes clear that she considers desire to increase both before and after the menstrual period. These cyclic variations are apparently not due to estrogen level, however (Waxenberg, 1969). Waxenberg (1969) reports that Johnson and Masters have found a lack of consistent coincidence in any large majority of women of peak responsiveness with either the estrogenic phase of the menstrual cycle or the time of menses.

Udrey and Morris (1968) studied the actual sexual behavior of women rather than their dreams or reported desires. Their samples were forty married nonwhite women and 48 middle-class women. They found rates of intercourse and orgasm at one point in the cycle were from two to six times the rates at other points in the cycle. The highest rates of intercourse and orgasm occurred about the time of ovulation. These results are fairly consistent with those of an early study by McCance, Luff, and Widdowson (1937). When subjects were given artificial progestins, the depression in sexual activity after the mid-cycle was abolished. The authors attribute this to a wiping out of the usual luteal peak of endogenous progesterone (Udry and Morris, in press).

An increase in sexuality at ovulation occurs among infrahuman primates (Michael, 1965; Michael, 1968; Rowell, 1967). In a natural situation, the infrahuman female in a sexually receptive phase will frequently exhaust the sexual capacity of more than one male (Rowell, 1967). It has been supposed that the continual sexuality of the human female is what has permitted monogamy, but the fact that human females do not experience strong cyclic pressure to sexuality would seem to be of greater importance.

ORGASM

The matter of female orgastic capacity has been extremely controversial. There has even been debate as to whether the physical capacity for orgasm exists in all women. Terman (1938) found very little correlation between orgastic capacity and psychological variables, leading him to the conclusion that the capacity for orgasm is probably innate. Elkan (1948) suggested that orgasm is an evolving trait that is not found in lower animals and hence may be biologically missing in some women. While evidence regarding orgasm in female animals is by no means complete, the Kinsey study (1965) pointed out that there is definite evidence of orgasm in at least some females in some species. Proper surveys, however, have not yet been conducted. Elkan's argument does not appear to be well taken.

There are, however, considerable numbers of women who do not experience orgasm in sexual relations. Dickinson and Beam (1931) summarized their findings among patients in Dickinson's gynecological practice. Two of five women had orgasm; two of five had it never or rarely or used to have it but do not now, and one in five had it sometimes or sometimes with clitoral stimulation. In a study of 153 normal women, seven per cent never had orgasm; over 23 per cent were inadequate in their sexual adjustment, and only 38 per cent were judged completely adequate in sexual adjustment (Landis, Landis, and Bolles, 1940). One third of Terman's (1938) sample rarely or never reached climax. In the age range of twenty-one to thirty, Chesser (1956) found 65 per cent of a sample of English women reported orgasm frequently or always and 50 per cent said they had a lot of sexual satisfaction. In the over-fifty age group, almost half still reported orgasm frequently or always and 25 per cent said they had a lot of sexual satisfaction. The Kinsey study (1965) found that 10 per cent of women did not have orgasm in marital intercourse. It was estimated that the average woman has orgasm in 70 to 77 per cent of marital coitus, increasing from 63 per cent the first year to 85 per cent the twentieth year of marriage. None of the data is consistent with the contention of Bergler and Kroger (1954) that at least 75 per cent of women are frigid, that is, have no coital orgasm. The closest finding to this high figure of 75 per cent may be the 60 per cent that Dickinson and Beam (1931) found did not definitely have orgasm. The greater agreement may be based on the fact that in both cases, the figures are based on private gynecological patients. Such a sample, of course, contains many more people with problems than a cross-section of the general population.

There are some obvious factors affecting orgasm that should not be forgotten. Johnson and Masters (1964) expressed the opinion that the two major deterrents to female sexual responsiveness are fatigue and preoccupation. Kegel (1952) pointed out the factor of poor muscle tone, especially due to obstetrical damage and childbirth. He views sexual perception, like control of the bladder, as an acquired or learned function. He believes that the pubococcygeal muscle, which has inserts in the vaginal wall and provides bladder control, has a sensory perceptual function, probably through specialized proprioceptors. Kegel reported that cases with a perivaginal muscular contractile strength of 20mm Hg or more have few sexual complaints. Of 123 women placed on a program to exercise this muscle, 78 had thus far reported orgasms for the first time. (The exercise is basically contraction such as to shut off a stream of urine.) This is a relatively high improvement rate, considering the simple and fairly inexpensive character of the treatment, especially when contrasted with psychotherapy. Kegel believes that psychic problems are the result, not the cause, of coital problems, but it is probable that causation can work both ways. Schaefer (1969) concludes that psychosexual satisfaction appears to be a learned experience. The learning can develop either for pleasure or against pleasure. Simon and Gagnon (1969) also stress learning factors in sexual development. Masters and Johnson (1970, p. 297), however, state that it ". . . seems more accurate to consider female orgasmic response as an *acceptance* of naturally occurring stimuli that have been given erotic significance by an individual sexual value system than to depict it as a learned response."

Social and Psychological Correlates of Orgasm

Unlike Terman (1938), Kinsey (Kinsey, Pomeroy, Martin, and Gebhard, 1965) found a number of correlations between orgasm capacity and psychological and social factors. Social class, however, related less to female than male sex behavior. Rainwater (1966) has pointed out that there is greater cross-class agreement on standards of female sexual behavior which may account for the apparent lack of social influence. Devoutness in all religious faiths, especially among the Catholics, depressed orgastic response in women. Decade of birth was a significant factor. In the four decades covered by the Kinsey research, there was an increase of five to six per cent in the percentage of women with orgastic response. The authors attributed this to decreased repression, but improved health and well-being among women may also be a cause. These may also be factors in the finding that orgastic capacity correlated positively with education and socioeconomic status. Lower-class women showed less orgastic response (Kinsey, Pomeroy, Martin, and Gebhard, 1965). Thirty to 37 per cent of a sample of English working-class wives reported always having orgasm (Woodside, 1948). It is difficult to compare statistics from the various studies, but this seems somewhat low.

In addition to obvious factors of poorer health and fatigue, just why lower-class women should have lower orgastic response is an interesting question. Rainwater (1966) found that forty per cent of the wives in lower-class marriages that were sharply segregated in sex role spontaneously complained that their husbands were inconsiderate sexually. Among this group, the double standard is strong and an effort is made to keep girls in ignorance of sexual matters. Lower-class white mothers do not discuss sex with their daughters, usually not even menstruation (Rainwater, 1966). As one young father described his wife to a poverty worker, "She's so scared I hate to do it to her."

Lower-class sexual behavior is a complex matter, however, and there is another group of girls who know a good deal about sex very early. This is most likely to be at the lowest levels of society. Evidence of sex shock has been found among them (Frank, Harrison, Hellersberg, Machover, and Steiner, 1951) . The Kinsey study (Kinsey, Pomeroy, Martin, and Gebhard, 1965) also found that traumatic sexual incidences occurred more often to lower-class girls. He found that 80 per cent of preadolescent sexual experience with an adult male resulted in fright or emotional upset, though not all to a serious extent. Hamilton (1929) reported a relationship between traumatic sexual experience and lack of orgasm. Dickinson and Beam (1931) reported that two thirds of their sample of 100 frigid women had had traumatic sexual experiences. It should be remembered, however, that what is traumatic for one person is not necessarily traumatic for another and that there are many cases on record of no apparent difficulty in adjustment among individuals with a history of sexual trauma. It is also true that in instances where no pain or violence is involved, the eventual effect on the child may depend more on the reaction of others to the event than on what actually happened. Despite all these qualifications, the fact remains that early traumatic experience apparently tends to have a negative effect on development and may be a factor in the lesser response of lower-class women.

Shope (1968) compared two groups of girls, orgastic and non-orgastic, matched for socioeconomic status, religious affiliation, age, term in college, and university grade average. All girls had had coitus at least fifteen times over a period of at least two months. He found that girls experiencing orgasm in their sexual relations were significantly less stable in terms of evenness of temperament than girls not experiencing orgasm. Generally, however, personality variables did not differentiate the groups. Girls with orgasm tended to feel that their mate's desire was equal to their own, and they did not feel so much that they were "giving in" to their mates. They seemed to have the ability to discuss sex freely and did not feel inhibited sexually. Interestingly, they also pretended orgasm significantly more often than the nonorgastic group.

Gebhard (1966) reanalyzed the original Kinsey study data to provide further information on factors in marital orgasm. He found that the percentage of women who have orgasm correlated with the extremes of happy and unhappy marriage, though there was little correlation in the middle range. Among the extremely happy marriages, only four per cent of the wives were not experiencing orgasm. He also found a correlation between length of foreplay and orgasm. In instances of foreplay of twenty-one or more minutes, only eight per cent of the wives had no orgasm. Less than one minute of penile intromission was rarely sufficient. On the other hand, when the duration of intercourse was sixteen or more minutes, only five per cent of the wives failed to reach orgasm. Gebhard concluded that neurophysiologic and unconscious psychological factors probably account for only five to ten percentage points' variation in orgasm capacity.

A rare experimental study of female sexual responsiveness is that of Fisher and Osofsky (1967). They found that sexual responsiveness correlated with a feeling of increased body prominence following gynecological examination, and that capacity for orgasm showed a consistent negative correlation with hostility. They also found a positive correlation between orality and sexual response, possibly providing some experimental support for Bergler's (1958) view of the importance of orality in the sexual adjustment of women. Among frigid women, Cooper (1969) found many immature, self-centered personalities, but he stresses that frigidity is not an homogeneous disorder. *In toto,* the presence of so much evidence of psychological, social, and physical correlates of orgastic response encourages agreement with the Kinsey study and Ellis (1908) that there probably are no innately frigid women.

Masochism and the Psychoanalytic View of Frigidity

Among the analysts, Bergler may perhaps best represent the type of viewpoint which Kinsey and his colleagues have been most at pains to discount. Bergler presented a much narrower view of normal adult sexuality than Kinsey and his co-workers have been willing to accept, since he, as well as most psychoanalysts, believed that normal sexual activity should usually culminate in coital orgasm. Furthermore, Bergler (1958) estimated that 75 per cent of women are frigid and stressed the psychological factor in frigidity. His main point was that during intercourse, a woman must unconsciously repeat the receptive role of the passive baby without resentment and grievance. He attributed frigidity problems primarily to the oral level, not Oedipal. He thought that because normal passivity is very close to neurotic masochistic passivity, defensive reactions may be aroused which interfere with proper receptivity. Clearly Bergler's views are mostly in error. He may be correct, however, that when there is a psychological factor affecting orgasm, it is more likely to stem from the conflicts of the oral stage than from the Oedipal stage.

Hart (1961) has pointed out that passivity is feared when it is equated with masochism or with helplessness. Unfortunately Deutsch (1944) has probably contributed to this faulty equation by stressing the need for a degree of masochism in women. In frequency of actual masochistic sexual perversions, there is apparently no significant difference between the sexes (Hamilton, 1929; Kinsey, Pomeroy, Martin, Gebhard, 1965), and Deutsch certainly does not mean that masochistic perversion is normal or necessary in women. In a later edition of her work, Deutsch added a footnote specifically denying that she thinks the desire to be raped and humiliated is normal in women, a view attributed to her by Horney (1939). Deutsch explained that she views the proper governing of mascohism as one of a woman's main psychological tasks. However, her writings have been considerably less than lucid on this point. For example, in saying that since reproduction involves pain, women must endow pain with pleasure, she suggests the inevitability of masochism. The question of pain and reproduction will be taken up in a later chapter. Suffice it to say here that pain does not always accompany reproduction and though it often does, the masochistic solution of endowing pain with pleasure is certainly not the only one, and there is no evidence that it is usual or even frequent.

May (1968) studied sex differences in stories made up to specially selected pictures. He interpreted his findings as showing greater masochism in women, but the findings are subject to so many alternate interpretations that they can not be regarded as sufficient to establish the point. There seems to be a serious semantic problem in the use of the term "masochism." It has such dark connotations that it would seem best to limit its use to the more restricted sense of pleasure in pain. It seems farfetched to label a sequence of suffering followed by joy as evidence of masochism in the way that May does. Such a sequence could also be attributed to greater awareness and conformity to the convention of having a happy ending every time.

Vaginal Versus Clitoral Orgasm

So far, no very precise definition of orgasm has been considered. Masters and Johnson (1965a, 1965b, 1966) have provided a definition in the form of minute descriptions of the anatomical and physiological sexual response in women. The stages of sexual response in the human female as they describe it are the following: the excitement phase, the plateau phase, the orgasm phase, and the resolution phase. These phases are paralleled in the male. In the female excitement phase, which may last from a few minutes to hours, the vagina moistens quickly with drops of clear fluid and the upper two-thirds balloons open; the nipples of the breasts usually become erect and the clitoris often increases in size. In the plateau phase, of thirty seconds' to three minutes' duration, the skin flushes; the breasts become about twenty-five per cent larger; the shaft of the clitoris retracts into its prepuce; the vagina balloons further and its transudate becomes more copious, and the uterus contracts as in labor. All this is accompanied by hypervenilation. In the orgasmic phase, lasting three to fifteen seconds, there are contractions of the lower vagina while contractions of the uterus continue. The resolution phase, of ten to fifteen minutes' duration, involves return of these organs to their initial state. The two unfailing signs of the occurrence of an orgasm were found to be tumescence and corrugation of the areolae of the breasts and involuntary contractions of the outer third of the vagina.

From an anatomic point of view, there was no difference in orgasm whether induced by clitoral area, vaginal, or breast stimulation. Their data provides no evidence for two orgasms, a vaginal and a clitoral one. Much ink has been spilled in this controversy. It originates in the statements of Freud that in the process of maturation, the young girl must give up her sexual investment in the clitoris and transfer it to the vagina, simultaneously switching from an active, masculine orientation to a passive, feminine sexual orientation. Deutsch's emphasis on female passivity stems from this notion. Analysts, including most prominently Bergler, have held that the absence of capacity for vaginal orgasm is a sign of abnormality. While it is not entirely clear what is meant by vaginal orgasm, a minimum criterion would certainly be an orgasm ultimately brought about by intravaginal intercourse. Inability to obtain orgasm in this way is considered abnormal by analysts; vaginal orgasms are thought to be more satisfying experiences providing more thorough and long-lasting sexual relief.

The Kinsey study (Kinsey, Pomeroy, Martin, and Gebhard, 1965) argued that it makes no sense to talk of a vaginal orgasm, since orgasm involves the whole body, not just either the clitoris or the vagina. Orgasm is essentially the result of rhythmic stimulation. The point was strongly made that no distinction could be drawn between a clitoral and a vaginal orgasm. However, one can certainly correctly speak of orgasm from clitoral stimulation as opposed to orgasm from intravaginal intercourse. The term coital orgasm seems adequate to describe the latter. For the most part, analysts believe that barring physical factors, women who cannot attain coital orgasm are abnormal and do not accept their femininity.

The Kinsey study's emphasis on whether or not the vagina responds to stimulation is not entirely to the point, since in some instances, women are so frozen with fear at penetration that pleasurable response of any kind is impossible. Nonetheless, the Kinsey study takes up the question of the sensitivity of the vagina. In trying to refute the idea of a vaginal orgasm, Kinsey and his colleagues cited as evidence lack of response to stroking of the vagina with a glass rod. As Bergler and Kroger (1954) rightly point out, this experiment is hardly comparable to intercourse. Equally beside the point, the Kinsey group cited the fact that physicians routinely cauterize the cervix without anesthesia as further evidence of the absence of feeling in the vagina and the impossibility of sources of pleasure there. Kroger, an experienced gynecologist, dismissed as nonsense the idea that this was a painless procedure. The Kinsey group undoubtedly would have come to a different conclusion themselves had they asked women how they felt about being cauterized. Just as it is absurd to speak as though orgasm takes place only in the vagina, it is also absurd to suppose that the vagina is uninvolved in orgasm. It decidedly is involved (Masters and Johnson, 1966). However, Freud's notion of female sexuality switching from masculinity (clitoris) to femininity (vagina) is clearly mistaken.

The Masters and Johnson data, while ruling out types of orgasm differing in anatomic characteristics, do not entirely rule out variation in orgasms which could be appropriately divided into types on the basis of neurological or psychological response (Schaefer, 1969). A few comments of Masters and Johnson suggest that they, in fact, found some differences in orgasms brought about by stimulation of the clitoris and those brought about by intercourse. For example, orgasm obtained by masturbatory stimulation of the clitoris caused more contraction of the gluteal muscles than orgasm obtained by intravaginal stimulation. They also concluded on the basis of their sample that "sexually mature women" are not content with only one orgasmic experience during episodes of *clitoral* manipulation. They prefer two or three orgasmic expressions before reaching satiation, with many preferring five to twenty, stopping only with physical exhaustion

(1965b). No desire for repeated orgasms from intravaginal stimulation was reported.

Marmor (1963) takes the position that the difference between the so-called clitoral and vaginal orgasm is explicable not in terms of the different origin or location of the orgastic response but in the different intensity of it and in the degree to which cortical factors are contributory. He sees the clitoral orgasm as a spinal one, while the vaginal orgasm has greater cortical facilitation. Benedek (1959b) seems to take a similar view.

There have been consistent psychological reports of variation in orgasm, contrasting such adjectives as "superficial" with "deeper and more sweeping" (Schaefer, 1969). Kegel (1952), for example, found that such changes in verbal report were correlated with increased sexual response during intercourse brought about by improved muscular strength and tone. Bergler has also stated that one orgasm is not as good as another, apparently in its effects of creating psychological well being. Evidence relevant to this point is notably lacking. Rheingold (1964) provides some rare insight into female frigidity from the male point of view. His descriptions of the feelings and reactions of the man with a frigid wife make it clear that frigidity is no fun for the male either, a point perhaps too often forgotten.

Need for Orgasm

The Kinsey study has emphasized that there are greater individual differences among women compared to men with regard to the strength and continuity of their sexual needs. While information on the effects of abstinence is not very complete, Kinsey noted that many women had long periods with no sexual activity, a rare event among men. Mervin Freedman (1967) was surprised by the ability of many young Vassar women to forego sexual expression completely without sign of strain or stress. Wallin (1960) obtained questionnaire data from 540 wives regarding orgasm as a condition of enjoyment of intercourse. He concluded that orgasm was not necessary for enjoyment of coitus, and whether or not lack of orgasm is experienced as frustrating is socially or culturally determined. Johnson and Masters (1964) claim that many women never experience orgastic release from sexual tensions and do not need such release.

While these statements are a welcome and necessary counter to the cult of the orgasm, in the interest of accuracy, some qualification is necessary. It is one thing to say that women do not necesssarily need orgasm or sexual stimulation, but there is definite evidence that sexual stimulation without orgasm is unpleasant for many and can even be harmful. Kinsey (1965) found that among women who petted but did not obtain orgasm, 26 per cent reported groin pain, and 51 per cent nervousness. Masters and Johnson (1965a) reported twelve hours of vasocongestion following sexual arousal without orgasm and not followed by sleep. Presumably with sleep, detumescence would take somewhat less time. Vasocongestion may be an important causal factor in cystic changes of the breast, ovary, and uterus (Taylor 1949a, 1949b, 1949c). Even without cystic changes, women frequently reported pain in these areas as a result of vasocongestion. There are other causal factors of vasocongestion besides what Taylor called unphysiologic sexual behavior. These are constitutional anomalies of the pelvic venous system, especially on the left side; damage to the pelvic veins from inflammation or from childbirth, and too much standing. Taylor considered dyspareunia (pain during intercourse) to be the most important cause in the continuation of the congestion syndrome. Among 105 women in their twenties and thirties with the syndrome, 31 showed a definite psychiatric symptoms. Taylor believed that the syndrome caused the nervousness, but it is more likely that "nervous" reactions are causal in both directions. A nervous, neurotic woman might be more inclined to develop the syndrome, and the pain, discomforts, and lack of satisfaction inherent in the symptoms undoubtedly contribute further to the development of nervous symptoms. For example, in the course of the syndrome, menstrual disorders and pain, as well as frigidity and dyspareunia, tended to develop. The point here seems to be that women who are continually aroused sexually and are unrelieved by orgasm are likely to become quite uncomfortable, and if other unfavorable factors are also present, they may even show adverse somatic developments. Of course, occasional unrelieved arousal allowed to wear off in sleep has no such ill effects.

VIRGINITY

Virginity quite clearly no longer remains an unquestioned value of our culture. The merits of premarital sexual activity have been increasingly debated in recent years. The Kinsey study (Kinsey, Pomeroy, Martin, and Gebhard, 1965) contended that there is probably a partial causal relationship between premarital orgasm and marital orgasm, a view that Bell (1966), for example, has accepted. Marital orgasm is also of some importance in marital happiness. Terman (1963) found a correlation of .26 between wife's orgasm adequacy and total marital happiness score. Are we to suppose that premarital relations will promote marital happiness?

The virgin state may have certain psychological characteristics, but it has not been the subject of much systematic study. Ladner (1968) has concluded that the transition from virgin to nonvirgin is the most crucial stage of psychosexual development. Among thirty lower-class adolescent black girls, there were two distinct groups. The virgins were more immature, obedient to parental authority and held strong beliefs about morality. They tended to romanticize relations with their boyfriends. The nonvirgins tended to be more sophisticated, rebellious, and autonomous and inclined to become deeply involved in interpersonal relations.

Bromley and Britten (1938) pointed out that the virginal girl does not label any specific feeling as referable to sexual impulse. Certainly it is easier for virgins to be unaware of their sexual feelings and it is easier for women than men to have this kind of confusion. Obvious anatomic and cultural factors are involved. This splitting off of the responsible recognition of sexual feeling is characteristic of hysteria, which occurs more often in females than in males. Lack of conscious integration of sexual feelings and/or lack of experience can result in dangerously provocative behavior or blasé unawareness of sexual intentions or implications. A certain amount of this is acceptable as normal girlish naivete. A tendency to repress sexuality is probably more important as a causal factor in this kind of naivete than virginity per se. But then, lack of experience makes it much easier to maintain repressions.

Virginity is still valued as a wifely prerequisite by a definite minority of college men. A double standard was readily admitted by 24 per cent of a sample of college men (Reiss, 1962). Cultural preference for expression of equalitarianism is again indicated by Reiss's finding that a more subtle measure of attitude indicated that 39 per cent of the males adhered to the double standard. Ehrmann (1959) found 33 per cent of his sample of college men held the double standard. Both of these authors pointed out that males will frequently specifically deny holding a double standard in order to encourage greater sexual cooperation from their dates.

Packard (1968) found that while the idea that a spouse might have had previous sexual experience did not "seriously" trouble either sex, a majority of males said it would trouble them "some." In London, 64 per cent of a large sample of adolescent boys wanted to marry a virgin (Schofield, 1965). It would seem, then, that quite apart from moral or religious considerations, young girls are being realistic in placing some value on their virginity. If women were to become dominant, Coleman (1966) suggests that a less severe sex code would be adopted, since women would no longer need to conserve their exchange value.

PREMARITAL RELATIONS

Kinsey (1965) supposed that premarital relations might have a favorable effect on later marital adjustment in that a girl could gain experience at an earlier age and under conditions of less significance for her life. That is, if the sexual adjustment were poor, she could dissolve the relationship with much less trouble than dissolving a marriage. The ambiguities of the Kinsey book, however, cause some difficulty with this point. At more than one place in the book, the much less controversial opinion is expressed that the relationship between premarital orgasm and postmarital orgasm is probably not a causal one but due to selection factors. The more responsive women would be more likely to have premarital relations and having reached orgastic responsiveness, would be likely to retain it in their marital life. It should be noted that the women who did not have orgasms in their premarital relations did more poorly than the virgins in obtaining marital orgastic responsiveness.

Another possible explanation of the premarital-postmarital orgasm correlation rests on the fact that apparently the variables of premarital relations, class, and marital orgasm are all interrelated. Only 38 per cent of the lower socioeconomic group had premarital coitus compared to 56 per cent of the upper group, and the percentage of women with marital orgasm is less over all years of marriage among lower-class women. The crucial variable here may be class or some correlate of class, such as fatigue or less-emancipated ideas rather than premarital experience.

Lack of support from other studies makes it even less likely that a true, causal relationship exists between premarital relations and marital orgasm. Burgess and Wallin (1953) found that marital orgasm was not related to having had orgasm before marriage. Popenoe (1961) found that at the start of marriage, only 28 per cent of virgins compared to 39 per cent of nonvirgins experienced orgasm, but even this difference dwindled in less than a year. Eventually 85 per cent of both groups experienced orgasm. Kanin and Howard (1958) used satisfaction with marital coitus as a measure of the effects of premarital coitus. After the first few days, little effect was discernible. They note that 18 per cent of those with premarital coitus reported problems, often sex-related, beginning with the honeymoon.

The more general question of the relationship between premarital sexual relations and marital adjustment is also of interest. If Kinsey and those who have quoted him since are correct that premarital relations promote marital orgasm, one would expect also a positive relationship between premarital relations and marital adjustment. Support for this proposition, however, is scanty. In a sample of 100 normal and 100 mentally ill women, a positive relationship was found between marital adjustment and premarital intercourse (Landis, Landis, and Bolles, 1940). Terman (1938) found no statistically significant relationship. Davis

(1929) found a significant relationship between virginity and marital success; Locke (1951) also reported a similar finding, but it was statistically significant only for men.

The Burgess and Wallin (1953) results are interesting in that they have been frequently used in a rather misleading manner to support the position that premarital relations promote marital success. This conclusion was based on the finding that nine tenths of the couples who had had premarital sexual relations and *who eventually married* reported that the premarital sexual experience helped strengthen their relationship. The subjects of the sample were probably more unconventional than the general population, but it is questionable that this interpretation of the results is correct even for this population. First of all, more of the couples who had had premarital relations broke their engagement. They were no longer in the sample to be asked what effect they felt premarital relations had on their relationship. The total group of couples having premarital relations obtained a significantly lower engagement success score and significantly fewer of the men desired no change in their partner. Kirkendall (1961b) found only 30 of 688 premarital liaisons strengthened by sexual relations. He found that where it did no harm, the relationship was usually so strong that it could not really be strengthened.

Shope (1967) found a low positive relationship between virginity and predicted marital happiness, as well as sexual adjustment. Reevey (1963) also found a large significant difference between the college women considered to be good marital bets and poor marital bets. The latter were involved in much more intimate premarital behavior. The overall impression reviewing the literature is that it is highly questionable that there is a causal relationship between premarital relations, even with orgasm, and marital orgasm. Moreover, if one is ultimately more concerned with marital happiness than marital orgasm, the evidence suggests that there is a tendency for virginity to be related to marital happiness. Again, the relationship is probably not solely and directly causal but may be the result also of related factors such as greater conventionality, religious conviction, and emotional security.

Still more doubt that premarital relations are conducive to

healthy development is raised by the findings of Halleck (1967) that of the girls coming for campus psychiatric help, a disproportionate number were having premarital relations. This author pointed out that in some situations today, girls are exposed to greater pressures for sexuality than for chastity. Swenson (1967) found that a sample of 25 coeds in therapy had significantly less social activity but significantly more sexual experience compared to a matched sample of 25 other coeds. Within the control group, girls having intercourse reported significantly more psychosomatic problems.

SUMMARY

There is considerable evidence that sex drive (motivation to seek and initiate sexual activity) is greater among men than among women, though the sexes overlap on this characteristic. This difference appears to be based on innate factors, and accentuated by learning mediated by cultural factors. In fact, differences in degree of sexual motivation may exist before puberty as well. In potential for sexual *response,* however, women have more orgastic capacity than men and it seems probable that all or nearly all women have the physical potential for orgasm. Women typically become sexually responsive somewhat later in life than men, and their sexual behavior is more mediated by affection. Research on cyclic variation in sexual desire and behavior is inconclusive at this time. Much evidence suggests increased sexual desire before and after the menstrual period but recent data indicates increased coitus and orgasm in the middle of the cycle.

The Masters and Johnson data (1966) must surely end the vaginal versus clitoral orgasm controversy. However, although orgasms may not vary anatomically, they may vary psychologically, or they may even vary in their central nervous system effects. The need for orgasm has been exaggerated, but it nonetheless remains true that continual arousal without orgasm causes psychic and physical discomfort. Unconscious conflicts as causes of frigidity appear to have been overemphasized, and sexual masochism is no more frequent in women than in men. Judging from the evidence regarding premarital sexuality, the new sexual freedom of women appears to be a mixed blessing. It seems doubtful that premarital sexuality is as beneficial as has been implied. In fact, the evidence suggests quite the opposite.

Chapter 9

PREGNANCY

PREGNANCY IS THE CAPACITY which most uniquely differentiates women from men. It is an extremely important event in the life of a woman and her family, and the course of the pregnancy has effects for good or ill on the unborn child she carries within. From a theoretical point of view, pregnancy is interesting because of the psychosomatic and biobehavioral effects which it can manifest. Empirical studies of the psychology of pregnancy have only recently been pursued with vigor. This relative neglect may well be a reflection of androcentric bias; pregnancy does not trigger masculine interest. Androcentric bias is certainly reflected in the Freudian hypothesis that having a baby represents compensation for lack of a penis. As seen in Chapter 3, there is little to support this general line of thinking, though no study bearing directly on Freud's sour grapes hypothesis was found.

This phallic overemphasis in the psychology of women may also have led to the general lack of attention given to the psychology of the doll. The doll ordinarily becomes the focus of the little girl's attention at a very early age and helps to develop a positive orientation toward future sex-role function. In later years, some aspects of the psychology of the doll are transferred to the purse. The purse, however, is nearly always interpreted in the context of a sexual symbol, ignoring its significance as a child symbol, something valuable to be carried about and not to be lost.

ACCEPTANCE OF PREGNANCY

Newson and Newson (1963) point out that women are under great time pressure to bear children. Prescribed childbearing behavior, at least in England, regards it as "too bad" to have an infant before age twenty-one, but a woman with no child by age twenty-six feels left out. People, especially women, are supposed to like children and want to have children, and for the most part they do. Expressions to the contrary are taboo in our culture and are generally regarded as shocking. While far more people want more children than want fewer (Pohlman, 1969), the fact is that children are not always wanted. It was found that 17 percent of white couples had more children than they wanted; the percentage was 23 per cent among those married ten or more years. Among nonwhite couples, 31 per cent had more children than they had wanted (Whelpton, Campbell, and Paterson, 1966). In an American sample of mothers from a low-income group, only slightly over half clearly wanted their children (Cobliner, 1965). Among a fairly unbiased sample of 278 pregnant Scottish women, 41 per cent did not want the pregnancy, 18 per cent did not mind, and 41 per cent desired it (Scott, Illsley, and Biles, 1956). In a sample of 212 student wife primiparae (women pregnant the first time), 64 per cent stated they had been happy about their pregnancies (Poffenberger, Poffenberger, and Landis, 1952). Gordon (1967) found that 80 per cent of women were happy about their first one or two children, but only 31 per cent were happy about the fourth or more. In a sample of middle-class wives, he found a change from a general acceptance figure of 55 per cent to 72 per cent after the availability of oral contraceptives. The figures for the happy acceptance of a child can be seen to range rather widely from only 31 per cent for those having their fourth or more child (Gordon, 1967) to the high figure of 83 per cent (Whelpton, Campbell, and Petterson, 1966). The latter figure is probably higher than some of the others because it is based on subjects from a more favored economic group and it is based on how people felt about their children some time after they were born. More negative figures are gained from on-the-spot assessment of the pregnant woman's attitude. Favorable economic circumstances and planning of the pregnancy appear to be factors increasing acceptance.

Among 5,293 white, nonprison women, the main sample of the Kinsey study, one fifth to one quarter had had an induced abortion at some point in their lifetime (Gebhard, Pomeroy, Martin, and Christenson, 1958). Ford (1945) concluded that the widespread restrictions on abortion among primitive peoples suggest that women are motivated to commit abortion. Many primitive peoples are not so different from their civilized counterparts as some romanticized accounts of the "natural" mother would have us believe (Soichet, 1959) .

FACTORS IN THE ATTITUDES OF PREGNANT WOMEN

There are some studies which investigate more fully the causal factors in the attitudes of pregnant women. In 1937, Despres reported on the attitudes of 100 primiparae. She found that the women with the most favorable attitudes toward their pregnancies were significantly different from women, with the least favorable attitudes in being less neurotic, and having had a closer relationship with their mothers, a happier home life, better marital adjustment, and economic security. Hamilton (1955) also found that those with the smoother, tranquil pregnancies had a better sexual and marital adjustment with fewer sources of guilt and negative bodily experience in the past. Likewise Grimm and Venet (1966; Grimm, 1969) found that among 124 "normal" middle-class pregnant women, desire for their particular pregnancy was related positively to social class and negatively to parity. Desire for this pregnancy was also positively associated with relative lack of neurotic symptoms and relative satisfaction with husband and life in general. Grimm points out that neurotic symptoms were less closely associated with lack of desire for the pregnancy than were the variables relating to reality circumstances at the time. It appears to be the old story—the rich get richer and the poor get poorer.

Sears, Maccoby, and Levin (1957) found that twice as many mothers were more pleased with the first pregnancy; delight was greater when the age gap between children was greater and when the sex of the new arrival was different from the preceding sequence. An initially negative attitude often becomes more positive by the time of the baby's arrival (Hall and Mohr, 1933; Klein, Potter, and Dyk, 1950; Winokur and Werboff, 1956.)

HORMONE CHANGES OF PREGNANCY

Some further information about the hormone changes of pregnancy may be helpful in evaluating the biobehavioral aspects of psychological state during pregnancy. Estrogen increases rapidly after the last missed menstrual period, the greatest rise occurring in the sixth to twentieth weeks. This is undoubtedly responsible for the increased sense of smell reported by some of Hamilton's subjects (1955). By the time of labor urinary excretion of estrogens has increased one hundredfold to one thousandfold, depending on the particular estrogen under consideration (Brown, 1956). Estrogens are known to increase energy metabolism, to promote growth of the uterus and a thick, rich epithelium; to assure the acidity of vaginal fluid, thereby retarding bacteria and fungus growth; to stimulate the increased thyroid and adrenal secretions of pregnancy, and to have a generally anabolic effect increasing protein content in bone, skin, and body (Lloyd and Leathem, 1964).

The synthesis of progesterone increases from 30 mg per day in the luteal phase of the menstrual cycle, to 200-300 mg per day during pregnancy. The preovulatory blood plasma level is very low—1 μg /100ml. In the second half of pregnancy, the blood plasma level of progesterone rises to 14-15 μg/ml (Hamburg, 1966). It stays high during the first stage of labor but is much lower in the second stage (Hamburg, Moos, and Yalom, 1968). Progesterone is known to have a sedative effect; electroencephalographic activity appears to be typically slowed during pregnancy, apparently due to progesterone (Gibbs and Reid, 1942; Gyermik, Genther, and Fleming, 1967). Slowing and slight impairment of cognitive functioning have been reported (Hamilton, 1955; Kane, Lipton, and Ewing, 1969), but little systematic study has been made of this topic. The gestagens, including progesterone, have effects on the breasts, and endometrium, and are responsible for the increase in bodily temperature during the first part of pregnancy (Lloyd and Leathem, 1964). Thyroid and the adrenal steroids increase. There are other changes known and undoubtedly still others to be discovered, but even less is known about their behavioral effects, so there appears little point in going into further physiological detail. As can be seen, the tremendous hormonal changes could easily underlie emotional lability, but the unusually high hormone levels, once achieved and steadily maintained, could support a pervading sense of well being.

EMOTIONAL STATE DURING PREGNANCY

There has not seemed to be much agreement about emotional state during pregnancy. Opinions range from pregnancy as a time of "vegetative calm" (Benedek, 1959b) to pregnancy as a crisis state (Bibring, Dwyer, Huntington, and Valenstein, 1961; Taylor, 1962). In the crisis view, pregnancy is seen as a time of physiological stress, like puberty and menopause. The fundamental changes associated with pregnancy are believed to create problems not only for the ill or neurotic but for the normal woman as well. All women are believed to become more anxious and regressed (returning to earlier, simpler, more childlike modes of adjustment). Compulsive women are the one exception; they are merely supposed to become more compulsive. The resolution of these conflicts is viewed as extending into the postpartum period.

A special part of the pregnancy adjustment is thought to be a reorientation of the pregnant woman toward her own mother. Some support for this may be seen in the finding of Hamilton (1955) that eight of twelve women became closer to their mothers as a result of pregnancy. Five of the twelve women moved closer to their mothers-in-law. The crucial factor here seemed to be whether the mother-in-law had a possessive or liberating attitude toward her married son. In no case did a poor relationship with a mother-in-law improve with the pregnancy. This generally positive view of mother-daughter relations is in sharp contrast to the exaggerated and dismal picture Rheingold (1964) paints of the mother-daughter relation during pregnancy and after. This important topic, however, deserves more intensive study.

Benedek (1959b) sees pregnancy as a developmental stage and as a period of "vegetative calm," an intensification of the progesterone phase. Some support for this view may be found in the study of Hooke and Marks (1962), who concluded that pregnancy is a period of unusual well being. This conclusion was based on a sample of twenty-four Minnesota Multiphasic Personality Inventories taken in the eighth month of pregnancy. There was no significant increase in the percentage of abnormal profiles, but the fact there were significant increases compared to a normative group in five of the nine scales measuring abnormal psychological tendencies is hardly consistent with an interpretation of unusual well being. While the changes were not in scales measuring depression and anxiety, the changes can be interpreted as showing greater bodily concern, feelings of resentment, sensitivity, and emotional lability. If pregnancy truly promoted a sense of well being, surely one would have expected significant decreases, not increases, in these feelings. An additional argument that Hooke and Marks raise in order to buttress their case is quite interesting —the fact that psychiatric hospital admissions fall during pregnancy (Pugh, Jerath, Schmidt, and Reed, 1963). Before delivery, Paffenbarger (1964) found the ratio of hospital admission for psychosis compared to neurosis to be one to two, but after parturition, the ratio reversed and there were two psychotics admitted for every neurotic. Apparently there is an increase of milder emotional changes during pregnancy but a decrease in more severe reactions (Kane, Lipton, and Ewing, 1969).

Caplan (1960) describes the period from the end of the first trimester to the seventh or eighth month of pregnancy as a time of introversion and passivity. Women are described as lazy, cow-like, and in need of love and affection. These changes he considers most characteristic of pregnancy. While the pregnant woman's dependency may be a nuisance to the rest of the family, Caplan feels that the need is legitimate and the family should adjust accordingly. From the end of the first trimester to three to four weeks postpartum Caplan claims that conflicts—usually unconscious—come to the fore paradoxically without the usual accompanying anxiety. He believes that this gives pregnant women a temporary, misleading appearance of almost psychotic disturbance.

Hanford (1968) sees the first part of pregnancy as conflict ridden, while conflict declines during the middle period. During the last part of pregnancy, fear of labor increases. Excretion of 17-hydroxycorticosteroids seems to parallel this pattern. Hanford concluded that any factor increasing stress may have a potential adverse effect on pregnancy.

Several of the studies of emotional state during pregnancy were made with subjects from lower socioeconomic groups. These studies are especially interesting, since they shed some light on how life begins for the poor. One of the earliest direct empirical studies of emotional state during pregnancy is that of Hall and Mohr (1933) who interviewed sixty-six women awaiting birth. Most of the pregnancies in this low-income group were unplanned and fourteen of the mothers were not reconciled to it; ten had attempted abortion. Twenty-eight had economic worries, while sixteen had fears regarding heredity. In general, the account is a terrible catalogue of depression and superstitious fears. Hurst and Strousse (1938) interviewing another group of one hundred poor women found that only three were less anxious during pregnancy, twenty-two were the same, and the remaining seventy-five were more anxious. Seventy-five per cent had economic worries, sixteen per cent phobias of various sorts, 7 per cent anxiety about the husband, and 10 per cent anxiety about other family members. Forty of the fifty followed after delivery were no longer worried so much, even though their troubles were the same. In the course of psychiatric interviews of a similar sample of one hundred pregnant women, Thompson (1942) found many emotional problems and a great need to talk. Hamilton (1955) reached the same conclusions. Klein, Potter, and Dyk (1950) closely observed a group of twenty-seven pregnant women and found that all but three showed mood changes, though not usually marked. Those with a previous tendency to instability showed the most marked changes. However, they saw no instance of euphoria or unusually good spirits. Most of this group, again, were severely disadvantaged. One would not expect such a black picture with less disadvantaged subjects. Hamilton (1955), for example, found that even though fears and anxiety increased in thirteen of the fourteen women she studied, moods of elation also occurred in those women living in a secure relationship with their husbands.

Riffaterre (1965) found significantly more depression as measured by the Rorschach, though not by the Minnesota Multiphasic Personality Inventory in a sample of pregnant Jewish women compared to a nonpregnant control group. Two hundred and twelve student wives questioned a few weeks to two and one-half years after their first delivery, reported a significant increase in emotional upset during pregnancy compared to the prior period, with another increase in the second half of pregnancy (Poffenberger, Poffenberger, and Landis, 1952). Tobin (1957) had one thousand postpartum patients fill in questionnaires. During their pregnancy, 68 per cent of the recently pregnant women admitted crying spells for no reason, compared to 5 per cent among a group of five hundred patient controls; 84 per cent admitted to the blues compared to 26 per cent in the controls; 61 per cent reported extreme irritability compared to 8 per cent in the controls. After birth, 63 per cent of the mothers admitted crying or depression. Only 12 per cent of the mothers admitted having such symptoms when not pregnant. Tobin concluded that emotional changes are part and parcel of a normal pregnancy on a biochemical basis and recommended that women be warned to expect this so they would not worry about it.

PARITY AND PSYCHOLOGICAL ADJUSTMENT

It has generally been supposed that for multiparae, an easier psychological adjustment parallels the easier physical task of childbirth. Clearly labor is shorter and easier for multiparae, but Grimm (1969) questions the greater ease of psychological adjustment. Erickson (1965) found that primiparae showed significantly more fear for themselves and the baby, but that they were less irritable than multiparae. Winokur and Werboff (1956) found the primiparae in their sample of 124 were less obviously apprehensive than the multiparae. For this reason, separation of primiparae from multiparae has been recommended in educational and treatment programs. Cohen (1966) found that compared to primiparae, emotional problems related to pregnancy were about fifty per cent greater in a sample of middle class, Protestant multiparae. While those expecting their third baby felt more secure and sure of themselves than those expecting their first, during labor, multiparae were reported to be more fearful about their own survival and about having deformed babies than primiparae (Larsen *et al.,* 1966). As discussed in the next chapter, it is also by no means clear that multiparae have an easier time during the postpartum period. Grimm (1969) concludes that women with several children simply do not get enough support, psychologically and realistically, from those around them.

EMOTIONS AT DIFFERENT STAGES OF PREGNANCY

Emotional changes may be very much dependent on the stage of pregnancy. During the first trimester, Bushnell (1961) found fatigue, nausea, and loss of appetite in forty-seven of a series of fifty-five women. He came to the conclusion that the women were depressed and consequently treated them with amphetamines. Napping and total sleep time increased during the first trimester (Karacan, 1968). Erickson (1967) followed a small group of women, using daily symptom check lists in order to study longitudinal trends during pregnancy. She found nausea, vomiting, headache, decreased sex desire, and euphoria frequently reported during the first four months of pregnancy and rarely mentioned later. Fatigue, depression, irritability, and anxiety were frequently reported in the first four to five months and in the last month of pregnancy. Backache, increased appetite, tension, and increased sex desire were complaints not particular to any phase of pregnancy. Insomnia was a continual problem, showing a sharp increase during the last four weeks. Swollen limbs, short breath, and groin pain were not a problem till the last month of pregnancy. Ten out of 14 of Hamilton's subjects (1955) complained of fatigue and sleeplessness in the last month. Five complained of frequent need to urinate, physical restlessness, backache, clumsiness. Five, who were also those with obsessive fears, showed bursts of activity in the last two weeks. The activity seemed to have an anxiety-reducing function.

Grimm (1961), studying a sample of 200, found an increase in tension in the last half of the last trimester. In a 1966 study, she found less neuroticism at sixteen weeks, more enthusiasm about the pregnancy, and fewer somatic symptoms. It was also during this middle period of pregnancy that Eron (1953) failed to find any difference between pregnant women and controls on anxiety indicators measured by the Thematic Apperception Test. A Russian study has reported more stable conditioned reflexes in animals during middle pregnancy (Nemtsova, Morachevskaia, and Andreeva, 1958). Apparently this is the time of "vegetative calm." Later on, at thirty-six weeks, Grimm (1966) reported somatic and emotional symptoms merging as one factor and a new factor of sex adjustment appearing. The group as a whole did not become more neurotic or depressed with pregnancy. Situational stress correlated .32 with neuroticism, and .33 with somatic symptoms. McConnell and Daston (1961) found increased feelings of body penetrability during the eighth and ninth months of pregnancy; these significantly decreased after delivery when the women apparently felt more integrated and less vulnerable. The body barrier score, which is believed to measure more fixed personality characteristics, showed no significant change.

RELATION OF SYMPTOMS AND ATTITUDES

Zemlick and Watson (1953) made an intensive study of fifteen subjects. They found a significant relationship between emotional adjustment during pregnancy and the frequency, duration, and intensity of psychosomatic symptoms. Those women with favorable attitudes early in pregnancy were apt to be well adjusted and to have fewer somatic complaints in pregnancy. None of the measured variables predicted severe pathological symptoms such as hyperemesis (pernicious vomiting), continuous bleeding, albuminuria, or premature delivery. Hamilton (1955) found nausea, persistent food cravings, obsessive fears, moodiness, and depression significantly related to sexual anxiety. Brown (1964) also found more bodily symptoms in those women with more worries, anxiety, neuroticism, and differences with their husbands. Another study (Zuckerman, Nurnberger, Gardiner, Vandiveer, Barrett, and den Breeijen, 1963) assessed anxiety and somatic complaints monthly beginning in the fourth or fifth month. They also found a significant positive relation between somatic complaints during pregnancy and manifest anxiety, marital conflict, and indirect indicators of conflict, particularly dreams.

Rosengren (1961, 1962a, 1962b) has studied pregnancy from the point of view of the woman's tendency to adopt a sick role. This tendency has been generally found to be more marked in the lower classes, in those changing social status, and in those women of the higher classes with low self esteem. While Rosengren excluded obviously ill individuals from his sample, lacking a more refined control for actual sickness, one cannot be sure that those who adopted a sick role were not, in fact, sick in some milder degree. Social disarticulation and low social status appear again as important variables in studies of postpartum psychotic reactions and toxemia.

So far as emotional state in pregnancy is concerned, the weight of the evidence suggests that it is not generally a period of unusual well being. However, such feelings occur in some women during middle pregnancy and there may be a decrease in psychotic reactions during pregnancy. Milder emotional disturbances, however, apparently increase, especially during the last six weeks.

DEPENDENCY DURING PREGNANCY

Benedek (1959b) and Bibring (1959) have characterized pregnancy as a time of increased dependency and even regression. Wenner (1966) observed fifty-seven normal and neurotic patients on this point and reported her opinion that the women with more mature forms of dependency did not regress, nor did those immature women whose dependency needs were met. She concluded that regression is not characteristic of pregnancy so long as one does not label a realistic increase in the need for help as regression. Hook and Marks (1962) found significantly less dependency among the pregnant women of their small sample. Assuming that food cravings during pregnancy are the result of increased dependency needs, and assuming that food taboos protect women from the danger of increased weight, Ayres (1967) predicted and found that the strength of dependency indulgence in a culture was significantly correlated with the number of foods tabooed during pregnancy.

That women may require more help during pregnancy, childbirth, and the first postpartum weeks is scarcely to be denied. Women who pride themselves on self-sufficiency may be made anxious by this (Hamilton, 1955), as well as women who have not learned to trust people and women who cannot be sure they have help available. Whether women typically become more dependent beyond the requirements of reality is an open question. Conflicts about having to rely on others have not been carefully investigated, but hints of the importance of this area appear repeatedly in the studies on habitual abortion, toxemia, and adverse postpartum reactions.

SEXUAL DESIRE DURING PREGNANCY

Modifications of sexual desire have also been said to occur during pregnancy. The effect of sexual activity on pregnancy is a question of great importance, but it is not a psychological one. Suffice it to say that many physicians believe that intercourse has an adverse effect and sometimes prohibit it in the first three months of pregnancy and frequently prohibit it in the last month or two. This is not a modern medical innovation, since nearly all the sixty-four primitive tribes which Ford (1945) studied forbade sexual intercourse during the last month of pregnancy, with varying restrictions before that. Ayres (1967) found that fourteen of thirty-six societies had no sexual restrictions during pregnancy; twelve forbade intercourse for the entire pregnancy, and three placed restrictions only on the last four to eight weeks. Ford points out that there is some increased risk of infection during pregnancy and that the uterine contractions of orgasm may precipitate labor. These facts undoubtedly help account for the prevalence of the taboo. Masters and Johnson (1966) emphasize that these dangers are generally exaggerated, however.

Erickson (1967) found a decrease in female sex desire during the first few months of pregnancy. Robertson (1946) found a relationship between excessive nausea and vomiting during early pregnancy and unwanted sexual relations. Far from seeing abnormal psychological tendencies in this, Horsley (1966) suggests that vomiting during early pregnancy is a natural protective device to limit sexual activity and thus decrease the probability of miscarriage. Landis and Landis (1958), in their study of 212 couples, found that one fourth of the wives noticed a marked decrease in sex desire while less than one fifth noticed an increase. Pregnancy had no effect on sexual adjustment for 58 per cent; 24 per cent found their sexual adjustment better, and 18 per cent found it worse. As pregnancy progressed, both husband and wife had less desire. Many said it did not seem right to continue sexual relations (Landis, Landis, and Poffenberger, 1950).

Masters and Johnson (1966) observed sexual relations of six women during their pregnancies. Four of the six complained of cramping and aching after orgasm in the first trimester. There was an increase in sex drive in the second trimester, with a concomitant increase in vaginal lubrication. In the second and third trimesters, vasocongestion brought on by sexual relations declined slowly, especially in multiparae. In the last three months, the vasocongestion sometimes did not go down at all, resulting in continuation of sexual tension in spite of marked and satisfying orgasm.

In a larger sample of 111 pregnant women interviewed at intervals during and after pregnancy, only a few reported increased sexual interest during the first trimester, while the rest found either no change or decreased desire attributable to nausea, fatigue, or fear. After the first trimester, all but 19 of 101 women reported an increase in desire. In the last trimester, 31 of 40 nulliparae (women who have never given viable birth) were advised to abstain from intercourse; 33 of the 40 lost interest in sex. Forty-six of 61 parous women were also restricted; 41 of them also lost interest. Twenty of the 111 said their husbands lost interest in intercourse. Sixty-eight of the 77 women for whom coition was interdicted worried about their husbands. Masters and Johnson question the need for routine prohibition of sexual relations. They feel that in many cases it is an unnecessary additional strain to marital and personal adjustment, since the occasional complications may be easily remedied by modern medicine.

PSEUDOCYESIS

The actual effects of attitudes and emotions on conception and on pregnancy has long been a subject of interest and speculation. Only recently has sufficient evidence accumulated to permit some scientific evaluation of the question. Aspects of the topic have been considered in two reviews (Grimm, 1967; McDonald, 1968). Since ancient times, however, one of the most dramatic and convincing illustrations of the potentialities of psychic influence has been the case of pseudocyesis, or false pregnancy. Cases of pseudocyesis not only falsely believe they are pregnant but show an almost complete simulation of the pregnancy state—breast changes, amenorrhea, nausea, uterus growth and softening of the cervix, obvious abdominal swelling, even a positive pregnancy test; labor may also be simulated. Once the woman is convinced that she is not pregnant, all these typical signs and symptoms of pregnancy disappear. Grimm (1967) concluded that there is no question but that this is a psychological phenomenon governed by the not-always-unambivalent wish to have a child.

PSYCHOLOGICAL CORRELATES OF INFERTILITY

The negative effects of psychological motivation on fertility have been more difficult to pin down. Benedek (1952b) has suggested that infertility is a somatic defense against the stresses of pregnancy and motherhood. She feels that infertile women tend to be either very hostile or childish and immature. Rakoff's (1963) observations on amenorrhea after severe shock are of interest in suggesting both the complexity of the matter and the importance of psychological factors. He found several different endocrine patterns, and discovered blocking factors at three different levels—the hypothalamic pituitary, ovarian, and endometrial levels. Rakoff emphasized the relative ineffectiveness of physical, hormonal treatment in that tissues were somehow able to remain unresponsive to large doses of hormones, while readily responding to smaller doses after psychotherapy or situational change.

Grimm (1967) concluded that there was almost no research designed to answer the question of psychological factors in infertility and that the available evidence did not provide very strong support for the hypothesis. Most of the articles on this topic tend to be impressionistic and contain no data, but there are several studies not included in Grimm's review which provide positive support for a relationship between psychological factors and infertility. In one study (Eisner, 1963), five judges blindly compared the Rorschachs of twenty women who were functionally infertile (infertile with no known physical cause) with those of twenty multiparae matched for age and socioeconomic status. The judges agreed that the infertile women showed significantly more schizoid responses, sex responses, and ice and snow responses to Card

VII of the Rorschach. The ice and snow responses were interpreted as a specific sign of frigidity. In Rorschach circles, Card VII is known as the mother card, and at another level these responses can also be interpreted as showing failure to develop trust and intimacy in the earliest relation with the mother. The infertile women were preoccupied with sex and disturbed in feminine role. The author concluded that while some of their disturbance may have been caused by their failure to have children, it was implausible that this alone could cause the schizophrenic-like adjustment seen in the Rorschach protocols. She believes that it is justifiable to conclude that psychological disturbance is a causal factor of infertility.

All functionally infertile women, however, may not be this disturbed. It is doubtful that this group of women is representative, since more normal infertile women may accept their state and not come (or be pushed) to a special clinic for help. Sample biasing was suspected in a study of secondary amenorrhea (Kelley, Daniels, Poe, Eassner, Monroe, 1954). (Failure to menstruate usually also results in infertility, so studies of secondary amenorrhea are related to the study of fertility problems.) A group of women treated for secondary amenorrhea were compared to two control groups. They were found to be characterized by psychosexual immaturity, oral conflict, and schizoid thinking. The authors' suspicion of a biased sample is supported by the results of studies of more representative samples (Osofsky and Fisher, 1967; Shanan, Brzezinski, Sulmen, and Sharon, 1965). Neither of these studies, discussed in Chapter 7, found such psychopathology in their subjects with amenorrhea. In fact, the latter study concluded that amenorrhea is not a symptom, but merely one possible reaction to stress.

One study of infertility failed to exclude women infertile from a known physical cause. Consequently, no relationship was demonstrated between infertility and psychological variables (Seward, Wagner, Heinrich, Block, and Myerhoff, 1965.) Belatedly, the authors contrasted nine of the original forty-one individuals judged high in organic causation with nine patients judged low in organic causation of their sterility. Six of the nine "low-organic" patients had had homosexual experience compared to none in the "high-organic" group. The "low organics" also had less orgastic capacity.

Authors of two dissertations also found significant psychological differences consistent with the positive findings of the previous studies. Brody (1955) found functionally infertile women were significantly different from fertile women in viewing the mother as a punishing figure as rated from projective test data. They were also significantly different from the women infertile from a physical cause in having more masculine and aggressive traits. Laitman (1958) found that functionally infertile women showed significantly more need for encouragement and emotional support than fertile women. Contrary to the conclusion of Grimm, (1967), the weight of the evidence now seems clearly in favor of the hypothesis that psychological factors can be causal in some cases of infertility.

By now it should be clear that if all the conjectures about psychological influence on reproductive functioning are true, there is hardly a woman alive whose reproductive functioning has not been influenced by psychological factors at some time in her life. This influence should not necessarily be regarded as a sign of neurosis or even as a negative factor but ordinarily as providing a woman with more control, albeit usually at an unconscious level, over the functioning of her body.

SPONTANEOUS ABORTION

The Hopi Indians are said to believe that women can produce abortion at will, but Devereux (1955) generally found among primitives an emphasis on the difficulty of producing abortions. He cautions that the Hopi ease of abortion may have been facilitated by associated venereal disease. The question of psychological influence in cases of spontaneous abortion has been somewhat more fully studied than psychological influence in infertility. Spontaneous abortion is not an uncommon experience; it occurred at some time in the life of about 25 per cent of the Kinsey sample and ended about 16 per cent of the conceptions (Gebhard, Pomeroy, Martin, and Christenson, 1958).

A group in Nova Scotia has produced some of the best and most systematic research on the question of habitual abortion (three successive spontaneous abortions). They have simultaneously evaluated physical factors including hormone levels and psychiatric data but provided no quantification of the latter. They have found hormonal support to be generally adequate (Tupper and Weil, 1962), though they found significantly lower levels of estrogen and progesterone in aborters, while chorionic gonadotrophin, 17-ketosteroids and hydroxy-corticoids showed greater quantitative fluctuations (Weil and Tupper, 1960). These fluctuations were often in response to psychological factors and frequently presaged a miscarriage, as is well illustrated in their case-history report (Weil and Stewart, 1957). In a 1957 study (Tupper, Moya, Stewart, Weil, and Gray, 1957), they found that forty-four of a hundred spontaneous aborters were basically dependent and immature. They had trouble making decisions, anxiety, confusion about their sex role, and even ignorance about sex. Another group of forty-four were superficially quite opposite—an independent, frustrated type with mixed feelings about the feminine role. These women tended to be married to understanding but neurotic husbands whom the wives tried to shield from inconvenience. The remainder of the one hundred were a mixed group including neurotics and "shiftless" individuals.

A later study of eighteen habitual aborters given the Rorschach and other tests (Weil and Tupper, 1960) revealed a picture of a group of women described by the authors as excessively independent and self controlled, but unable to achieve real independence and still less rebellion. Phrased in terms less loaded with clinical jargon, the authors appear to be describing women who show inappropriate and conspicuous acts of independent behavior, while at the same time giving evidence of strong dependency needs. The women were also described as operating on the basis of behaving in order to survive. As children, lack of conformity would have resulted in withdrawal of what little affection their mothers had to give them. Most of them wanted to get pregnant because their husbands wanted a child or because they thought that having a child was the main thing for a woman to do. Although their sex lives were satisfactory, sexual identification was said to be confused. Unable to compete with an efficient, hard-working, self-sacrificing mother, they identified with the father. Their independence was more like aloofness and conveyed an attitude of, "To hell with you." There was a lack of social participation which may have been partially a function of the fact that thirteen of the eighteen had been brought up in another locale. The pregnancy was seen as a threat.

In a second study, Tupper and Weil (1962) characterized two main personality types as especially prone to habitual abortion—the immature and the excessively independent. These two types were found to be especially likely to abort in the presence of certain stresses: an absent husband, lack of interest shown by the husband, or lack of interest shown by the doctor or other relatives. A striking aspect of these descriptions is the way they generally fit with the picture of psychosexually disturbed women described by Bergler (1958). As a causal factor, he emphasized disturbance in the oral stage which is thought to be the life period when basic attitudes about trust are established. The usual types to emerge from disturbance at this level are considered to be an immature dependent type, and the very opposite, a reactively independent type. However, the evidence indicates that tactual and body contact are much more crucial than orality in causing these developments (Bronfenbrenner, 1968). Rheingold (1964) has suggested that the many and varied disturbances of feminine function tend to be related and to stem from the same source—disturbance in the early relationship to the mother. Evidence of interrelation of reproductive disorders can be gleaned from the literature (McDonald, 1968), but a well-controlled, systematic study of this question is lacking.

The Nova Scotia group has successfully treated habitual aborters with psychotherapy of a simple supportive type, not lengthy or complicated analyses or uncovering therapy. An American group has also obtained gratifying results with the use of a similar kind of psychotherapy. Generally, research on the effectiveness of psychotherapy has been hampered by the lack of objective, adequate criteria. But in this instance in which the criterion is very clear-cut (the baby either is or is not carried to term), psychotherapy has been clearly established to be significantly more effective than no treatment or ordinary obstetric care (Grimm, 1962; Mann, 1956; Mann and Grimm, 1962). The results of the American studies show considerable consistency with those of the Nova Scotia group. Mann (1959) described one group of habitual aborters as women who grew up with a dominant, overprotective mother who encouraged dependency. The father, for one reason or another, was unable to provide help. Another group aborted in guilty response to specific problems such as a past criminal abortion. Some of these women had guilt feelings fostered by the father who encouraged and then punished sexual acting out (Mann, 1957).

Grimm (1962) has reported the most thorough, objective evidence of a psychological factor in habitual abortion. She gave the Wechsler Bellevue Intelligence Test, Rorschach, and Thematic Apperception Test to seventy habitual aborters and thirty-five normal controls similar in background variables. The habitual aborters were significantly less able to size up social situations, and plan and anticipate correctly; they had poorer emotional control and more conformity and compliance, which Grimm has aptly described as "self-compromising compliance," greater tension regarding hostile feeling, stronger feelings of dependency, and greater guilt. These same signs also significantly differentiated a small organic group of aborters from the less organic group. After successful therapy, a group of eighteen previously habitual aborters showed a statistically significant change on these factors in the normal direction. It should be noted that all these studies exclude from the experimental group women who abort for obvious physical reasons. All in all, the data suggest psychic factors as a causal element, but Grimm (1967) modestly concluded that it has not been conclusively demonstrated that psychological factors cause abortion proneness, nor has the possibility been ruled out that abortions have led to psychic disturbance.

NAUSEA AND VOMITING

Nausea and vomiting during pregnancy is another area in which psychological factors have been suspected. Grimm (1967) points out that there is no question that there are biochemical changes occurring in pregnancy, particularly in the early stages, that could in part account for nausea and vomiting. It must also be realized that the fact that severe vomiting has been relieved by hypnosis (Kroger and De Lee, 1946) is no evidence that the vomiting has a psychological cause, since many physiologic functions may be dramatically altered by hypnosis.

Robertson (1946) believes that excessive vomiting represents an expression of disgust. Of fifty-seven vomiters, forty were frigid women attempting to deal with unwanted coitus; this was true of only four of forty-three controls. Twenty of the fifty-seven vomiters had an undue attachment to their mothers, compared to only four of the controls. It should be noted that Robertson's data shows a relationship between vomiting and unwanted coitus in frigid women, not simply a relationship between vomiting and frigidity. Coppen (1959) did not test for this specific point, but he found no significant differences in sexual functioning between vomiters and normal subjects. There were also no significant differences between the groups in neurotic symptoms before or during pregnancy, attitudes to pregnancy, extroversion, or emotionally disturbing events during pregnancy. The vomiters were, however, slightly but significantly more masculine in build.

Fifty-five per cent of a sample of 212 normal student wives reported nausea. There was no relationship between intent to become pregnant and nausea (Poffenberger, Poffenberger, and Landis, 1952), a finding confirmed as well in a Swedish population (Nilsson, Kaij, Jacobson, 1967). A French study (Chertok, Mondzain, and Bonnaud, 1963) has suggested that ambivalence toward pregnancy, rather than simple acceptance or rejection, is the crucial variable leading to excessive vomiting. Even though the hypothesis was formulated after observing half the sample, three impartial judges reevaluating the same data did not find statistically significant evidence of ambivalence. Another French study found that twenty-two of twenty-four women with uncontrolled vomiting in the first three to four months of pregnancy were emotionally immature, especially in relation to their mothers (Barrucand, 1968). Shuttleworth (1954) found and cross-validated a significant relationship between the hypochondriasis score on the Minnesota Multiphasic Personality Inventory and vomiting, but the increased bodily concern indicated by the higher hypochondriasis score may have been a result rather than a cause of the vomiting.

Subjects with persistent and/or severe vomiting show somewhat more substantial evidence of psychological influence. A group of prolonged vomiters showed a significantly higher incidence of bodily symptoms prior to pregnancy, and more interpersonal, economic, and occupational stress during pregnancy compared to a normal control group. Harvey and Sherfey (1954) compared the results of interviews and Rorschach tests from twenty hyperemesis patients with fourteen normal pregnant women. It is not clear, however, that evaluations were made blindly. Evaluating individuals without knowledge of whether they are in the control group or the abnormal group protects against the experimenter's biases affecting his interpretation. Among the hyperemesis patients, they found more history of gastrointestinal distress in response to emotional stress; they also found dysmenorrhea in eighteen of the twenty, and all twenty were said to be completely frigid. The hyperemesis patients were more immature and passively compliant in relation to their mothers, more anxious and tense in pregnancy. It is unclear, however, that all of these differences represent significant deviations from the fourteen controls. Guze, Majerius and their colleagues (1959, 1960) followed up hyperemesis patients for two to four years after the affected pregnancy and found they were not significantly different from control subjects in psychiatric illness, gastrointestinal symptoms, abnormalities of pregnancy, attitudes to menstruation, pregnancy, sex, husband, or mother. They concluded that there is no evidence for a persistent psychiatric condition.

It still seems possible to agree with Grimm (1967) in her conclusion that nausea and vomiting in early pregnancy are not a sign of maladjustment or rejection of the pregnancy. However, even the evidence of psychological involvement in cases of severe vomiting is less than convincing, though on the other hand, the evidence does not permit this possibility to be ruled out. Newton (1963) gives the incidence of vomiting among the Navaho Indians as 14 per cent, certainly low compared to American women. However, it is just as possible that they suppress a "natural" tendency to throw up as that other American women exaggerate it. Factors such as secondary gain and attitudes of pregnancy rejection have probably been overstressed as causal factors, especially in comparison to more realistic situational stress factors. Tylden (1968) points out that hospital ward attitudes are incongruously punitive toward hyperemesis patients. She concluded from her observations that hyperemesis represents a psychosomatic cry of help with strong indication for supportive psychotherapy. She does not believe the hyperemesis patient is rejecting her baby, but rather that she needs protection.

PSYCHOLOGICAL FACTORS IN TOXEMIA

The toxemias of pregnancy, while usually capable of being well controlled by good prenatal care, remain a leading cause of death and injury to mother and baby. The disorder consists of one or more of the following prominent symptoms: water retention causing edema and excessive weight gain, hypertension, and proteinuria. Convulsions are symptomatic of an advanced state of the disorder. The causes of toxemia are not well understood, and it is the subject of hot medical controversy. Ringrose (1961) briefly lists some of the many theories of its etiology.

Dalton (1964) believes that toxemia is one of a group of disorders of electrolyte balance including premenstrual tension, glaucoma, periodic paralysis, depression, migraine, and some forms of epilepsy. A relationship between the premenstrual syndrome and toxemia, for example, is suggested by her estimate that the premenstrual syndrome occurs in about 32 per cent of a random group of women, but about 86 to 88 per cent in a group of women previously suffering from toxemia. On the other hand the fact that young, unwed primiparae more frequently develop toxemias of pregnancy has been cited as evidence for an emotional factor (Salerno, 1962). This hypothesis would attribute the reaction to excessive hormone, for example aldosterone, produced in response to emotional stress. In any case, in a carefully controlled study of 128 subjects, using injections of progesterone, a natural antagonist of aldosterone, Dalton was able to achieve a significant decrease in high blood pressure, edema, and albuminuria—the symptoms of toxemia. It may merely be that very young girls more frequently do not have sufficient physical maturity to sustain proper hormone balance throughout their pregnancy, or it may indeed be that under certain bodily conditions, emotional stress can be a factor in causing the toxemia reaction by triggering hormone change.

One of the earliest studies (McNeile and Page, 1939) of the psychologic factor in toxemia contrasted normal, preeclampsic (toxemia not so severe as to have caused convulsions), and hypertensive patients in their responses to a set of standard psychiatric questions. While no statistical tests were applied, large and obvious differences were found between the hypertensives and the normals. The authors concluded that there was evidence of a psychological component in hypertension but no evidence of it in the toxemias. Studies since 1939 include a broader range of more precisely measured variables and do not agree with this conclussion. Coppen (1958) compared fifty primiparae with preeclamptic toxemia with fifty controls matched for age, parity, and time in pregnancy. The subjects were studied by means of psychiatric interview, the Maudsley Personality Inventory, and anthropometric measurements. Toxemics had significantly more emotionally disturbed menarche, premenstrual tension, poor sex adjustment, psychiatric symptoms during pregnancy, and disturbed feelings about it, more heartburn and afternoon vomiting during pregnancy, high neuroticism score on the Maudsley, and abnormal androgyne score indicating masculinity of build. Some of these differences, such as increased psychiatric symptoms and heartburn, may be attributable to the toxemia itself, since patients were examined after they had been affected by the disorder. Studies in which subjects are selected after they have developed the disorder being studied are called retrospective. All retrospective studies suffer from the common defect that it is not always clear what is the cause and what is the result of the disorder. Studies which avoid this design fault are called prospective.

Soichet (1959) likewise did a retrospective study, interviewing forty-three toxemic women and sixty-nine control subjects. The data of this study, however, were not quantified, and statistical tests were not used. It seemed to Soichet that the toxemic women were ambivalent toward their pregnancy; they wanted to prove they were women, but they felt inferior in the area of sex and procreation. They had more tendency to see pregnancy as a shame or sin. They seemed to feel guilty in the eyes of their unborn baby, with this guilt releasing the self-destructive forces of toxemia. Soichet believes toxemia is a defense against guilt arising from a secret, distorted meaning of pregnancy. He further supports this speculation by the fact that questionnaires to mental institutions revealed only two preeclampsic cases among seven hundred sixty-seven pregnant schizophrenics. The schizophrenic women presumably used other defenses and therefore did not need a psychosomatic defense such as toxemia. It is unclear whether this is in conflict with Salerno's (1958) report that toxemia is frequent in schizophrenic patients especially primiparae and especially occurring before the first psychotic episode. Salerno presented no data to support his view.

Ringrose (1961a) in a prospective study of toxemia found that the average score of forty-one unmarried, white toxemic patients on the Minnesota Multiphasic Personality Inventory (MMPI) was in the normal range. There were however, significant differences between those who later developed preeclampsia and those who did not in the percentage with one or more scores in the abnormal range (over 70). A second sample of forty-one MMPI profiles of indigent Negro women (1961b) apparently partly obtained after the disorder had developed, showed the very high figure of 46 per cent, with one or more scores in the abnormal range (above 70). Eighty-five per cent had one or more scores over 60, but it is somewhat misleading to categorize these all as abnormal personalities as Ringrose did. A score of 60 might not represent a reliable deviation, and it is not in accord with usual clinical practice to classify all such profiles as abnormal.

In another retrospective study (Hetzel, Bruer, Poidevin, 1961), the toxemic group had significantly more stressful life situations during pregnancy than a control group. The differentiating stresses included economic, occupational, and interpersonal stresses, a husband who was an inadequate provider, and/or who rejected his wife after pregnancy. There was no significant difference in attitudes to sex, menstruation, or conception, or in sex satisfaction, though the authors say that this variable may not have been accurately measured; nor were there significant differences in the obstetrical history of the mothers of toxemic patients and control subjects.

An excellent prospective study (Glick, Salerno, Royce, 1965) found that preeclampsic patients showed a significantly higher incidence of the following: (a) abnormal childhood history of emotional disorder, especially enuresis, (b) a state of being single, divorced, widowed, or separated rather than married and with husband, and (c) previous history of abortion. Brown (1964), though he found no relationship between anxiety and toxemia, found significant correlations with variables concerning the husband. Taking the evidence as a whole, it would appear that there is a significant relationship between psychological factors and the development of preeclampsia.

Brewer (1966) strongly holds the view that at least one type of toxemia is caused by malnutrition. As partial evidence, he points out that toxemia is more prevalent in the lowest socioeconomic group. In his definition of toxemia, however, he mentions vomiting, abdominal pain, and headache as frequently occurring. These symptoms were not characteristic of the patients in the studies just considered, and it is possible that Brewer is dealing with a somewhat different disorder. While he reports that he was nearly able to eliminate this type of toxemia by prenatal care stressing proper diet, Brewer had no control for the effect of his own personality on these women. Increased stress of all sorts is more common in the lowest socioeconomic group, and the effect of intervention by the care of a dramatic and dedicated physician might significantly increase the pregnant woman's feeling of security during her pregnancy.

On the other hand, the psychological studies have not controlled the factor of diet. Faulty eating could be a correlate of neuroticism, either through general mental disorganization and lack of caring, or overscrupulous following of the doctor's orders against eating. If the doctor prescribes the patient's diet with an eye to her weight gain, and the woman weighs more because she is retaining water, a vicious cycle might be set up in which toxemia is increased by physician-induced starvation. Even though starving, a neurotic, fearful patient with low self esteem might find it very difficult to rebel against her doctor or disregard his instructions. Brewer makes a plea for others to replicate his study. Quite clearly, a study controlling both diet and psychological factors is needed.

PREMATURE DELIVERY

Much less information was found regarding prematurity; however, one study found statistically significant differences between thirty mothers delivering prematurely for no accountable medical reason and thirty control women who delivered at term (Blau, Slaff, Easton, Welkowitz, Springarn, and Cohen, 1963). Examined one to three days postpartum, the mothers of premature babies received significantly different ratings in attitudes to pregnancy, femininity, maturity, and social-familial relations. They had more negative attitudes toward pregnancy, conscious feelings of hostility and rejection of the pregnancy. They were more immature and narcissistic. They had made more attempts to abort. This retrospective study certainly suggests a psychological factor in premature birth, but it will require further confirmation, particularly with prospective investigation.

SUMMARY

The data in this chapter are remarkable in the extent to which they document the mutual influence of mind and body. Hormonal changes of pregnancy may underlie the emotional changes which are frequently observed. On the other hand, poor attitudes and environmental factors can contribute to adverse mental and physical symptoms. There is evidence that psychological attitudes may be causal in some cases of infertility, prematurity, spontaneous abortion, and toxemia. In contrast, the role of pregnancy rejection and secondary gain in producing nausea and vomiting during pregnancy appears to have been exaggerated. Psychological factors and situational stress may have a role in severe cases.

These tentative conclusions of psychosomatic influence on reproductive functioning will require much more verification, however, before they are accepted by obstetricians. In any case, psychosomatic reactions, for example infertility or spontaneous abortion, should not necessarily be considered neurotic. There are, after all, circumstances in which pregnancy is not in the best interest of the mother or potential child, the most stark example being residence in a concentration camp.

Chapter 10

MOTHERHOOD

In recent years, motherhood and parentcraft have absorbed the attention of educated women in an unprecedented way. Most of them did not derive their interest or knowledge about motherhood and child rearing from their education but from popular sources. In many ways they have been uncritical about this information. Two salient aspects of the childbearing fashion have been natural childbirth and breast-feeding. Read (1944), an English physician, has held that childbirth was not meant to be painful and that except in unusual cases, the pain comes from tension caused by fear. His object has been to train mothers to give birth without fear, pain, or the necessity of heavy drugging. Read appears to have had a thoroughly healthy influence in reducing the tendency to use heavy doses of drugs in childbirth, a practice dangerous to the infant. His ideas and similar ones of other writers have known worldwide popularity and have prompted Parker (1960) to label it as a philosophy of childbirth. Many adherents certainly do have something of the aspect of the true believer. Breast-feeding, too, has tended to assume cult-like proportions. This chapter will give special attention to these topics, as well as present a systematic review of the psychology of labor, childbirth, and postpartum reactions and adjustments.

The topic of motherhood in the sense of child rearing is for the most part not considered, since this topic would surely deserve a book of its own. Mom is likely to remain indispensable. Bronfenbrenner (1968) has concluded that maternal care (not merely sufficient stimulation) is crucial to normal psychological development. David (1965), reviewing variables associated with mental health, notes the importance attributed to maternal warmth. He comments that Mom has returned to professional favor and that there is less tendency to worry about the evils of overprotection.

HORMONAL CHANGES OF CHILDBIRTH

The hormonal changes of childbirth are the most drastic in a woman's lifetime. They begin shortly before delivery when, for example, progesterone drops sharply in relation to estrogen. Blood levels of progesterone remain high during the first stage of labor. Thirty per cent of women experience an extreme fall in progesterone from 15-20 $\mu g/100$ ml of blood plasma to 3-5 $\mu g/100$ ml in just a few days or even hours (Hamburg, 1966; Hamburg, Moos, and Yalom, 1968). Perception of hormonal changes may account for the fact that many women sense that labor is imminent. The lowered progesterone level unblocks the action of oxytocin which is believed responsible for initiating the contractions of labor and delivery (Zarrow, 1961). At childbirth, the level of estrogens changes as well, returning to normal in five to twenty-five days (Brown, 1956). Much remains unknown about the processes initiating labor. One investigator (Kazzaz, 1965) successfully predicted onset of delivery in thirteen of sixteen pregnant women on the basis of their feelings, thought, and fantasies about the fetus during pregnancy. The conclusion was that emotional factors caused the hormonal changes that result in the onset of labor. It remains to be seen, however, whether further studies will confirm this finding.

FEAR OF CHILDBIRTH AND ITS CONSEQUENCES

Fear seems to be very common before delivery. Sixty-three per cent of a group of normal middle-class primiparae feared labor and childbirth, and 41 per cent worried about the health and normality of their unborn child (Poffenberger, Poffenberger, and Landis, 1952). Ford (1945) concluded that fear of difficult delivery "haunts" primitive women; methods to insure easy delivery were found in thirty-five of the sixty-four tribes studied. Kartchner (1950), on the basis of interviews with five hundred women entering the hospital for delivery, states that the fear of death is always present. Hamilton (1955) confirmed this in only two of fourteen subjects.

Psychological factors such as fear have been suspected of adversely affecting the course of labor. Grimm (1967), however, concluded that in general, emotional adjustment and attitudes are related to adjustment or psychological response in labor but not to efficiency of uterine action or other abnormalities of labor. Several of the studies discussed in the last chapter showed results consistent with her conclusion (Grimm and Venet, 1966; Shuttleworth, 1954; Stewart and Scott, 1953; Winokur and Werboff, 1956; Zuckerman, Nurnberger, Gardiner, Vandiveer, Barrett, and den Breeijen, 1963). In addition, Eysenck (1961) found that neither neuroticism nor extroversion predicted labor. McDonald (1965) gave the Thematic Apperception Test and the Minnesota Multiphasic Personality Inventory to 107 lower-middle-class unwed mothers. Dividing the group by the obstetrician's rating of a normal or abnormal delivery, there were no statistically significant differences between the groups. The Zemlick and Watson study (1953) of fifteen subjects also reported negative findings.

Jeffcoate (1965) has shown that the physical factors of height and age of mother, weight and position of infant are significant variables in abnormal uterine action. He believes that a psychological interpretation of uterine dysfunction is untenable, since one delivery cures the dysfunction in 83 per cent of the cases. A weakness of the studies of psychological effect has been failure to control adequately for physical factors. Kann (1955) discusses this problem and points out some other physical factors affecting birth, such as the malleability of the infant's head. Better control of relevant physical variables would probably result in more consistent demonstration of a psychological effect. This effect may be present as an important factor in only a small minority of cases that need to be separated from those whose labor is disrupted by more physical factors.

Because of the fact that these physical factors have not been adequately controlled and because of the presence of various observations and studies which suggest that emotional factors can and do influence labor, Grimm's (1967) conclusion to the contrary seems premature. Having cited the negative evidence, it seems appropriate now to evaluate more thoroughly the positive evidence of a psychological effect.

Interest in this question has been stimulated by the common observation that arrival at the hospital has an inhibiting effect on the progress of labor (Hamilton, 1955). Fear has been shown to be effective in disrupting the labor of mice (Newton, Foshee, and Newton, 1966; Newton, Peeler, and Newton, 1968). A group of human mothers with prolonged labor (more than twenty-four hours) showed a significantly higher incidence of bodily symptoms prior to pregnancy and greater economic and occupational stress during pregnancy (Hetzel, Bruer, and Poidevin, 1961).

Grimm (1961) found a significant relationship between tension and the length of the second stage of labor in multiparae. (The second stage of labor extends from completion of cervical dilation until delivery). The eleven subjects with extreme tension had significantly more deformed or dead babies. Grimm was understandably reluctant to be too impressed with these findings, since most of the results of the study were negative. There was no relationship between psychological variables and complications of labor or its length in primiparae. Furthermore, it was not possible to replicate the positive relationship which had been reported between measures of denial of pregnancy, sex identification and normality of delivery room record (Davids and De Vault, 1960; Davids, DeVault, and Talmadge, 1961). The latter study also reported that a normal delivery group showed significantly less anxiety in the seventh month of pregnancy, compared to an abnormal delivery group.

Erickson (1965) also found significant psychological differences between a group of multiparae with complications of labor and a group without, and she also did not find these differences with primiparae. It may not be coincidental that these two studies (Erickson, 1965; Grimm, 1961) show a greater tendency for positive results with multiparae than with primiparae. It seems likely that failure to control for physical causes of complications is a more serious methodological flaw in the case of primiparae than in the case of multiparae. Primiparae probably have more complications of labor deriving from physical rather than psychological sources. Failure to weed these individuals from the experimental group may have obscured evidence of a psychological effect. Erickson's multiparae group with labor complications showed significant differences compared to a group with normal labor on the following variables: fear for self, fear for the baby, irritability and tension, depression and withdrawal, poorer health in pregnancy, longer first and second stages of labor, infants of less weight, and infants with lower Apgar Index (measure of well-being at birth).

Other reports showing a psychological influence on labor include a dissertation (Crawford, 1969) and an excellent prospective study which found a significant relationship between negative emotional factors and inertia in labor or fetal asphyxia and inertia together, but not fetal asphyxia alone (Engström, Geijerstam, Holmberg, and Uhrus, 1964). In another study (Kapp, Hornstein, and Graham, 1963), eighteen primiparae with inefficient uterine action were compared with forty-three controls. The interviewer was kept in ignorance as to whether a subject was a control or one with abnormal labor. Using very simple scales, the investigators found significant differences in attitude to motherhood, sex and marriage, relation to mother, adjustment to pregnancy, concept of early home life, predelivery concept of labor, habitual neurotic bodily complaints, habitual anxieties, worries and fears, attitude to first menses, and attitude to the father of the child. A weakness of the study is, however, that data was obtained in the postpartum period and the results could have been affected by the differential experience in labor, rather than being solely a function of preexisting attitudes.

In another study of eighty-six white, lower-class women the Minnesota Multiphasic Personality Inventory, Taylor Anxiety Scale, Kent Intelligence Test and Interpersonal Check List were given in the second trimester of pregnancy (McDonald and Christakos, 1963). After delivery, the group was divided into normal and abnormal groups on the basis of abnormalities of pregnancy, delivery, or the fetus. The abnormal group was at a high anxiety level compared to college norms and was significantly more anxious than the normal group. The abnormal group had significantly more deviant scores on the Minnesota Multiphasic Personality Inventory. It is unclear whether it is the same group of subjects or a different sample of eighty-six in which the abnormal group also showed a significantly higher IPAT Anxiety Scale score and significantly less repression and denial compared with intellectualization and obsessive defenses as measured by the Minnesota Multiphasic Personality Inventory (McDonald, Gynther, and Christakos, 1963). It should be noted that these latter defenses are more characteristic of males than females and that the hysteroid women are probably able to obtain more relief from fear by depending on the authority and reassurance of the medical personnel than the other women. A significant correlation (.61) was found between total anxiety scores and labor times, but length of labor also correlated significantly (.62) with birth weight. The abnormal group had a significantly higher ratio of boy babies. This finding is a good example of the need for more adequate control of physical variables which would aid interpretation of the results.

Cramond (1954), using the Minnesota Multiphasic Personality Inventory, found that compared to matched controls, a group of fifty married patients with difficult labor could be characterized as having suppressed their feelings rather than expressing them openly. Scott and Thomson (1956) interpreted the results of their study as being consistent with Cramond's hypothesis. Cramond's ideas are also somewhat consistent with the silent terror reported by Watson (1959) who interviewed postpartum a group of twenty-five black women who had had prolonged labor. Also included in the group of studies, offering at least some indication of positive results, should be the study of Klein, Potter, and Dyk (1950). In summary, on balance there appear to be more studies favoring than opposing the hypothesis that psychological factors can influence the physical course of labor. Certainly the current state of evidence does not permit this possibility to be ruled out, especially since negative studies may well be the result of failure to control relevant variables.

CHILDBIRTH TRAINING

The literature on the effectiveness of childbirth training might be expected to provide additional clues as to the presence or absence of psychological influence on the birth process. An extensive review of these studies, however, will not be given here because of their poor quality and tangential relevance. Grimm (1967) reviewed the literature on the effectiveness of childbirth training and concluded that the length of labor and occurrences of complications are probably not much affected by programs of preparation or education but that less medication is given and spontaneous delivery is more likely. Grimm notes, however, that these changes may be a function of the policy of the doctor or the medical setting as much as of the preparation of the patient, since the variable of medical care has often not been controlled. Another important uncontrolled variable is that of volunteering for class instruction.

A key issue of the whole childbirth-training controversy centers around the question of pain. Read (1944) claims that if women were not so tense and fearful, childbirth, though hard work, would not be painful except in unusual cases. (This view is not stressed by Bing (1967) who uses techniques, similar to reciprocal inhibition, based on learning theory.) Hamilton (1955), on the basis of her observations of labor, emphatically rejects the notion that it is merely hard work. She pointed out that screaming, vomiting, moaning, hair pulling, self-biting, self-scratching, head banging, and begging for medication are behaviors that bespeak of pain, not mere hard work. In a sample of five thousand European women (Malcovati, Fornari, and Miraglia, 1965) 10.5 per cent reported no pain during labor; 77 per cent reported mild to bearable pain, and 12.5 per cent reported insupportable pain.

Some overly enthusiastic supporters of "natural" childbirth have cited the supposed easy, joyful births of primitive women to contrast with those of decadent, civilized women. A woman squatting by the path to give birth and then racing to catch up with her friends is a typical example of this ecstatic vision. More sober and impartial reviews indicate that such occurrences are rare in any primitive group and that while the women of some tribes seem to experience less pain than American women, most experience as much and some even more (Ford, 1945; Freedman and Ferguson, 1950; McCammon, 1951). The Freedman and Ferguson study of primitive cultures concluded that the fact that childbirth pain can be increased or decreased by environmental manipulation should not blind us to the physiological reality of its sources or the universality of its existence.

In fact, discussions of childbirth pain suffer from a general distortion of the understanding of pain and of psychological influence on pain, or for that matter on other symptoms. Too often, professional people as well as laymen err in believing that if hypnosis, suggestion, or a placebo can remove pain or a symptom, then it was psychological and not physical in its source. Usually there is a connotation of legitimacy to the latter, while psychologically caused symptoms or ailments are seen as akin to moral weakness and are sometimes punitively treated by doctor, family, and friends alike. A Johns Hopkins study (Lasagna, Mosteller, Felsinger, and Beecher, 1954) is one of the best challenges to this view. They studied the response to placebos of sixty-nine patients suffering from postoperative pain. It is important to note that in this instance there is an undeniable physical source of the pain. Fifty-five per cent of the patients sometimes had their pain relieved by placebo; 14 per cent were consistently relieved, and 31 per cent were consistently unrelieved. Those whose pain was consistently unrelieved were nearly as abnormal in personality as those who consistently responded to the placebo. Those responding to placebos were outgoing, dependent, and emotionally expressive, while those who did not respond deviated from normal in being unusually rigid and overcontrolled emotionally.

In theory, it should certainly be possible to decrease childbirth pain in most patients by either placebo, strong suggestion, or hypnosis. (Conditioning techniques (Bing, 1967) also depend on other factors for their effectiveness). The effectiveness of pain relief would be expected to depend on the personality of the woman, the suggestive force, and the absence of countersuggestion. Emotional objections to attempts to evaluate childbirth education doubtless derive from the fact that questioning its effectiveness produces countersuggestions. These, in turn, reduce the force of the suggestion, possibly even threatening its total effectiveness. Conditions of minimal suggestive force such as a woman trained in relaxation left by herself during labor to listen to the screams of other women would not be expected to produce such effective results as conditions of maximal suggestive force such as a woman trained to relax under hypnosis by the obstetrician and accompanied throughout labor and delivered by this same individual. In these circumstances, the physician is in an optimal position to screen out countersuggestions. Davidson (1962) personally managed her patients in this way and found a significantly shorter first stage of labor and less need for analgesics in a hypnotized group compared to either a physiotherapy or "usual-practice" control group. This was true even though she loaded the hypnosis group with the older primiparae and other difficult patients. By personally managing her patients, she achieved superior results.

Special training for childbirth seems to be most beneficial for those of lower educational attainment (Bergström-Walan, 1963); amount of education and higher social class seem to be positively related to good comportment during labor (Kartchner, 1950; Werts, Gardiner, Mitchell, Thompson, Oliver, 1965). (Good comportment during labor refers to cooperating with medical personnel and not causing trouble.) Generally speaking, the effectiveness of childbirth training programs in reducing pain and fear will probably depend upon how effectively the positive suggestions can be maintained, though some training techniques doubtless owe some of their effect to utilization of principles of learning (reciprocal inhibition).

THE EXPERIENCE OF CHILDBIRTH

Having considered what effect the attitudes and feelings of the mother have on childbirth, it is time to reverse the question and evaluate what effect childbirth has on the mother. One dramatic finding is that of Jeffcoate (1965), who reported that one third of a sample of women who experienced the prolonged pain of severe inertia in delivery never had another child. Various meanings of childbirth have been discussed by psychoanalysts. These are as follows: separation and loss of vital energy (Lampl-de Groot, 1933); expelling a bad thing by violent, incoordinate labor; or retaining the fetus in order to conceal badness (Jones, 1942). Zilboorg (1957) mentions obsessive-compulsive women who wish to retain the fetus permanently. He emphasizes the masochistic delight of pain which he seems to think is characteristic of women in childbirth. Deutsch (1944) cites childbirth as an experience which influences development of masochistic tendencies. She does not accept Read's view that childbirth pain is largely from tension. No empirical evidence of masochistic pleasure in childbirth was found (Hamilton, 1955).

Some women are actually terrified to give birth. Fodor (1949) studied the dreams of women before and after childbirth and concluded that a morbid fear of childbearing arises from a prospective identification of the self with the child in the womb. All distinction is lost, and it is as if the mother were giving birth to herself, hence she has dreams and fears of suffocation. Fodor states that the mother's understanding of the part her own birth plays in her attitudes toward childbearing results in almost miraculous relief from difficult delivery. Previous abortions or guilt about injuring her mother at her own birth are other important factors. Hall (1967) finds evidence for Fodor's views in examples from adult dreams that look like references to the fetal state. He suggests that dreaming may well be the first mental activity.

POSTPARTUM EMOTIONAL CHANGES

Emotional changes during the postpartum period are so common as to have gained the nickname "baby blues." The argument that emotional changes following childbirth could not be physically based because no such behavior is observed in animals seriously misjudges the sensitivity and caution of our animal friends. The bitch is suspicious of all but the most familiar of the family, the hen hides her eggs and chicks as well; puss becomes surly (Schneirla, Rosenblatt, and Tobach, 1963), and if you bother her too much, she will move her kittens to a new hiding place. While the langur mother allows her infant to be passed about after birth (Jay, 1963), a baboon mother will not allow others to have her infant for the first month (De Vore, 1963).

Among human mothers, the usual postpartum syndrome as described by experienced nurses includes the following: (a) lack of energy and fatigability, (b) episodes of crying, (c) fears, especially regarding the baby, (d) mental confusion and inefficiency, (c) headaches, estimated to range from 30 per cent to very common, (f) insomnia, an occasional or very rare symptom, (g) worry about physical state, especially constipation and stitches, (h) a negative, touchy attitude toward the husband, reported in about 50 per cent. In contrast to this usual picture, insomnia is almost always present as a prodromal symptom of severe disturbance (Hamilton, 1962).

Gordon and Gordon (1959) estimate that 30 per cent of normal women have some emotional upset following childbirth. Sixty per cent of a sample of fifty lower class women showed depression in the postpartum period (Pleshette, Asch, and Chase, 1956). In a sample of 467 European women, 25 per cent had six or more postpartum mental symptoms and another 20 per cent had four to six symptoms (Jacobson, Kaij, and Nilsson, 1965).

A recent study (Yalom, Lunde, Moos, and Hamburg, 1968) points out that the crying in the postpartum period does not necessarily represent depression but may indicate sensitivity and lability. Sixty-seven per cent of a sample of thirty-nine reported crying of five or more minutes. The episodes were fairly evenly distributed over a ten-day postpartum period, with a slight increase from the fifth to tenth days. There was no absence of symptoms, as has sometimes been reported, during the first forty-eight hours. Seventy-three per cent of the multiparae reported previous postpartum depressions. Persistent postpartum depression correlated significantly with infections, lower parity, longer interval since the last pregnancy, and younger age of menarche. Another group with brief depression showed significant correlations with the length and difficulty of labor (Hamburg, Moos, and Yalom, 1968). These authors found no significant decrease in performance on memory tasks from the prenatal level, but it is unclear if practice effects were controlled for.

Of 25 subjects examined nine days postpartum, Robin (1962) found emotional lability in sixteen and short depression in nineteen. Response to the Thematic Apperception Test was significantly different from a control group and consistent with depression. Significant impairment was noted on the Shipley Hart-ford, an intelligence measure and test of mental efficiency. Robin concluded that postpartum emotional changes are endogeneous and organically determined, an opinion shared by many others (Hamilton, 1962; Hemphill, 1952; Paffenbarger, 1961; Ryle, 1961).

PARITY AND POSTPARTUM ADJUSTMENT

It is commonly said that, "The first one is the hardest," but research findings do not entirely support this picture. While Gordon and Gordon (1960) found psychological disturbance in the postpartum period significantly more frequent after the first birth, and lower parity was found to be related to depression after childbirth (Yalom, Lunde, Moos, and Hamburg, 1968), other studies find a more troubled adjustment for women who already have children. Larsen (1966) found that stress was apparently greatest for those mothers who already had at least two children. These women reported more fatigue during and after pregnancy. They became more fearful with each successive pregnancy, and increasingly annoyed by too much company and interference by relatives and neighbors. Problems of housework and routine tended to multiply. A Scandinavian study also found increased postpartum mental symptoms with parity but not in all women. They suggest that only some women are adversely affected by parity (Kaij, Jacobson, Nilsson, 1967). Grimm (1969) reported results of a study of lower-income women (Pavenstadt, 1965). After two or three children, they actually showed a lower level of maturity and adjustment than they had at the time of the initial testing early in their first pregnancy. The investigators accounted for this apparent downhill course in terms of the patients' economic insecurity and prospects of a life of drudgery and involuntary childbearing. One must agree with Grimm that longitudinal studies of normal women before, during, and after the child-rearing period are needed.

The studies of Gordon (1957), Gordon and Gordon (1967, 1965, 1960, 1959, 1957), and Thomas and Gordon (1959) make an exceedingly useful contribution to this problem of adverse postpartum reactions. They found the following factors to be significantly related to emotional disturbance arising from childbearing: (a) coming from a home broken by death or other separation, (b) a history of emotional disorder in self, parents, or immediate family, (c) history of previous severe physical illness or physical complication of pregnancy, (d) marital differences in religion or age, (e) rising or falling on the economic or social ladder, a factor also associated with pregnancy disturbance by Rosengren, (f) recent move to the suburbs, (g) older parents, (h) unplanned pregnancy or a female child, (i) acute strains in the period of childbearing such as a change of residence, husband away from home, or no outside help from the family or practical nurse. Primiparity and lower social class were also predisposing factors. While personal insecurity related to background sensitization was found to be important, problems and stresses of the immediate situation, which they misleadingly call maternal-role conflict, were found to be even more important in creating emotional disturbance. Based on these findings, they provided advice and guidance to a group of new mothers and found that only two per cent of them had emotional problems at the half-year mark, compared to 28 per cent of a group of control mothers. The babies of the instructed mothers had significantly less irritability, feeding, and sleeping problems. The beneficial results could still be statistically shown four to six years later in both the mother and child.

POSTPARTUM PSYCHOSIS

There is a special danger of psychosis following childbirth (Pugh, Jerath, Schmidt, and Reed, 1963) ; Gordon and Gordon (1957) give the probability of puerperal psychosis as 1 in 400, with the probability of a neurotic or other abnormal mental reaction as five times as high. Shainess (1966) points out that like battle fatigue, postpartum reactions show the factors of exhaustion and role change. Hamilton (1962) defines three basic viewpoints about psychoses following childbirth. These are as follows: (a) no relationship to parturition (Foundeur, Fixsen, Triebel, and White, 1957), (b) the psychogenic view of Zilboorg (1928) that frigidity and homosexuality are important factors, a view Hamilton states has not been sustained by several studies, and (c) the physiological viewpoint.

The first viewpoint is reflected in the fact that in recent years, puerperal psychosis has been excluded from the psychiatric nomenclature on the grounds that it does not represent a disease entity. The wide acceptance of this view would have been more appropriate if accompanied by equal scepticism about other "disease" entities in the nomenclature. In any case, recent studies have raised this question more strongly once again. Paffenbarger (1964), for example, reported that while the onset of predelivery psychoses is scattered evenly through the pregnancy, postpartum psychoses cluster about the delivery. In his sample of 314, all had a short lucid period after delivery, 34 per cent were psychotic by the end of the first month and 80 per cent by the end of the first six weeks. It has been said that there is no more such a thing as a puerperal psychosis than a college psychosis, but it is doubtful that there is so close a time relationship between psychosis and entry into college. Citing similar findings, Tetlow (1955) concluded that it is silly to say these psychoses have nothing to do with childbirth. In agreement with several other investigators, he concluded that history of mental disturbance in self or family is a predisposing factor (Gordon, 1957; Jansson, 1963; Paffenbarger, 1961; Paffenbarger, 1964; Seager, 1960). While all psychoses after childbirth are not of one pattern, the conclusion that they are unrelated to childbirth is untenable, and the conclusion that no segment of these is causally related to changes in physiology seems premature. On the other hand, the symptomatology of the psychoses is certainly diverse, though there is evidence of more affective disturbance and "organic looking" symptoms such as confusion and perplexity (Jacob, 1943; Jansson, 1963; Protheroe, 1969).

Markham (1961) makes a more recent contribution to the psychoanalytic view with her impressions based on a comparison of eleven women who became psychotic after childbirth with eleven who did not. The former were specifically characterized by a symbiotic dependent tie with their mothers while simultaneously experiencing anal-sadistic impulses toward them. She reported considerable depression also in the controls and much the same emotional feelings and conflicts, but the nonpsychotic women showed more intellectual and emotional control and more resilience and resourceful use of defenses. The data of this study are not quantified, and one also cannot be sure that the differences noted are not merely those between the psychotic and the nonpsychotic rather than prior characteristics which differentially affect the development of puerperal psychosis.

Observations have been made on the role of family relationships in puerperal psychosis. Lomas (1959) reported on twelve cases. The families were nuclear; that is, they consisted of just the parents and children and were somewhat isolated from other relatives. The wife was usually frigid and was dominated and controlled by her husband. He was, in fact, ineffectual and needy, and Lomas supposed that the wife selected him for that reason. When the wife wanted a real baby, there was trouble because the husband was unable to provide the necessary emotional support. Another study of fifteen postpartum psychotic and neurotic reactions (Daniels and Lessow, 1964) found that each of the patients had a single intense, childishly dependent relationship with a mother, husband, or mother-in-law. Often a woman would switch such a relationship from her mother to her husband. Typically the wife was overly dependent, while the husband was controlling and overprotective. Yet a third study (Beach, Henley, Peterson, and Farr, 1955) reports eight cases of overprotective husbands who, though good providers, typically made their wives feel inadequate and then in times of real stress assumed a passive role. They tended to compete with their wives in the feminine role, often assuming credit for the baby themselves. They were a sort of counterpart of the castrating female. There is an interesting consistency to the finding of domineering, emotionally undermining husbands. It is impossible to know if these findings are truly independent, since objective means of measurement were not described. Furthermore, it should be noted that the small numbers of subjects and absence of controls make their findings only suggestive.

The third viewpoint about psychoses following childbirth that Hamilton defined was the physiological one. He cited Paffenbarger (1961) as one of the best examples of this point of view, since he found no correlation of postpartum psychosis with the "potentially more psychological variables" such as past reproductive record or age at marriage. Subtle signs indicating physical factors were statistically significant. These included greater age, longer interval since last pregnancy, one week less gestation period; higher incidence of headache, respiratory illness, hypertension, and dystocia; and lower birth weight of the infants. These factors were generally confirmed in a later study (1964) in which it was also shown that the infant's low weight at birth was not typical of the mother's previous pregnancies. Some of these findings confirm those from studies of less severe disturbance. The Gordon team had found previous illness and greater age to be factors, and longer interval since the last pregnancy was a significant factor in the study of Yalom, Lunde, Moos, and Hamburg (1968). Paffenbarger found that recurrence of psychosis was one in three in subsequent pregnancies, and the psychoses were of the same type. Baker (1965) reported a recurrence rate of six sevenths for puerperal schizophrenia, a very black picture indeed.

In addition to the work of Paffenbarger, results of some Scandinavian studies have been suggestive of physiological causation. Direct comparisons are difficult, however, since the studies do not deal solely with postpartum psychosis. A retrospective study of 467 mothers (Jacobson, Kaij, and Nilsson, 1965) found significant relations between frequency and mental symptoms and such physical symptoms as slowed involution of the uterus, genital pains, dyspareunia, and dysmenorrhea. There were also significant relations with previous spontaneous abortion and nausea in pregnancy. Mental symptoms did not relate to length of breast feeding or lactation trouble.

In another sample of 861 (Nilsson, Kaij, and Jacobson, 1967), a significant relationship was found between number of mental symptoms postpartum and delayed involution, change in the duration of the menstrual cycle, genital pains, and sexual disturbances. The authors concluded that a definite relation exists between mental illness and somatic disturbances in connection with pregnancy, delivery, and the postpartum period. A significant relationship was also found between mental symptoms before and during pregnancy and after pregnancy. Those with the highest frequency of mental symptoms in pregnancy had a significantly higher frequency of unplanned pregnancy, worsened economic circumstances as a result of pregnancy, more spontaneous abortion, nausea and vomiting, lactation trouble, delayed return to normal weight, or weight increase after partus. In neither study were complications of delivery related to psychological history. Tod (1964), in a prospective study, also found postpartum depressions to be preceded by symptoms during the pregnancy, in this case, pathological anxiety.

In another retrospective Scandinavian study, Jansson (1963) investigated all women of one locale hospitalized for psychiatric disturbance during the interval from twenty weeks pregnant to one year after delivery. These women hospitalized during the years 1952 to 1956 were followed up six to eight years later. While there was no significant difference in the frequency of pathological heredity between the psychiatric control group and the childbearing group, the latter was significantly different from the normal control group. Their previous mental disturbances were also more associated with childbearing than was the case among the psychiatric control group. The childbearing group did not differ from the normal control group in marital relations or sexual life, age, parity, or complications of delivery, but they had had significantly more previous somatic illness, and their babies weighed significantly less. The last finding was twice reported by Paffenbarger (1964, 1961). The most frequent time of onset of symptoms was in the month after delivery when 33 per cent became ill. Eighty-five per cent of the patients showed depression, 45 per cent anancastic symptoms (obsessive-compulsive), 30 per cent confusion, and 4 per cent manic symptoms. The psychiatric control group differed significantly in having fewer symptoms of depression, and vegetative-hypochondrical, anancastic, asthenic-emotional, and confusional symptoms. Those patients with onset of symptoms one month before delivery to three months after showed the most difference in symptoms from the psychiatric controls. Jansson considers the factors of increased risk as age over thirty, illegitimacy, previous psychiatric hospital care (especially if connected with childbirth), and vulnerable personality.

In a later study (Jansson and Selldén, 1966), the hypothesis that the greater amount of confusional symptoms in postpartum disturbance might be attributable to brain injury was not supported by electroencephalogram comparisons with control groups. They suggest that fatigue may be responsible for the multiple signs of mental inefficiency they had noted. It is puzzling that while organic-like symptoms are frequently noted in the postpartum period, changes in electroencephalograms are not demonstrated (Jansson and Selldén, 1966); Melges, 1968); and intellectual impairment has not been consistently shown. While Robin (1962) reported intellectual impairment even in normal subjects, Melges (1968) found no difference from controls in serial sevens or digit span despite the fact that he reported confusion in 92 per cent of his subjects. He concluded that the confusion noted in these postpartum psychiatric patients is from identity diffusion but that hormonal changes may make some women more vulnerable to breakdown under this stress. Opinion seems to be moving toward the view that postpartum psychoses can be attributed to increased environmental stress in association with lack of rebound due to biochemical changes which help trigger illness particularly in susceptible women (Protheroe, 1969; Treadway, Kane Jarrahi-Zadeh, and Lipton, 1969).

Fortunately, severe mental disturbance following childbirth is a rare occurrence, but milder disturbances are all too common. While the Gordon team has supplied some practical help in the way of minimizing adverse mental reactions following childbirth, the basic etiology remains obscure. Further study of the role of physiological factors appears to be promising, especially in view of recent case reports of psychosis following withdrawal of contraceptive pills which simulate a pregnancy effect in the body (Keeler, Kane, and Daly, 1964; Wallach, 1968).

POSTPARTUM SEXUAL ADJUSTMENT

The postpartum period is also frequently characterized by a change in sexual adjustment. In the sample of 212 student couples, there was significantly less sexual desire after birth than in early pregnancy. Poor health and fear of another labor and childbirth were significantly related to poorer sexual adjustment after birth (Landis, Poffenberger, and Poffenberger, 1950). Masters and Johnson (1966) found that although four of six subjects reported eroticism when seen four to five weeks after delivery, their physiologic responses—vasocongestion of major and minor labia, lubrication, distention of the inner two thirds of the vaginal barrel—were, in fact, reduced in rapidity and intensity. The walls of the vagina, especially in the nursing mothers, were thin, like those of a senile woman. The sex skin color was lighter and there were fewer contractions in orgasm. At the six- to eight-week check, the picture was much the same. At three months, the subjects were normal again, though the nonnursing mothers were ahead of the others. Masters and Johnson believe hormonal factors probably account for these changes. In their larger sample studied only by interview, 47 of 101 showed a low level of sexuality. Factors in producing this were fatigue, fear, pain, and vaginal discharge.

Masters and Johnson (1966) suggest that postpartum medical advice should be more individualized, since many women are sufficiently healed for sexual relations before the standard rule of six weeks and they often wish to resume normal marital relations. Seventy-one of the husbands interviewed had had intercourse medically proscribed; 18 admitted extra-marital activity. Husbands may manifest the strain in other ways. In one instance, this author treated a husband with a neurotic conversion reaction directly brought on by temptation to adultery.

BREAST-FEEDING

Breast-Feeding and Postpartum Sexuality

While 47 of 101 mothers studied by Masters and Johnson (1966) showed a low level of sexuality in the postpartum period, the 24 nursing mothers showed a higher level of sexual tension than in the pre-pregnancy period. However, it will be recalled that there was some evidence of slower recovery of physiologic sexual response in nursing mothers. Six of the 24 mothers felt guilty in regard to sexual arousal during nursing; 16 of 25 who rejected nursing had husbands who rejected it. While steroid starvation may result in excessive fatigue and emotional instability in postpartum women, Masters and Johnson (1966) conclude this would not be the case for nursing women. According to Hytten (1959), however, fatigue is no stranger to the nursing mother. He found most nursing mothers excessively tired at three months postpartum. Only 2 of 106 mothers studied had no troubles to report and they were living with their mothers. Two thirds of the women gave up breast-feeding.

Lactating women have distinctive hormonal characteristics, and while they may be rich in some hormones, Brown (1956) found the level of estrogens low, averaging in the range of the early postmenstrual phase. Low estrogen undoubtedly contributes to the weakened physiological sexual response, as this hormone is responsible for the vitality of the tissues involved. This information lends some support to the notion that there is a physiological basis for conflict between the maternal and heterosexual roles. When the menstrual cycle returns, the mother will probably again be fertile. The periodic irritability accompanying the cycle may function to loosen dependency ties with existing offspring.

In primitive societies, survival of the infant is almost completely dependent on the mother's ability to nurse him, and the average age of weaning is between three and four (Ford, 1945). Under these circumstances, the infant frequently remains with the mother almost continually and is nursed at any time, day or night. Intercourse is generally forbidden during the nursing period, since a new pregnancy would deprive the existing baby of proper nurture. Suppression of fertility during lactation is a relative matter. It is often supposed that primitive women have little trouble with nursing, but Ford pointed out that the existence of many techniques for improving and increasing the milk supply suggest that milk scarcity is as frequent a problem for them as for the modern mother. Unlike the modern American woman, they do not expect each child to survive in a rosy state of health; many of their babies simply die.

The infant's sucking at the breast results in the production of prolactin, oxytocin, and probably ACTH. While oxytocin is sometimes credited with starting the milk flow, the so called let-down reflex, more recent opinion suggests that oxytocin only helps maintain the prolactin which is responsible for forming the milk (Meites, Nicoll, and Talwalker, 1963). Oxytocin is involved in the human sexual orgasm, and the presence of oxytocin may account for the ready sexual arousal during nursing. Conversely, intercourse may result in the inadvertent production of a stream of milk.

Emotional Requirements of Breast-feeding

The passivity of the nursing experience has generally been stressed, and much emphasis has been placed on a woman's capacity to be passive. It is true that the mother must be able to accept the milk coming out without any specific willing of it and also that she must be able to accept the concomitant sensual sensations of the nursing experience. The coming out of the milk, however, does not entirely qualify as a low-energy, passive experience as there is an active, forceful expulsion of the milk. In fact it has been recommended that the term "milk-ejection reflex" should be substituted for the term "let-down reflex" (Cowie and Foley, 1961).

Emotions are definitely able to influence the milk flow (Newton, 1955). Fear, shame, embarrassment, or worry can inhibit the milk-ejection reflex so that milk does not come out of a breast full of milk. Naturally this is very frustrating to the baby, and it can also be physically uncomfortable for the mother since it may lead to breast engorgement.

The Breast-feeding Experience

Reassurances given mothers are frequently not very precise. Newton (1955) points out that it is inaccurate to state that bottle feeding is nearly the same as breast-feeding so long as the mother holds her baby while feeding him. The involvement of the mother's whole body as well as the baby's body creates a definitely different kind of relationship. Mother and infant become a much more intimate unit. Quantities of prolactin are produced in the mother during breast-feeding. Very little is known about the effects of this hormone on human behavior, but in animals it is known to be important in facilitating maternal behavior. Animal maternal behavior, however, is highly dependent on learning. During breast-feeding, oxytocin acts on the uterus causing contractions for up to twenty minutes after a feeding. Breast-feeding thus counteracts uterine hemorrhage and aids the involution of the uterus. The stimulation of the nipple and the mother's need for the baby to provide physical relief by emptying the breast are additional factors which make breast-feeding a special experience. Furthermore, the milk-ejection reflex may become conditioned to various cues. The cry of a baby, for example, may come to initiate the flow of milk automatically. Usually this is convenient, but not if it is a movie scene of a baby that has elicited the milk.

Breast-feeding, Hormones, and Nurturance

The question of the contribution of breast-feeding and/or hormones to nurturant behavior has been largely uninvestigated among humans. In a first approach to the problem, neither nursing mice nor human mothers were found to differ significantly in many aspects of maternal care from their nonnursing counterparts (Newton, Peeler, and Rawlins, 1968). They did differ in certain behaviors, however, which suggested a greater need for body contact with the offspring among the nursing mice and human mothers. This may be a result of the learned pleasure of nursing.

Levy (1942) approached the problem of nurturance and hormones not by studying the hormones crucial to breast-feeding but by studying the relationship of the length of the menstrual period and maternal behavior judged from fantasy and verbal report. He found a .58 correlation between these two variables.

Peskin (1968) replicated this study with improvements. Use of longitudinal data permitted indication of directionality of causal influence and a more direct measure of maternal performance was made. The fifty-five subjects had been part of the Berkeley longitudinal study and had not differed from each other in length of the menstrual period during adolescence. At age thirty, those fifteen subjects with a menstrual period of four or fewer days were contrasted with those eleven having a period of six or more days. There were no differences between the groups in other relevant social and physical variables nor in the number of children. Compared to the women who later had long menstrual periods, the women with short periods had been more masculine and competitive during adolescence rather than conforming, somatizing, and feminine. Thus it appears that attitude determined length of menstrual flow rather than that a physiological factor determined attitude. The more masculine women, however, were rated at age thirty as more maternal, more attractive, and competent in their sex role. Obviously it makes no sense to talk to masculine women as being more maternal. Peskin explains that the "masculine" women were more effective, directing their energy more to action while the "feminine" women tended to direct their energy toward their bodies (somatization). This study serves to underscore once more the fact that the ideal of the culturally feminine woman is maladaptive. Peskin's results also lend no support to Levy's finding nor to the notion of a biobehavioral influence on maternal attitudes. On the other hand, correlates of the most relevant hormones such as those involved in breast-feeding were not measured by Peskin.

Among nonhuman primates, Butler (1953) found that multiparous rhesus monkey mothers had a higher preference for viewing infants than primiparous female monkeys. A primipara's motivation to view an infant increased if her infant was removed a few hours postpartum. Butler thought that this suggested a hormone influence on behavior. Spencer-Booth (1968) found that rhesus monkey mothers paid less attention to infants, compared to females who had not borne infants. Females were more interested in infants than were males. This sex difference in infant-directed behavior occurs before puberty (Chamove, Harlow, and Mitchell, 1967). Of fifteen pairs of preadolescent rhesus monkeys tested with a one-month-old infant, females showed significantly more positive social behavior and significantly less hostility to the infant than did males. The difference was present with monkeys reared only with their mothers and also in those monkeys who were reared only with peers. The authors concluded that the behavior appears to have a biological basis. They also point out that this sex difference is also often observed among monkeys in a natural field situation.

Prevalence of Breast-feeding

Breast-feeding has been generally on the decline. For example, in the United States, in 1946, 65 per cent of babies were getting some breast milk at the time they left the hospital; in 1956 the figure was 37 per cent. In Bristol, England the percentage of breast-feeding mothers dropped from 77 per cent to 36 per cent in twenty years (Mead and Newton, 1967). While an heroic revival has been attempted among American college-educated women, the fashion did not sustain one such sample of women very long, since the median duration of breast-feeding was less than three months (Salber, Stitt, and Babbott, 1959). In more recent years, the common use of birth control pills provides an additional complication, since the effects of these various compounds on nursing are not well understood. Some have estrogenic properties and may retard lactation as estrogen is known to do (Cowie and Foley, 1961).

Not only has there been variation in breast-feeding over the years, but there are also regional and class differences. Breast-feeding is less common in New England and more common in the Western states. Unlike the earlier days, breast-feeding is now more common in the upper socioeconomic groups in the United States and in England as well (Newson and Newson, 1963). On the basis of these findings, Robertson (1961) makes a plea for professional workers to consider cultural factors before interpreting refusal to nurse as purely personal idiosyncrasy or sign of emotional disturbance.

Attitudes and Willingness to Breast-feed

In a study of 110 young mothers, another set of investigators (Brown, Lieberman, Winson, and Pleshette, 1960) touched again on the erotic versus maternal split in concluding that our erotic culture makes it hard for women to identify with a madonna figure. While 80 per cent of the mothers would feed artificially again, only 67 per cent of those who breast-fed would do so again. This study and the importance of the role of the husband in choice of feeding method (Masters and Johnson, 1966) combine to suggest that conflict with heterosexual needs has been underrated as a source of resistance to breast-feeding. The sexual aspect of this heterosexual need is probably not so important as the more strictly security aspects of it. Many women, apparently with some reason (Masters and Johnson, 1966), are anxious during pregnancy and the postpartum period lest they lose their husbands. Since they often feel vulnerable and dependent upon their husbands at this time, it is not surprising that they are sensitive to anything which might appear to handicap their marital adjustment.

Benedek (1959b) undoubtedly represents many professional workers in her opinion that masculine women find it hard to be passive in breast-feeding. Although there are undoubtedly many such women who find the whole idea revoltingly cow-like, the hard, protruding breasts and spurting milk can lend themselves to active interpretations as well as passive ones. For example, one young woman with many masculine interests happily breast-fed and amused herself with "target practice" squirting at a mirror across the room. In this girl, the breast had apparently become a penis equivalent. Adams (1959) found more penis-envy disturbance in a breast-feeding group than in a bottle-feeding group. The bottle-feeding group, however, was no paragon of adjustment. They showed greater dependency, rejection of the child, dissatisfaction with their sex role, and psychosexual disturbance.

Newton (1955) interpreted choice of breast-feeding as a sign of good psychological adjustment. Questioned after birth, not surprisingly those women who felt labor had been hard significantly more often preferred artificial feeding and felt that men had a better time in life. One cannot be sure that having favorable or unfavorable attitudes toward femininity is not partially the result of whether or not the female functions go easily and happily rather than that women with poor attitudes toward femininity have disturbed physical function. Better evidence of such a relationship are the facts that primiparae who had wanted to breast-feed were more likely to have very short labors and to be successful in feeding.

These findings are consistent with those of Newson and Newson (1962) that it is fruitless to insist that women breast-feed. Women forced to breast-feed usually found or developed a physical reason for not continuing. Frequently the reason given was not having enough milk. On the other hand, it is a mistake to think that these kinds of data are adequate to support the opposite assertion so frequently encountered that, "If you really want to breast-feed, you will have enough milk."

Some Negative Aspects of Breast-feeding

American women have been subjected to a barrage of literature and advice exhorting them to breast-feed. Unfortunately, well-meaning authors generally confine themselves to making the case for breast-feeding, leaving the women to find out for themselves the negative possibilities. While a thorough consideration of the relative merits of breast-feeding is not relevant to the main theme of this book, a brief discussion of some salient points oversimplified in the popular literature may be of interest. Hytten (1959), for example, analyzed several hundred twenty-four-hour specimens of milk and found that one third of the women were producing milk inadequate in quantity, quality or both. Decline in quantity and quality were sharply related to age. He points out that breast-feeding is not cheaper, but only appears cheaper, and that most nursing mothers were excessively tired. He nonetheless concluded that satisfactory breast-feeding is by far the simplest and best method of infant feeding. This conclusion largely begs the question of the probability of *successful* breast-feeding for a given mother. *Successful* is often a crucial qualification. Mothers are told that breast-feeding decreases the likelihood of breast cancer, but the fact that it is *successful* breast-feeding which has this effect is often not mentioned.

Another study (Mellander, Vahlquist, and Melbin, 1959) agrees that if the mother's diet is deficient, so is the milk, and that breast-feeding is probably not a major factor in conferring immunity to newborn infants. Furthermore, it is not at all clear as yet that breast-feeding helps prevent development of allergies as is often alleged. A comparison of various factors of the physical development of children showed no especial advantage to breast-feeding. These Swedish authors nonetheless favored breast-feeding. They concluded that under the best conditions of sanitation and care, artificial feeding resulted in a slightly increased incidence of infection, proneness to deficiency disease, and possibly greater risk of allergy. These authors felt that most of the advantages would be attained by breast-feeding during the first three months. Under conditions of primitive or uncertain sanitation, the advantage of breast-feeding would be much greater.

McGeorge (1960) is even less favorable to breast-feeding, noting many of the difficulties already mentioned and pointing out that the milk passes on drugs the mother may be taking. He concluded that the psychological benefits are undecided and that breast-feeding should be discontinued the moment it shows signs of being a burden. Rheingold (1964) comes to a similar conclusion.

Psychological Effects of Breast-feeding

Many mothers have undoubtedly been induced to breast-feed on the basis that in this way, they would best fulfill the oral, sucking needs of their child and insure that he would become a psychologically mature individual and not remain fixated at the oral level. This argument has been used to induce mothers to nurse their children into the preschool years. There is considerable irony in the conclusion of Sears and Wise (1950) that a large part of oral drive is a learned or secondary drive. Thus the more satisfaction an infant gained from sucking, the more he would want to suck. Lengthy breast-feeding would thus be expected to increase the drive, not satisfy it. The characteristics of the orally fixated individual, for example as described by Glover (1956), are not without their charm, but this result may not be to everyone's liking and certainly does not correspond to the Freudian ideal of mature personality. Actually, evidence from nonhuman primates suggests that contact comfort is more important to the infant than sucking, though the latter is also important (Harlow, 1958; Harlow and Suomi, 1970; Harlow and Zimmerman, 1959).

McGeorge (1960) is basically correct that the findings of studies regarding the relative psychological benefits of breast-feeding versus artificial feeding have been equivocal. It is probable that failure to control for the quality of breast-feeding, its length, sex of the child, and type of weaning, to mention only a few relevant variables, has retarded more definitive answers. The longitudinal study of Heinstein (1963) controlled more variables and is more informative than earlier studies. She concluded that breast-feeding as such does not provide a psychologically better beginning to life. As Sears would predict, boys who were nursed for a long time showed signs of an oral-behavior syndrome. Warmth of the mother tended to be an important factor. Boys nursed fourteen months or more by a warm mother developed in a better than average way, while the opposite was true of boys similarly nursed by a cold mother. Girls, on the other hand, showed better adjustment when breast-feeding was combined with other favorable parental characteristics, but the daughters of cold, breast-feeding mothers were actually worse off than daughters of comparable mothers who had been artificially fed.

Brody (1956) also concluded from her observations that demand breast-feeding is no guarantee of successful motherhood. Rather than suggest specific techniques, she recommends the principles of sensitivity and consistency. Some writers have come to the firm conclusion that the evidence indicates that breast-feeding is no better for psychological adjustment than bottle feeding (Brim, 1959; Davis, 1965; Orlansky, 1949; Sewell, 1952). Certainly the evidence is not such that a mother need feel she is depriving her child if she chooses to bottle feed. If she is older, sickly, without much household help, or in a disruptive environment, she may well be doing herself, her family, and her child a favor by choosing to bottle feed. On the other hand, a woman living in conditions of questionable sanitation would be well advised to breast-feed if at all possible. Nostalgic sentiment is surely on the side of breast-feeding, but women should realize that a strict reading of the evidence at this time does not show the clear advantages suggested by popular literature.

MOTHERHOOD AS A DEVELOPMENTAL STAGE

Most research on mothering has concerned itself with the effects of mothering on children rather than the effects of children on mothers. Benedek (1959a) points out that parenthood is a developmental stage and that a parent relives her own childhood through her child. This may lead to more complete and thorough resolution of old conflicts resulting in superior levels of integration. On the other hand, it may result in the unwarranted projection of the parent's conflicts onto the child, adversely affecting his development.

Some of the pitfalls of research on mothering can be illustrated by a study which began with forty-two white, low-income primiparae and ended with fifteen (Zemlick, 1952; Zemlick, and Watson, 1953). Many subjects could not be induced to remain in the study, even though extra attention at the prenatal clinic was promised. One of the major conclusions of the study was that neurotic mothers show their rejection by overprotecting their infants. An anthropology student had independently rated the maternal behavior of the mothers; women classed as neurotic were rated as most attentively maternal. How could this be? It was also discovered that these same women had unusually disordered reproductive histories. The psychologist's experimental procedures of interviewing and testing may well have scared off the more normal women, leaving him with a special group who had had reproductive trouble in the past and were therefore more receptive to the promise of special medical attention. Rather than making any one of several more parsimonious interpretations, it was assumed that what the anthropologist had rated as good mothering was not good mothering but overprotection. Moreover, it was assumed that the overprotection masked rejection. The authors seem to have digested neither scientific methodology nor the keen observations of Levy (1966) on maternal overprotection. If indeed the mothers were overprotective, it is relevant that Levy found that overprotection was not necessarily accompanied by rejection and that difficulty becoming or remaining a mother often preceded overprotection.

Rubin (1967, 1967a) conducted an interview study of the process of becoming a mother. She made an intensive, longitudinal study of a few subjects and an extensive, cross-sectional study of a large number of subjects. The beginning point of role learning tended to be mimicry, a sort of magical and superficial musing about the role. Introjection, projection, and rejection were described as the processes of trying various behaviors for fit. Eventually this resulted in establishing an identity. Role play and fantasy were extensively used as learning vehicles. The girl's own mother was not desired as a model, since she was needed as a mother for nurturance. If the woman were separated from her mother spatially, a trip like a pilgrimage often occurred or food associated with the mother was ingested. Peers were the typical models. There was a considerable amount of grief work as old roles were discarded—bride, schoolgirl, career woman. After birth, grief work was involved in giving up the nurturant care of the girl's own mother or in giving up the exclusive attachment to a previous baby. The final adjustment did not occur until three to four weeks postpartum. The frequent rejection of mother as model found among women suffering from postpartum psychiatric reactions is apparently not so pathological as Melges (1968) supposed.

SUMMARY

While the cold, analytical scientific approach constitutes an almost comic contrast to motherhood, nonetheless, some useful information may be garnered from the investigations. It would seem that, techniques based on learning theory aside, Read's dream of painless, drugless childbirth can be realized only to the extent that physical factors and the intensity of positive suggestion permit. While the precise role of psychological factors in initiating and furthering the birth process is unclear, it seems likely that they have some influence. They may be crucially important in only a small percentage of births. The ease and advantage of breast-feeding appears to have been inflated in the popular literature, and ironically there is some evidence to suggest that mothers giving great sucking gratification increase the likelihood of the oral fixation they were trying to avoid. In any case, breast-feeding is clearly not a sure road to success as a mother.

The Gordon team has provided some precise advice on how to minimize adverse postpartum reactions. Emphasized are the following factors: the absolute necessity of planning for sufficient help and rest, avoiding change of residence for six months postpartum, and increases in emotional support and company, especially from the husband. Too often a new birth signals either a move to new quarters or an austerity program of more work less time home for dad, and economizing for mom on extra help and sitters. Such plans are penny wise and pound foolish, especially for those with adverse background factors. Postpartum mental changes are extremely common, though they rarely require medical care. The symptom of sleeplessness is an ominous one which apparently differentiates the more usual reactions from the serious ones. Once a postpartum psychotic reaction has occurred, estimates of recurrence ranged from one third to the high figure of six sevenths for puerperal schizophrenia.

Studies of normal mothering are surprisingly few. Little objective data is available concerning the correlates and antecedents of succorant behavior in women. While it seems highly unlikely that hormonal factors are crucial to mothering, the kind and extent of their importance is not known. Experience appears to be an important factor in good mothering. Techniques appear to be of little avail in improving care. Brody recommends instead the principles of sensitivity and consistency. Research on mother variables seems to be relatively neglected, and at this point it might well be more productive of improved child health than would increased child study.

Chapter 11

THE LATER YEARS

EACH YEAR THERE ARE MORE WOMEN living to older ages in the United States. They must face loss of reproductive capacity and major role changes as they lose the role of mother and often that of wife as well. One gains the impression that the identity problem in women is not so much in achieving identity but in mastering shifts in identity. Perhaps it could be better stated that a woman's identity must include the expectation of major shifts in role. The role shifts required by the life cycle are often made more difficult by concomitant subcultural changes caused by an out-group marital alliance, economic and class mobility, or geographic shifting. Despite the social problems implicit in these facts, comparatively little research has been devoted to this area. How do women feel about these life changes? How extensive and how severe are the symptoms of menopause? Are the symptoms physiologically based or a product of other troubles of these years, or are they only predominant in neurotic women?

MIDDLE-LIFE CHANGES

Frank (1956) makes the point that a role implies a reciprocal, complementary response from others and that others may hinder a woman from making appropriate changes in her role behavior. The obvious case is the husband who resists his wife's expansion of the role of wife and mother when this role has dessicated. Frank points out that even without the problem of role changes, women have more difficult role requirements than men. Women already feel impelled to meet a variety of roles—wife, mother, daughter—and these role requirements sometimes conflict with each other. The husband is more likely to slough off his equivalent social responsibilities, sometimes to his wife. Women are often so involved with others that they cannot easily disengage themselves. Another problem which Frank sees as pressing heavily on the middle-aged American woman is the glamour cult.

Loss of the maternal role is a jolt to many women. A national, stratified sample of 569 women was queried about what made them feel useful (Weiss and Samuelson, 1958). Seventy-five per cent of those women with preschool children, and 40 per cent of those with school-age children referred to the family, but the percentage dropped off markedly when there were no children to care for. Of the older, unmarried women even 22 per cent of those who had jobs said nothing made them feel useful and important. Bart (1968) studied 533 women between ages forty and fifty-nine entering a psychiatric hospital for the first time. The diagnosis of depression was most frequently associated with traditionally oriented women who had lost maternal roles in which they were overprotective or overinvolved. Such depression was more common in Jewish mothers. In a sample of one hundred alcoholic women, Curlee (1969) found twenty-one in whom the excessive drinking was related to a middle-age identity crisis. These women were experiencing a change in, or challenge to, their roles as wives or mothers. Curlee points out that for women, identity crisis is frequently associated with menopause, loss of a husband, or the children leaving home.

A small sample from a larger survey study puts the problem of postparental life in a more normal and happier perspective (Deutscher, 1968). Among thirty-three couples whose children had left home, half of the twenty-eight wives intensively interviewed felt that the postparental phase was "better" than the preceding phases. Four thought it was as "bad" or "worse;" opinions of the rest fell in between. The husbands were also generally favorable to the postparental phase of their lives. The couples felt they had less work, more freedom, and a more amiable marital relationship. The troubles of those who reacted unfavorably to the postparental period seemed to center about menopause, physical disabilities, feeling a failure, and inability to fill the gap left by departing children. Axelson (1960) also found that parents reported an increase in satisfaction compared to the time when their children were in high school, though they registered a significant increase in loneliness.

In a study of opinion about aging, women from ages forty to

sixty-five found some virtues in aging. They viewed themselves as gaining in power what they gave up in sweetness (Neugarten, 1956). They saw the young woman as bland, passive, tied to her mother, nice, pleasant, and sweet. Even if she were a career girl, she was seen as dependent and passive. When she married, she was seen as taking on a collaborative role with her husband. At middle age, however, women were considered stronger than their husbands, and more dominant than young people. They were more self confident and inner directed; they saw themselves now as the judge, not the judged. While they were viewed as dominant, they were also viewed as dependent. The dependency needs tended to be met more by the children—especially the daughter—than by the husband. These older women did not seem to envy the young women or see them in a more desirable position. The men sampled agreed essentially with this picture of women but emphasized the older women as being active and authoritative in the family, while the male was seen as passive. In a later study, Neugarten and Gutman (1968) concluded that women, as they age, seem to become more tolerant of their own aggressive, egocentric impulses, whereas men appear to become more accepting of their own nurturant and affiliative impulses. At more advanced ages, the ego qualities of both sexes seem to become more constricted—more detached from the mastery of affairs and less in control of impulse life.

BECOMING A GRANDMOTHER

Neugarten and Weinstein (1968) has studied the reactions of seventy middle-class couples to being grandparents. The sample was all from the Chicago area and skewed with regard to religious affiliation, with 40 per cent Jewish, 48 per cent Protestant, and 12 per cent Catholic. The age range of the grandmothers was from the early fifties to the mid-sixties. The majority of the grandparents expressed only comfort, satisfaction, and pleasure with the role. A sizeable number seemed to be idealizing the role of grandparenthood and to have high expectations of the grandchild in the future. About one third of the sample expressed some discomfort or disappointment. Sometimes they had trouble thinking of themselves as a grandparent. In some instances, there was conflict with the parents with regard to the rearing of the grandchild; some grandparents were indifferent to caretaking or responsibility in reference to the grandchild. Grandmothers (29 of 70) significantly more often than grandfathers felt a sense of biological renewal through the grandchildren. In spite of the fact that their grandchildren were fairly close by, 27 per cent of the grandmothers and 29 per cent of the grandfathers in this sample reported feeling relatively remote from the grandchildren and acknowledged relatively little effect of grandparenthood on their own lives. The authors report little evidence of the old authority relation to the grandparents. The new styles of "fun seekers" or "distant figures" had been adopted by over half of all the cases in this sample. The "fun seeker" was like a playmate to the children, while the "distant figure" was characterized as an intermittent Santa Claus. Only 5 per cent of a sample of midwestern grandparents regularly cared for grandchildren. Albrecht (1954) remarked that if there were cases of excessive love, they were well concealed.

BECOMING A WIDOW

After age sixty-five, 19 per cent of men and 53 per cent of women are widowed (Riley, Foner, Hess, and Toby, 1969). The severity of the trauma is suggested by the fact that thirteen months after being widowed, 21 per cent of a sample of Boston widows and 32 per cent of sample of Sydney widows were judged to have sustained a marked health deterioration compared to controls (Maddison and Viola, 1968). The widow is expected to resume her previous level of activity, not to withdraw from role participation. They are respected for being independent and typically live alone near children but not with them. The financial support of widows is very small, and it is largely through peer support that individuals seek reassurance, release from stress, and a renewed sense of identity (Riley, Foner, Hess, and Toby, 1969). In general, the aging process seemed harder on women than on men, and widowers and widows were especially unhappy (Guren, Veroff, and Feld, 1960).

THE CLIMACTERIUM

The climacterium, or cessation and atrophy of the organs of reproduction, is variously greeted with joy or sadness, depending on the individual woman's attitude toward this aspect of her sexual functioning. Since most women have long ago learned to value their female functions, unadulterated joy or relief is undoubtedly a rare reaction. Many women, however, have the wisdom to accept and enjoy each season of life. The female of the human species is the only one known to have a true menopause (Riopelle and Rogers, 1965). Menopause refers only to cessation of menstruation while climacterium refers to all the changes of ovarian decline. In two thirds of women, menopause occurs between the ages of forty-five and fifty-five; half of the rest cease menstruating before and half later (Grollman, 1964). Menopause itself is not a very good index of hormone state. What happens biologically is that the ovaries cease to function, resulting in a discontinuation of the menstrual period. Fertility is eventually lost, though it may continue for a year or two after menstruation ceases. The ovaries no longer produce estrogen and of course not progesterone either. There is an increase in the hormones which stimulate the gonads; these originally were thought to cause some of the uncomfortable symptoms of menopause, but these symptoms are now attributed to the estrogen deficiency per se (Lloyd and Leathem, 1964). While males show only a slight and regular decline of their sex typical hormones from thirty to ninety, females show a more abrupt decline in estrogens, though it begins gradually enough in the mid-thirties (Brown and Matthews, 1962; Lloyd and Leathem, 1964; Wilson and Wilson, 1963). While nearly all the other glands function the same or nearly the same regardless of age, estrogen production in the postmenopausal woman is one sixth of its previous level. It is as low or lower than in the last days of the menstrual period (Brown and Matthew, 1962).

ESTROGEN EFFECTS

The more subtle consequences of this decline in estrogen are many. The breasts and genital tissues atrophy. The uterus becomes smaller and the vaginal mucosa becomes thin and less resistant to bacterial infection. These weakened tissues may cause or aggravate stress incontinence and may also cause dyspareunia (painful sexual relations). Regular sexual relations, however, seems to help maintain the vagina in good condition (Rubin, 1966). Two ladies in their sixties with a lifetime history of twice weekly sexual relations retained good lubrication without hormone replacement (Masters and Johnson, 1966). Actually, the skin and mucous membranes in all parts of the body are affected by estrogen decline and tend to become dry and lose elasticity. The shine and glow of a woman's appearance is adversely affected. Hair on the head and vulva may become sparse. Estrogen acts to increase protein anabolism and its decrease results in a loss of nitrogen, the basic factor in these tissue changes. The muscles lose strength and tend to stiffen; protein is lost from the bones, resulting in osteoporosis and the so-called dowager's hump. These bone changes may cause or contribute to low-back pain, arthralgias, and atrophic arthritis. The decline in estrogen also may contribute to the build-up of cholesterol in the blood and consequent hypertension. The decreased energy output may result in an accumulation of fat. Loss of estrogen disrupts the entire system; it is involved in carbohydrate metabolism and may be responsible for the increase in diabetes with age (Wilson and Wilson, 1963). Disruptions of autonomic activities include digestion and, most prominently of all, the vascular system. In some way, estrogen alters the vascular contractility (Lloyd and Leathem, 1964), and its absence can cause the characteristic hot flushes (a feeling of warmth, sweating, and flushing). While estrogen is implicated in all these changes, it may be only one factor, and the exact mechanism is frequently unclear.

The Wilson team (1963) also believes that estrogen loss may be directly responsible for depression and negativism. Others have thought hormonal changes might cause depression indirectly through loss of attractiveness, and there is no doubt that many women of menopausal age are depressed simply because of their troubles. Whether or not hormone deficiency can cause depression directly is by no means established, but the many reports of failure of hormonal treatments to alter mental states of the involutional period do not constitute irrefutable evidence that hormonal decline did not play a direct role in triggering the mental reaction. Intervening changes may make replacement of the deficiency insufficient. The Wilson team (1963) is firmly on the side of replacement of estrogen to prevent and correct this catalogue of ills. They point out that during the Roman Empire, the life expectancy of a woman was twenty-three; in the fourteenth century it was thirty-three; in 1900, it was forty-eight, and today it is seventy-five. They believe that this radical change requires radical reevaluation of previous attitudes about aging. Their views, however, are distinctly controversial. Masters (1956) seems to be in favor of replacement therapy, and many individual physicians are as well, though they tend to be cautious in their claims of what benefits may be expected. It is especially important to understand that fertility is not restored and aging is not prevented. Specific ills may be ameliorated, however.

INCIDENCE OF MENOPAUSAL SYMPTOMS

One of the better studies of the incidence of menopausal symptoms was done in England in 1933 (Barrett, Cullis, Fairfield, and Nicholson, 1933). Questionnaire returns were gathered from over one thousand women ages twenty-nine to ninety-one who had had no menses for five or more years. A nonpatient sample was used which made the results more representative of the general population. However, some of the data is probably not very exact because it depended solely on the memory and self-report of the women. Overall, 14 per cent of the women reported no symptoms during the menopausal period, and 21 per cent had only hot flushes. Ten per cent were briefly incapacitated by their symptoms. Married women had significantly more symptoms than single women. The most common symptom was the hot flush, occurring in 62 per cent, and lasting two years in the majority, though continuing indefinitely in many women. Forty-five per cent of the women had headaches, 40 per cent giddiness, 34 per cent obesity, 31 per cent nervous instability, 24 per cent rheumatic pain, and 21 per cent uterine hemorrhage. The seven per cent of women with ten or more pregnancies had significantly more symptoms, with the exception of nervous instability, which was not affected by the number of pregnancies. Fifty-eight per cent of the total sample reported having had menstrual trouble, and there was a significant relation between menstrual and menopausal abnormality.

Neugarten and Kraines (1965) report the responses of 460 American women ages thirteen to sixty-four to a checklist of twenty-eight menopause symptoms. The highest frequency of emotional symptoms was during adolescence; the highest frequency of somatic symptoms was during the menopause. Menopausal and nonmenopausal women of the same age could be significantly differentiated on the basis of the following endocrine-related symptoms: vasomotor manifestations, paresthesia, formication (crawling sensation of the skin), irritability and nervousness, melancholia, heavy menstrual flow (occurring in 51 per cent), breast pain, and feeling of suffocation. [Interestingly, suffocation is prominently mentioned in postpartum nightmares (Fodor, 1949.] Vertigo, insomnia, and fatigue did not differentiate the two groups. During the postmenopausal period, ages fifty-five to sixty-four, Neugarten and Kraines found many fewer symptoms, indicating a marked recovery in spite of low endocrine status.

EMOTIONAL REACTIONS TO MENOPAUSE

In another study (Neugarten, Wood, Kraines, and Loomis, 1963), it was found that women of the upper socioeconomic group do not fear menopause, though about half of all women questioned felt menopause was unpleasant. The older women reported a more positive attitude to the menopause; some women reported being more vigorous afterward. These authors found no evidence of the closing-of-the-gates feeling that Deutsch (1945) reports as typical of women in this phase of life.

Neugarten (1968) expresses the opinion that the timing of the climacterium did not order or explain the data which she had gathered on women during the middle and late years of life. She suggests that biologically based developmental components in personality may not be so important in the later years as in earlier years. While Neugarten and Kraines (1965) found more emotional symptoms during adolescence than during the menopause, it should be noted that menarche, for example, also did not have clear psychological effects as *the* organizing event in a young girl's life (see Chapter 6). Neugarten does not deny the importance of menopause or other biological factors in adult personality, but she points out that a woman's illness, for example, or that of her husband, may be of greater importance.

There are very few good studies of menopause. The last study to be reported is not a very adequate one but will perhaps illustrate some shortcomings of research design. A psychiatric work-up of fifty menopausal, low-income women was undertaken to investigate personality during menopause. Some subjects had been referred for psychiatric evaluation, but twenty-seven women were examined only as a result of the study. Depression was found in forty-one of the fifty, but the depression was of a reactive sort.* These women had many marital and situational difficulties and these seemed to be the source of the depression. Guilt feelings were conspicuously lacking and the premorbid personality was not like that of women developing involutional psychiatric reactions (Stern and Prados, 1946). Some of the most severely disturbed women were those whose menopause had been brought on artificially by hysterectomy. The authors suggest that this operation itself was probably undertaken as a cure for hysterical or psychosomatic involvement of the reproductive system.

Despite much time, money and effort, this study makes little contribution to our understanding of menopausal reactions. The subjects do not represent any clear population, since they are a lumping of women whose menopause had been brought on artificially, women in menopause without obvious psychiatric reaction, and women whose symptoms were obvious enough to prompt psychiatric referral. Even more serious is the fact that there is no control group. Without a control group, it is impossible to guess whether the depression found can be attributed to age, lower-class status, situational difficulties, or menopause. For example, it is

*Reactive depression refers to one brought on by situational stresses; other types of depression appear to be based more on loss or on physiological change.

not possible to conclude that menopause depression is characteristically reactive, because the variable of social class has not been controlled. It is known that there is a relationship between social class and type of mental symptoms. The obsessive neurotic usually thought to be the personality type preceding involutional reactions would be expected to be rare in the lower class.

Accurate data is so scanty that it is difficult to form many firm conclusions about the psychology of menopause. The fact that significant differences (Neugarten and Kraines, 1965) were found between menopausal and nonmenopausal women of the same age indicates that there are symptoms specific to menopause and that these are not merely a function of age. The decline in emotional symptoms from their high point during adolescence prompted Neugarten and Kraines to comment that the mature women were better able to handle the physiologic stress. The authors of the influential text of Weiss and English (1957) believe only neurotic women have many symptoms during menopause. It has even been suggested that though neurotic women do have more symptoms, it is not because they complain more nor because of their faulty attitudes but because they have higher hormonal requirements and therefore suffer more with the change (Shorr, 1942). Greenhill (1946) reported that only 41 per cent of one hundred normal, nonneurotic women complained of symptoms that might be mild autonomic lability, mild tension, or depression during the menopause. It is not clear, however, how he decided whether a woman was neurotic. He expressed the opinion that women who are neurotic before menopause get worse then.

An unusually well-controlled study of the effects of sex hormones on aged women showed significant improvement, compared to a placebo control group, in motivation, mental flexibility, and aspects of memory (Caldwell, 1954; Caldwell and Watson, 1952). Mood did not improve, perhaps because of the limited opportunity of the environment in a home for the aged. The subjects had a less than average history of mental stability. To obtain significant improvements, even if of only one or two years' duration, is a promising finding.

The evidence at this time is not sufficient to clarify how much of the symptoms of the menopausal period and later life are attributable to situational difficulties, neurotic attitudes, identity crises, and/or hormonal deficiencies, but hormonal deficiencies are clearly responsible for some of them. It used to be believed that involutional psychotic reactions were brought on by hormonal changes. Etiological emphasis, however, has shifted almost entirely in favor of mental conflict factors. These include faulty prior personality, especially compulsive, rigid, and/or narcissistic character and the more immediate conflict factors of aging and role changes. The contribution of hormone changes in producing psychotic reactions in this period has therefore been little studied recently.

SUMMARY

It would seem that while neither getting older nor being old is favorably viewed by the young, those actually going through the experience find compensations. There are many role changes which may challenge a woman's adjustment during middle life, such as becoming a childless, infertile woman, or perhaps becoming a widow. Becoming a grandmother appears not to present much problem. Menopause is viewed as unpleasant by about half of women. For many women, however, it is not a decisive psychological event. There are symptoms specific to menopause, but is unclear how common they are. The figure given by Greenhill (1946) that 41 per cent of women have unpleasant symptoms would definitely be low since it excludes neurotics, and by some standards, a large percentage of the population today is neurotic. Many women become more vigorous after menopause, but the extent and proportion of recovery is not clear. The studies indicating the beneficial effects of hormone replacement appear to offer a boon to aging women. While it is too soon to know the extent and severity of the side effects of estrogen treatment, there appears to be every likelihood that women will not only be living longer but living better.

Chapter 12

SUMMARY AND CONCLUSIONS

WOMEN BEGIN LIFE with cells that are fundamentally different from men. In the course of development, this causes anatomic differences and other differences as well. Anatomy is but a part of destiny. Girls develop physically faster than do boys, and the difference in maturation rate which is only about a month at birth becomes nearly two years at puberty. The extent of female accelerated mental development is not agreed upon, but girls show precocious language development. The boys eventually catch up, but even as adults, women retain a slight average superiority in verbal facility. Women are constitutionally less strong muscularly than men and are less physically active, beginning at a very early age. While the battle of the sexes in terms of which is smarter has tended to die down in recent years, the more specific question of whether or not women are as capable of analysis as men is as hot a question as ever. The small average sex difference in analytical skill seems to involve only spatial tasks. The causes of sex differences in space perception and in cognitive approach have not been established.

Males are clearly more physically aggressive than females and have the dominant authority in all societies. Male aggressive qualities are undoubtedly less adaptive today than in days of yore, but nonetheless they remain a definite factor in the relation of the sexes. While the Victorian notion that women have no sex drive is clearly not true, women apparently have less sex drive than men. The difference is particularly obvious during adolescence when male sex drive is at its peak and female sexuality is apparently yet to be aroused. However, a childhood difference in sexuality may also exist. While women may be less driven to sexual behavior, they have greater capacity for orgastic response.

These sex differences in aggression and in sexual drive appear to have a biological basis, though they can be muted or exaggerated by cultural conditions. Generally, aggressiveness as a method of coping does not develop and is not culturally encouraged, since it is not seen as effective for a woman. Fear, on the other hand, is a more frequent admission in girls and women than in boys and men. There is no evidence that males are better adjusted generally than females. Differences in "emotionality" may be more apparent than real. Showing fear is not the male style, but it is the female style and may well be designed to elicit protection responses or chivalrous behavior. A frequent male response to circumstances that might cause anxiety in a woman is to express aggression instead, perhaps in the form of braggadocio, bluster, temper tantrum, or irritable behavior. These behaviors represent a denial of fear and refusal to show weakness. Between peer males, a show of weakness would certainly result in a loss of status and might even invite attack. The sexes are expected to conform to certain styles and patterns of behavior. He or she who is out of step elicits confusion if not scorn, anger, or ridicule.

As children, girls are less trouble, and more conformity is expected of them. On the average, they can be verbally reasoned with at an earlier age than boys. This method of discipline, especially compared with physical punishment, appears better suited to the development of a strong superego. Girls generally appear to show more conformity, guilt, and resistance to temptation. Since they do not have such great antisocial impulses to control, they are less tempted than males.

Girls, like boys, are fundamentally most attached to their mothers. While some girls show an Oedipal interest, the question has been raised as to what extent this is a function of marital disturbance and the father, rather than arising from the girl's biological instinctual development. Ordinarily girls are quite clear that they are girls, though they do not always like it. They are surprised and interested to learn that boys are different from girls and may be annoyed that they are not "fancier." The promise of new life, however, is usually sufficient to make them biologically content with their lot. The advantages and greater status of the male role, however, eventually become evident, and girls frequently wish they were boys. Envy of the male role is so prevalent and without clear relationship to psychopathology that it cannot be considered abnormal. Often cases of neurotic, "masculine" women have their roots not in penis envy but in a faulty early relationship with the mother such that trust does not develop. The resulting aloof, independent attitude is masculine only by happenstance. On the other hand, exaggerated aspects of "feminine" character development, especially extremes of dependence and passivity, are, associated with incompetence and poor performance as wives and mothers.

Masculinizing influences include having an older brother or brothers and/or an affectionate relationship with the father. While it has been stated that upper-middle-class girls remain confused for a longer time about sex role than girls from working-class families, it would probably be more accurate to say that upper-middle-class culture has a broadened sex-role definition in comparison to the working class. Generally speaking, this has been historically true. The periods of "freedom" for women almost always refer to "freedom" for women of the upper classes. The anomalous position of American women today becomes more understandable when viewed in terms of status changes in our culture. The leveling of classes and races has reduced the relative status of at least some women of the higher classes. Status barriers of sex have not decreased nearly so much as those of class and race. As producers of one of the few remaining important, unmanufactured products, women are conspicuously inefficient and do not share in the prestige of a highly technical society.

Efforts to present women as rounded-off men have generally been at pains to minimize any biological influence in women. This study does not deal with men; assuredly biological influences can be demonstrated in them as well, but they are not so complex as those in women. Menarche per se does not clearly have psychological effects, but the social effects of curvaceous maturation are pronounced. Beauty in women is a real and important variable related to their sense of well-being, dominance, and group status.

The cyclic changes of the menstrual cycle indicate biobehavioral effects which are so common that they cannot be considered neurotic. Psychosomatic influences are also in evidence. Psychological attitudes can stop menstruation. There is also some evidence suggesting a relationship between negative attitudes to femininity and discomforts of menstrual functioning, but direction of causality has not been clearly established. Primary dysmenorrhea appears to be physically caused. On the whole, while there probably are some women whose unhealthy attitudes make a significant contribution to their menstrual problems, this aspect has been overemphasized. General education about cyclic emotional changes would be helpful in reducing instances of extreme loss of control and undue interpersonal conflict.

Likewise, biobehavioral effects are noticeable during pregnancy. These effects and those of immediate marital, social, and economic stress have been consistently underemphasized in favor of unconscious motivation as explanations of adverse developments in pregnancy, especially in the case of severe nausea and vomiting. On the other hand, it is not possible to rule out psychological factors in some cases of prolonged labor, even though most prolonged labors are from physical causes. There is considerable evidence of a psychological influence in instances of habitual abortion without known organic cause and also some evidence of such an effect in functional infertility. It would appear that women have somewhat more control of their reproduction, albeit control at a rather primitive, unconscious level, than what had hitherto been supposed except in folklore.

Proper transition to motherhood appears to depend peculiarly on having a clear conscience in regard to one's own mother and on being in a sufficiently nurturant and protective environment. Nurture may come from the mother, the mother-in-law, or the husband, though the husband tends to be crucial, especially in the nuclear family arrangement so common now in the United States. Husbands are frequently unprepared for such a burden, particularly since sexual restrictions have already placed some strain on the marital bond. Women are frequently insecure at this point. Often decisions about breast-feeding are influenced by the wife's opinion of the husband's attitude. Bottle feeding, by binding the mother less closely to her baby, relieves a triangular threat to the marital relationship and allows the mother to feel and look more like her old self. Current American culture and mores are no longer conducive to successful breast-feeding.

The later, middle years of life are somewhat paradoxical in that for all the miseries expected of menopause, the picture emerges of a female figure more dominant (and also larger) than in the previous years of her life. Menopause itself, like menarche, does not appear to be a decisive psychological event. Role changes of the empty nest or widowhood appear to be more important. There is evidence, however, of symptoms specific to the climacterium, so that the assertion that only neurotic women have symptoms at this time is unsupported.

* * *

This review has been an attempt to see what the available scientific evidence could contribute to our understanding of women. While this is a restricted approach, it seemed one worthy of more complete consideration, since it has been so little pursued in systematic fashion. Many of the problems of women are merely the problems of people. We live today in a culture whose values in many ways run contrary to the welfare of human beings. Everyone suffers from these pressures. Women talk more about it and men kill themselves more on account of it. There has, however, been more change in the lives of women than in the lives of men.

Many emancipators had expected that women would increasingly pursue careers previously the province of the male sex. Instead, their hopes were buried in a recent bumper crop of babies proceeding in especially increased numbers from the better educated women. On the one hand, one can detect in this a defiant affirmation of humanity and human values, but nonetheless, one wonders, why not careers? It seems likely that most women have sensed what the evidence showed—that there is considerable hypocrisy, if not simply unwitting inconsistency, about the ideal of the equality of the sexes. For many people, espousal of the ideal merely represents conformity to social pressure and does not exist beyond a superficial level. Quite possibly, many women have deciphered the double talk and concluded that pursuing male careers is rarely worth the cost. Another aspect of the myth of sexual equality is that the double standard is dead. It is not, although again there is evidence of hypocrisy in that many apparently speak as though they hold a single, liberal standard of morality, although they do not.

A further reason for the failure of the emancipators may very well be insufficient appreciation of the deep-seated taboo against competition between the sexes. In general, women may pursue any activity without censure so long as it is perceived as not in competition with men. Thus women are praised, not censured, for taking over the usual tasks of men during war or other crisis. The welfare of mankind depends on the cooperation of the sexes. The activity and achievement patterns of both sexes have probably been largely determined by this very basic expectation of cooperation between the sexes. Role segregation by sex weighs not merely on women; men actually are more rigorously restricted in their role than are women. Who applauds the man who wishes to stay home and take care of the house and children while his wife works?

On the practical side, those who expected that women would increasingly pursue careers failed to reckon with the extent of class leveling which has increased the number of men from lower classes competing for positions in schools and jobs. Class leveling has also severely curtailed the quantity and quality of household help. Children cannot be reared by a labor-saving device. It is surprising that predominantly female unions and organizations devoted to the advancement and welfare of the female sex have not moved more effectively in the development of child-care facilities, emergency homemaker care, and home-maintenance services. Now that women live so long and are less needed for their child-bearing capacity, there certainly is increasing reason for them to assume roles other than wife and mother, at least part of the time. Improved methods of birth control and increasing knowledge of biobehavioral factors will help women achieve greater control over their bodies and their health.

In the Soviet Union, Communist ideology prescribes the equality of the sexes, but close inspection suggests that it is largely a freedom to do twice the work of men. While most women work,

80 per cent of them do physical work. Child-care facilities have long waiting lists and most women must make their own arrangements (Dodge, 1966). Sixty-five years ago the average life span of the Russian woman was two years less than that of the average man; now it is eight years less. This drastic reduction of the Soviet woman's life span has been attributed to, "The traumas of living conditions and working conditions." (*Kommunist,* 1963). In the lower grades, the sexes have been educationally separated for years. There is nothing like equality of the sexes in the positions of highest status in the Soviet Union. The much-publicized predominance of women in the medical profession is not so impressive when one discovers that most of these women are at a training and status level somewhere between our general practitioner and nurse. Most of the physicians at the equivalent level of training as American physicians are men (Dodge, 1966). The true picture of the status of women in the Soviet Union is not as it is usually conveyed in popular writings.

There is a welter of paradoxes emerging from this study. Among the lowest classes in the United States, learning is regarded as a feminine enterprise, and being bested by a woman in grades or intellectual activity is no especial shame. Cultural activity is viewed as a female province. In the upper-middle class, however, it is viewed as a male province primarily. Then, too, it is paradoxical that the liberal and democratic principles that promoted equalization of the sexes also promoted leveling of classes. In some parts of the world where there is less class leveling, one can see conspicuous examples of female career enterprise. These women are perceived as being of such high status that their participation in male role activities does not arouse general resentment. Furthermore, the greater technological and leadership needs in more backward countries allow women to view their role deviations as not in competition with men but in the service of the cooperative building toward progressive national goals. Women arising from milieus traditionally oppressive to women feel a greater sense of mission for female causes than do American women.

Equality of the sexes has not only been presented in the form of equality of opportunity and equality of value but also equality in the sense of sameness. Differences between the sexes have been minimized. A review of the evidence indicates that sexual equality in this sense is a pure myth. While men and women are more alike than different, they are nonetheless fundamentally different. Whenever there are differences, there is the possibility of making judgments of superiority and inferiority, but in a general way neither sex appears to have a clear edge. The motive for minimizing sex differences may well have been the lofty one of promoting harmony between the sexes; however, reality distortions are poor devices in the long run. Having looked at the evidence, the extent to which sex differences in development have been ignored in educational planning is surprising, though this may be in the process of being remedied. The answer here is probably to move toward more individualized instruction for boys and girls alike. It is also surprising that there has not been more consistent and systematic support for research and education about female functioning, pregnancy, childbirth, and child rearing. While authoritative treatment of these topics is difficult, if not impossible, such an effort might make women more resistant to fads and fashions promoted by popular magazines. These subjects seem to deserve much more attention than they are receiving in public education, especially considering the fact that sex education is now widely available.

The quality and quantity of the research reviewed varied considerably. While there was a surprising amount of good research on female sex life, there was very little on menopause. Research with women subjects is generally neglected (Carlson and Carlson, 1960), and the psychology of women is often assumed to parallel that of men. Nowhere is the folly of this more evident than in the review of Freud's theory of feminine development. The evidence suggests that it is misleading and almost totally false; however there is a relative dearth of data concerning psychoanalytic hypotheses. Even systematic case reports from psychoanalysts are lacking. It would seem that the "hard-headed" scientists have decided these questions are not worth investigating and that the psychoanalysts already know what is true anyway. The burden of proof, however rests upon the analysts. Research confirming or refuting psychoanalytic theory seems to have been spinning its wheels these many years, and meanwhile psychoanalytic concepts have become accepted as mental fixtures in the minds of much of the reading public.

BIBLIOGRAPHY

Abel, Theodora and Joffe, Natalie F. (1950) Cultural backgrounds of female puberty. *American Journal of Psychotherapy,* 4, 90-113.

Aberle, D. F., *et al.* (1963) The incest taboo and the mating pattern of animals. *American Anthropologist,* 65, 253-265.

Abraham, K. (1942) Manifestations of the female castration complex. In *Selected Papers.* London: Hogarth Press.

Adams, A. B. (1959) Choice of infant feeding technique as a function of maternal personality. *Journal of Consulting Psychology,* 23, 143-146.

Adams, E. B. and Sarason, I. G. (1963) Relation between anxiety in children and their parents. *Child Development,* 34, 237-246.

Adams, J. F. (1964) Adolescent personal problems as a function of age and sex. *Journal of Genetic Psychology,* 104, 207-214.

Adler, A. (1927) *Understanding human nature.* Garden City, New York: Garden City Publishing Company.

Albrecht, Ruth (1954) The parental responsibilities of grandparents. *Marriage and Family Living,* 16, 201-4.

Alpert, A. (1941) The latency period. *American Journal of Orthopsychiatry,* 11, 126-133.

Altman, M., Knowles, E., and Bull, H. D. (1941) A psychosomatic study of the sex cycle in women. *Psychosomatic Medicine,* 3, 199-225.

Ames, L. B., and Ilg, Frances L. (1964) Sex differences in test performance of matched girl-boy pairs in the 5-to-9-year-old age range. *Journal of Genetic Psychology,* 104, 25-34.

Ammons, R. B., and Ammons, H. S. (1949) Parent preferences in young children's doll-play interviews. *Journal of Abnormal and Social Psychology,* 44, 490-505.

Anastasi, Anne. (1958) *Differential Psychology: Individual and group differences in behavior, 3rd. ed.* New York: Macmillan.

Anastasi, Anne. (1949) *Differential psychology.* New York: Macmillan.

Anderson, I. H., Hughes, B. O., and Dixon, W. R. (1957) The rate of reading development and its relation to age of learning to read, sex, and intelligence. *Journal of Educational Research,* 50, 481-94.

Anderson, J. E. (1936) *The young child in the home.* New York: Appleton-Century.

Argyle, M. (1964) Introjection: A form of social learning. *British Journal of Psychology,* 55, 391-402.

Aronfreed, J. (1969) The concept of internalization. In D. A. Goslin (Ed.),

Handbook of socialization theory and research. Chicago: Rand McNally, pp. 263-324.

Aronfreed, J. (1968) *Conduct and conscience: The socialization of internalized control over behavior.* New York: Academic Press.

Astin, Helen. (1969) *The woman doctorate in America.* New York: Russell Sage Foundation.

Axelson, Leland J. (1960) Personal adjustments in the postparental period. *Marriage and Family Living,* 22, 66-70.

Ayres, Barbara. (1967) Pregnancy magic: A study of food taboos and sex avoidances. In Clellan S. Ford (Ed.) *Cross-cultural approaches.* New Haven: Human Relations Area Files Press.

Bach, G. R. (1945) Young children's play fantasies. *Psychological Monographs,* 59, No. 2.

Baker, A. A. (1965) Mother and baby unit for puerperal schizophrenia. In *1st International Congress of Psychosomatic Medicine and Childbirth.* Paris: Gauthier-Villars, 456-460.

Balow, I. H. (1963) Sex differences in first grade reading. *Elementary English,* 40, 303-6.

Bandura, A. (1969) Social-learning theory of identificatory processes. In D. A. Goslin (Ed.) *Handbook of socialization theory and research.* Chicago: Rand McNally, pp. 213-262.

Bandura, A. (1965) Vicarious processes: A case of no-trial learning. In L. Berkowitz (Ed.) *Advances in experimental social psychology.* Vol. 2. New York: Academic Press, pp. 1-55.

Bandura, A. (1962) Social learning through imitation. In M. R. Jones (Ed.) *Nebraska symposium on motivation.* Lincoln: University of Nebraska Press, pp. 211-269.

Bandura, Albert, and Walters, Richard H. (1963a) Aggression. In Harold W. Stevenson (Ed.) *Child psychology.* Chicago: University of Chicago Press, pp. 364-415.

Bandura, Albert, and Walters, Richard H. (1963b) *Social learning and personality development.* New York: Holt, Rinehart and Winston.

Barber, Theodore X., Calverley, D. S., Forgione, A., McPeake, J.D., Chaves, J. F., and Bowen, B. (1969) Five attempts to replicate the experimenter bias effect. *Journal of Consulting and Clinical Psychology,* 33, 1-6.

Barbu, Z. (1951) Studies in children's honesty. *Quarterly Bulletin of the British Psychological Society,* 2, 53-57.

Barnett, M. C. (1966) Vaginal awareness in the infancy and childhood of girls. *Journal of the American Psychoanalytic Association,* 14, 129-41

Barrett, L., Cullis, W., Fairfield, L., and Nicholson R. (1933) Investigations of the menopause in 1000 women. *Lancet,* 1, 106-108.

Barrucand, D. (1968) La psychogenèse des vomissements répétes de la femme enceinte. [The psychogenesis of repeated vomiting in the pregnant woman.] *Annales Médico-Psychologiques,* 2, 618-626. Abstract in *Psychological Abstracts.*

Barry, H., Bacon, Margaret K., and Child, I. L. (1957) A cross-cultural survey of some sex differences in socialization. *Journal of Abnormal and Social Psychology,* 55, 327-32.

Barschak, Erna. (1951) A study of happiness and unhappiness in the childhood and adolescence of girls in different cultures. *Journal of Psychology,* 32, 173-215.

Bart, Pauline B. (1968) Depression in middle-aged women: Some sociocultural factors. *Dissertation Abstracts,* 28, 4752.

Bayley, Nancy. (1967) Behavioral correlates of mental growth. *American Psychologist,* 1967, 23, 1-17.

Bayley, Nancy. (1956) Individual patterns of development. *Child Development,* 27, 45-74.

Bayley, Nancy, and Oden Melita H. (1955) The maintenance of intellectual ability in gifted adults. *Journal of Gerontology,* 10, 91-107.

Bayley, Nancy, and Schaefer, E. S. (1964) Correlations of maternal and child behaviors with the development of mental abilities. *Monographs Society for Research in Child Development,* 29.

Beach, F. A. (1958) Neural and chemical regulation of behavior. In Harry F. Harlow and Clinton N. Woolsey (Eds.) *Biological and biochemical bases of behavior.* Madison: University of Wisconsin Press.

Beach, F. A. (1956) Characteristics of masculine "sex drive". In M. R. Jones (Ed.) *Nebraska Symposium on Motivation.* Lincoln: University of Nebraska Press, pp. 1-32.

Beach, S. R., Henley, K., Peterson, A., and Farr, M. (1955) Husbands of women with postpartum psychosis. *Journal of Psychiatric Social Work,* 24, 165-169.

Beard, Mary. (1946) *Woman as a force in history.* New York: Macmillan.

Beard, Mary. (1931) *On understanding women.* London: Longmans, Green & Co.

Beavoir, Simone de. (1949) *The second sex.* New York: Bantam.

Becker, Gilbert. (1968) Ability to differentiate message from source and birth order and subject-sex interaction. *Psychological Reports,* 23, 658.

Bell, Robert R. (1966) *Premarital sex in a changing society.* Englewood Cliffs, New Jersey: Prentice-Hall.

Bell, R., and Costello, N. (1964) Three tests for sex differences in tactual sensitivity in the newborn. *Biologia Neonatorum,* 7, 335-47.

Bender, Lauretta, and Cramer, Joseph B. (1949) Sublimation and sexual gratification in the latency period of girls. In K. R. Eissler (Ed.) *Searchlights on delinquency.* New York: International Universities Press.

Bendig, A. W. (1959) College norms for and concurrent validity of Cattell's IPAT anxiety scale. *Psychological Newsletter of New York University,* 10, 263-267.

Benedek, Therese. (1959a) Parenthood as a developmental phase. *Journal of American Psychoanalytic Association,* 7, 389-417.

Benedek, Therese. (1959b) Sexual function in women and their disturbance. In Silvano Arieti (Ed.) *American Handbook of Psychiatry.* New York: Basic Books, 726-748.

Benedek, Therese. (1952a) *Psychosexual functions in women.* New York: Ronald Press.

Benedek, Therese. (1952b) Infertility as a psychosomatic defense. *Fertility and Sterility,* 3, 527-544.

Benedek, Therese, and Rubenstein, B. B. (1942) The sexual cycle in women. *Psychosomatic Medicine Monographs,* 3, Nos. 1 and 2.

Benedict, Ruth. (1938) Continuities and discontinuities in cultural conditioning. *Psychiatry,* 1, 161-167.

Benjamin, E. (1942) The Oedipus complex in childhood. *Nervous Child,* 2, 47-54.

Bennett, E. M., and Cohen, L. R. (1959) Men and women: personality patterns and contrasts. *Genetic Psychology Monographs,* 59, 101-155.

Bergler, Edmund. (1958) *Counterfeit-sex.* New York: Grune & Stratton.

Bergler, Edmund, and Kroger, William S. (1954) *Kinsey's myth of female sexuality.* New York: Grune & Stratton.

Bergström-Walan, Maj-Briht. (1963) Efficacy of education for childbirth. *Journal of Psychosomatic Research,* 7, 131-146.

Berkowitz, Leonard. (1962) *Aggression: A social psychological analysis.* New York: McGraw-Hill.

Bernick, N. (1965) The development of children's sexual attitudes as determined by pupil-dilation response. Unpublished doctoral dissertation. University of Chicago as cited in Kohlberg, 1966.

Berry, J. W. (1966) Temne and Eskimo perceptual skills. *International Journal of Psychology,* 1, 207-229.

Berry, J. L., and Martin, B. (1957) GSR reactivity as a function of anxiety, instructions, and sex. *Journal of Abnormal and Social Psychology,* 54, 9-12.

Bettelheim, Bruno. (1962) *Symbolic wounds.* New York: Collier Books.

Biaggio, Angela M. (1969) Internalized versus externalized guilt: A cross-cultural study. *Journal of Social Psychology,* 78, 147-149.

Bibring, Grete L. (1959) Some considerations of the psychological processes in pregnancy. *Psychoanalytic Study of the Child,* 14, New York: International Universities Press.

Bibring, Grete L., Dwyer, T. F., Huntington, D. S., and Valenstein, A. F. (1961) A study of the psychological processes in pregnancy and of the earliest mother-child relationship. *The Psychoanalytic Study of the Child,* 16. New York: International Universities Press.

Biller, Henry B. (1969) Maternal salience and feminine development in young girls. *Proceedings of the 77th Annual Convention of the American Psychological Association,* 4, 259-260.

Bing, Elizabeth. (1967) *Six practical lessons for an easier childbirth.* New York: Grossett & Dunlap.

Blau, A., Slaff, B., Easton, K., Welkowitz, J., Springarn, J., and Cohen, J. (1963) The psychogenic etiology of premature births: A preliminary report. *Psychosomatic Medicine,* 25, 201-211.

Blood, R. O. and Wolfe, D. M. (1960) *Husbands and wives: the dynamics of married living.* New York: Free Press of Glencoe.

Blos, Peter. (1962) *On adolescence.* New York: Free Press of Glencoe.

Blum, Gerald S. (1949) A study of psychoanalytic theory of psychosexual development. *Genetic Psychological Monographs,* 39, 3-99.

Boehm, Lenore and Nass, M. L. (1960) Social class differences in conscience development. Progress report, Jan. 30, 1960 as cited by Oetzel, 1966.

Bonaparte, Marie. (1965) *Female sexuality.* New York: Grove Press.

Borstelmann, L. J. (1961) Sex of experimenter and sex-typed behavior of young children. *Child Development,* 32, 519-24.

Bowlby, John. (1951) *Maternal care and mental health.* Geneva, Switzerland: World Health Organization.

Bradford, Jean L. (1968) Sex differences in anxiety. *Dissertation Abstracts,* 29, 1167.

Breuer, Josef and Freud, Sigmund (1957) *Studies on hysteria.* New York: Basic Books.

Brewer, John I. (1961) *Textbook of gynecology,* 3rd ed. Baltimore: Williams and Wilkins.

Brewer, Thomas H. (1966) *Metabolic toxemia of late pregnancy.* Springfield, Illinois: Charles C Thomas.

Briffault, Robert. (1927) *The mothers.* New York: Macmillan.

Brim, O. G., Jr. (1959) *Education for child-rearing.* New York: Russell Sage Foundation.

Brodbeck, Arthur J. (1954) Learning theory and identification: IV. Oedipal motivation as a determinant of conscious (sic) development. *Journal of Genetic Psychology,* 84, 219-27.

Broderick, C. B. and Fowler, S. E. (1961) New pattern of relationships between the sexes among preadolescents. *Marriage and Family Living,* 23, 27-30.

Brody, Harold. (1955) Psychologic factors associated with infertility in women; a comparative study of psychologic factors in women afflicted with infertility including groups with and without medical basis for their condition. *Dissertation Abstracts,* 15, 1253.

Brody, S. (1956) *Patterns of mothering: maternal influence during infancy.* New York: International Universities Press.

Bromley, Dorothy D. and Britten, Florence H. (1938) *Youth and sex. A study of 1300 college students.* New York: Harpers.

Bronfenbrenner, Urie. (1968) Early deprivation in mammals: A cross-species analysis. In Grant Newton and Seymour Levine (Eds.) *Early experience and behavior.* Springfield, Illinois: Charles C Thomas, pp. 627-764.

Bronfenbrenner, Urie. (1961) Parsons' theory of identification. In Max Black (Ed.) *The social theories of Talcott Parsons: A critical examination.* Englewood Cliffs, New Jersey: Prentice-Hall.

Bronfenbrenner, U. (1960a) Some familial antecedents of responsibility and leadership in adolescents. In L. Petrullo and B. M. Bass (Eds.) *Studies in leadership.* New York: Holt.

Bronfenbrenner, U. (1960b) Freudian theories of identification and their derivatives. *Child Development,* 31, 15-40.

Bronson, Gordon W. (1969) Fear of visual novelty: Developmental patterns in males and females. *Developmental Psychology,* 2, 33-40.

Broverman, D. (1969) Personal communication.

Broverman, D. M., Klaiber, E. L., Kobayashi, Y., and Vogel, W. (1968) Roles of activation and inhibition in sex differences in cognitive abilities, *Psychological Review,* 75, 23-50.

Broverman, Inge K., Broverman, D. M., Clarkson, F., Rosenkrantz, P. and Susan R. Vogel. (1970) Sex-role stereotypes and clinical judgments of mental health. *Journal of Consulting Psychology,* 34, 1-7.

Brown, D. G. (1962) Sex-role preference in children: Methodological problems. *Psychological Reports,* 11, 477-478.

Brown, D. G. (1957) Masculinity-femininity development in children. *Journal of Consulting Psychology,* 21, 197-202.

Brown, Daniel G. and Lynn, David B. (1966) Human sexual development: An outline of components and concepts. *Journal of Marriage and the Family,* 28, 155-165.

Brown, F., Lieberman, J., Winson, J., and Pleshette, Norman. (1960) Studies in choice of infant feeding by primiparas: Attitudinal factors and extraneous influences. *Psychosomatic Medicine,* 22, 421-429.

Brown, J. B. (1956) Urinary excretion of oestrogens during pregnancy, lactation, and re-establishment of menstruation. *Lancet,* 1, 704-707.

Brown, J. B. and Matthew, D. G. (1962) Application of urinary estrogen measurements to the problems of gynecology. *Recent Progress in Hormone Research,* 18, 337-385.

Brown, L. B. (1964) Anxiety in pregnancy. *British Journal of Medical Psychology,* 37, 47-57.

Brown, L. B. (1962) Social and attitudinal concomitants of illness in pregnancy. *British Journal of Medical Psychology,* 33, 311-322.

Brun-Gulbrandsen, Sverre. (1967) Sex roles and the socialization process. In Edmund Dahlström (Ed.) *The changing roles of men and women.* London: Gerald Duckworth.

Buckingham, B. R. and MacLatchy, J. (1930) The number abilities of children when they enter grade one. *Yearbook of the National Society for the Study of Education,* 29, 473-549.

Burgess, Ernest W. and Wallin, Paul. (1953) *Engagement and marriage.* New York: Lippincott.

Burian, Robert J. (1969) A study of the relationship between female body physique and a number of psycho-sexual-social correlates. *Dissertation Abstracts,* (10-A), 3666.

Bushnell, L. F. (1961) First trimester depression: A suggested treatment. *Obstetrics and Gynecology,* 18, 281.

Butler, R. A. (1953) Discrimination learning by rhesus monkeys to visual-exploration motivation. *Journal of Comparative Physiological Psychology,* 46, 95-98.

Byrne, D. (1965) Parental antecedents of authoritarianism. *Journal of Personality and Social Psychology,* 1, 369-373.

Caldwell, Bettye McDonald. (1945) An evaluation of psychological effects of sex hormone administration in aged women. II. Results after 18 months. *Journal of Gerontology,* 9, 168-174.

Caldwell, Bettye McDonald, and Watson, Robert I. (1952) An evaluation of psychologic effects of sex hormone administration in aged women. I. Results of therapy after six months. *Journal of Gerontology,* 7, 228-244.

Campbell, Elise H. (1939) The social-sex development of children. *Genetic Psychology Monographs,* 21, No. 4.

Caplan, G. (1960) Emotional implications of pregnancy and influences on family relationships. In Harold C. Stuart and Dane G. Prugh (Eds.) *The healthy child.* Cambridge: Harvard.

Carey, G. L. (1955) Reduction of sex difference in problem solving by improvement of attitude through group discussion. Unpublished doctoral dissertation, Stanford University.

Carlson, E. R. and Carlson, Rae. (1960) Male and female subjects in personality research. *Journal of Abnormal and Social Psychology,* 61, 482-483.

Casey, M. D., Street, D. R., Segall, L. J., and Blank, C. E. (1968) Patients with sex chromatin abnormality in two state hospitals. *Annals of Human Genetics,* 32, 53-63.

Chadwick, Mary. (1932) The psychological effects of menstruation. *Nervous and Mental Disease Monograph Series,* No. 56. New York: Nervous and Mental Disease Publishing Company.

Chamove, A. C., Harlow, H. F. and Mitchell, G. D. (1967) Sex differences in the infant-directed behavior of preadolescent rhesus monkeys. *Child Development,* 38, 329-335.

Chassequet-Smirgel, J., Luquet-Parat, C. J., Grunberger, B., McDougall, J., Torok, M. and David, C. (1970) *Female sexuality.* Ann Arbor: University of Michigan Press.

Chertok, L., Mondzain, M. L., and Bonnaud, M. (1963) Vomiting and the wish to have a child. *Psychosomatic Medicine,* 25, 13-18.

Chesser, Eustace. (1956) *The sexual, marital and family relationships of the English Woman,* Watford, England: Hutchinson's Medical Publications.

Childs, B. (1965) Genetic origins of some sex differences among human beings. *Pediatrics,* 35, 798-812.

Chodoff, P. (1966) A critique of Freud's theory of infantile sexuality. *American Journal of Psychiatry,* 123, 507-518.

Chomsky, N. (1968) Language and the mind. *Psychology Today,* 1 (9), 48-51, 66-68.

Clare, Jeanne E., and Kiser, Clyde V. (1951) Social and psychological factors affecting fertility XIV. Preference for children of given sex in relation to fertility. *Milbank Memorial Foundation Quarterly,* 29, 440-92.

Clemetson, C. Alan B., Blair, Lilian, and Brown, Albert B. (1962) Capillary strength and the menstrual cycle. *Annals of the New York Academy of Sciences,* 93, 277-300.

Cobliner, W. G. (1965) Some maternal attitudes towards conception. *Mental Hygiene,* 49, 550-557.

Cohen, M. B. (1966) Personal identity and sexual identity. *Psychiatry,* 29, 1-14.

Coleman, James. (1966) Female status and premarital sexual codes. *American Journal of Sociology,* 72, 217.

Coleman, James S. (1963) *The adolescent society.* New York: Free Press of Glencoe.

Conn, J. H. (1940) Children's reactions to the discovery of genital differences. *American Journal Orthopsychiatry,* 10, 747-54.

Connolly, C. J. (1950) *External morphology of the primate brain.* Springfield, Illinois: Charles C Thomas.

Cooper, Alan F. (1969) Some personality factors in frigidity. *Journal of Psychosomatic Research,* 13, 149-156.

Coppen, A. J. (1959) Vomiting of early pregnancy—psychological factors and body build. *Lancet,* 1, 172-173.

Coppen, Alec J. (1958) Psychosomatic aspects of pre-eclamptic toxaemia. *Journal of Psychosomatic Research,* 2, 241-265.

Coppen, A., and Kessel, N. (1963) Menstrual disorders and personality. *Acta Psychotherapeutica et Psychosomatica,* 11, 174-180.

Cosentino, F., and Heilbrun, A. B. (1964) Anxiety correlates of sex-role identity in college students. *Psychological Reports,* 14, 729-730.

Cowie, A. T., and Foley, S. J. (1961) The mammary gland and lactation. In William C. Young (Ed.) *Sex and internal secretions.* Baltimore: William and Wilkins, 3rd. ed.

Cramond, William A. (1954) Psychological aspects of uterine dysfunction. *Lancet,* 267, 1241-1245.

Crandall, Virginia C. (1967) Achievement behavior in young children. In Willard W. Hartup, and Smothergill, Nancy L. (Eds.) *The young child:*

Reviews of research. Washington, D. C.: National Association for the Education of Young Children, pp. 165-185.

Crandall, V. J., Orleans, S., Preston, A., and Rabson, A. (1958) The development of social compliance in young children. *Child Development,* 29, 429-44.

Crawford, Mary I. (1969) Physiological and behavioral cues to disturbances in childbirth. *Dissertation Abstracts,* 29, 2504-2505.

Crissman, P. (1942) Temporal change and sexual difference in moral judgments. *Journal of Social Psychology,* 16, 29-38.

Curlee, Joan. (1969) Alcoholism and the "empty nest." *Bulletin of the Menninger Clinic,* 33, 165-171.

Dahlström, Edmund and Liljeström, Rita. (1967) The family and married women at work. In Edmund Dahlström (Ed.) *The changing roles of men and women.* London: Gerald Duckworth, pp. 19-58.

Dalton, K. (1968) Ante-natal progesterone and intelligence. *British Journal of Psychiatry,* 114, 1377-1382.

Dalton, K. (1966) The influence of mother's menstruation on her child. *Proceedings of the Royal Society of Medicine,* 59, 1014.

Dalton, Katharina. (1964) *The premenstrual syndrome.* London: Heineman.

Dalton, K. (1960) Effect of menstruation on schoolgirls' weekly work. *British Medical Journal,* 1, 326.

D'Andrade, Roy G. (1966) Sex differences and cultural institutions. In Eleanor E. Maccoby. *The development of sex differences.* Stanford, California: Stanford University Press.

Daniels, Robert S. and Lessow, Herbert (1964) Severe postpartum reactions. An interpersonal view. *Psychosomatics,* 5, 21-26.

Darley, J. G. (1937) Tested maladjustment related to clinically diagnosed maladjustment. *Journal of Applied Psychology,* 21, 632-42.

Davids, Anthony, and De Vault, Spencer. (1960) Use of TAT and human figure drawings in research on personality, pregnancy, and perception. *Journal of Projective Techniques,* 24, 362-365.

Davids, A., De Vault, S., and Talmadge M. (1961) Psychological study of emotional factors in pregnancy. *Psychosomatic Medicine,* 23, 93-103.

Davidson, Helen H., and Gottleib, Lucille S. (1955) The emotional maturity of pre and post menarcheal girls. *Journal of Genetic Psychology,* 86, 261-266.

Davidson, J. A. (1962) An assessment of the value of hypnosis in pregnancy and labour. *British Medical Journal,* 2, 951-953.

Davis, Katharine B. (1929) *Factors in the sex life of twenty-two hundred women.* New York: Harper.

Davis, James A. (1965) *Education for positive mental health.* Chicago: Aldine.

DeLucia, Lenore A. (1963) The toy-preference test; a measure of sex-role identification. *Child Development,* 34, 107-117.

Despres, M. A. (1937) Favorable and unfavorable attitudes toward pregnancy in primiparae. *Journal of Genetic Psychology,* 51, 241-259.

Deutsch, Helene. (1945) *Psychology of women.* New York: Grune & Stratton, vol. 2.

Deutsch, Helene. (1944) *Psychology of women.* New York: Grune & Stratton, vol. 1.

Deutscher, Irwin. (1968) Postparental life. In Bernice L. Neugarten (Ed.) *Middle age and aging.* Chicago: University Chicago Press, 263-268.

Devereux, George. (1960) The female castration complex and its repercussions in modesty, appearance and courtship etiquette. *American Imago,* 17, 3-19.

Devereux, George. (1955) *A study of abortion in primitive societies.* New York: Julian.

DeVore, Irven. (1963) Mother-infant relations in free-ranging baboons. In Harriet L. Rheingold (Ed.) *Maternal behavior in mammals.* New York: John Wiley, pp. 305-335.

Diamond, Milton. (1968) Genetic-endocrine interactions and human psychosexuality. In Milton Diamond (Ed.) *Perspectives in reproduction and sexual behavior.* Bloomington: Indiana University Press, pp. 417-443.

Diamond, Milton. (1965) A critical evaluation of the ontogeny of human sexual behavior. *Quarterly Review of Biology,* 40, 147-175.

Dickinson, Robert and Beam, L. (1931) *A thousand marriages.* Baltimore: Williams & Wilkins.

Dinitz, S., Dynes, R. and Clarke, A. C. (1954) Preference for male or female children: traditional or affectional. *Marriage and Family Living,* 16, 128-30.

Dodge, Norton D. (1966) *Women in the Soviet economy.* Baltimore: Johns Hopkins.

Doherty, Anne. (1970) Influence of parental control on the development of feminine sex role and conscience. *Developmental Psychology,* 2, 157-158.

Dorfman, R., and Ungar, F. (1965) *Metabolism of steroid hormones.* New York: Academic Press.

Douvan, Elizabeth. (1960) Sex differences in adolescent character processes. *Merrill-Palmer Quarterly,* 6, 203-211.

Douvan, Elizabeth. (1957) Independence and identity in adolescence. *Children,* 4, 186-190.

Douvan, Elizabeth, and Adelson, Joseph. (1966) *The adolescent experience.* New York: Wiley.

Drellich, Marvin G., and Bieber, Irving. (1958). The psychologic importance of the uterus and its functions. *Journal of Nervous and Mental Diseases,* 126, 322-336.

Droege, R. C. (1967) Sex differences in aptitude maturation during high school. *Journal of Counseling Psychology,* 14, 407-411.

Droppelman, L. F., and Schaefer, E. S. (1963) Boys' and girls' reports of maternal and paternal behavior. *Journal of Abnormal and Social Psychology,* 67, 648-54.

Edel, Roberta R. (1968) What little Hans learned: Review of a learning theory approach. *Contemporary Psychoanalysis,* 4, 189-204.

Ehrhardt, A. A., Epstein, R. and Money, J. (1968) Fetal androgens and female gender identity in the early-treated adrenogenital syndrome. *Johns Hopkins Medical Journal,* 122, 160-167.

Ehrhardt, A. A., and Money, J. (1967) Progestin-induced hermaphroditism: IQ and psychosexual identity in a study of 10 girls. *Journal of Sex Research,* 3, 83-100.

Ehrmann, Winston. (1959) *Premarital dating behavior.* New York: Henry Holt.

Eichorn, Dorothy H. (1963) Biological correlates of behavior. In Harold W. Stevenson, Jerome Kagan and Charles Spiker (Eds.) *Child Psychology. Chicago:* University of Chicago Press, pp. 4-61.

Eisenman, Russell. (1967) Sex differences in moral judgment. *Perceptual and Motor Skills,* 24, 784.

Eisner, Betty G. (1963) Some psychological differences between fertile and infertile women. *Journal of Clinical Psychology,* 19, 391-395.

Elkan, E. (1948) Evolution of female orgastic ability—a biological survey. *International Journal of Sexology,* 2, 84-93.

Elliott, R., and McMichael, R. E. (1963) Effects of specific training on frame dependence. *Perceptual and Motor Skills,* 17, 363-367.

Ellis, Havelock. (1908) *Man and Woman.* New York: Scribner, 4th ed.

Ellis, N. W. and Last, S. L. (1953) Analysis of the normal electroencephalogram. *Lancet,* 1, 112-14.

Emmerich, W. (1959) Parental identification in young children. *Genetic Psychology Monographs,* 60, 257-308.

Engström, L., Geijerstam, G. Af, Holmberg, N. G., and Uhrus, K. (1964) A prospective study of the relationship between psycho-social factors and course of pregnancy and delivery. *Journal of Psychosomatic Research,* 8, 151-155.

Epstein, Cynthia. (1970) *Woman's place.* Berkeley: University of California.

Erickson, Marilyn T. (1967) Method for frequent assessment of symptomology during pregnancy. *Psychological Reports,* 20, 447-454.

Erickson, Marilyn T. (1965) Relationship between psychological attitudes during pregnancy and complications of pregnancy, labor, and delivery. *Proceedings of the 73rd Annual Convention of the American Psychological Association,* 213-214.

Erikson, Erik H. (1968) *Identity, youth and crisis.* New York: Norton.

Erikson, Erik H. (1963) *Childhood and society.* New York: Norton.

Erikson, Erik H. (1959) Identity and the life cycle. *Psychological Issues,* 1, No. 1.

Erikson, Erik H. (1951) Sex differences in the play configurations of pre-adolescents. *American Journal of Orthopsychiatry,* 21, 667-92.

Eron, L. D. (1953) Responses of women to the Thematic Apperception Test. *Journal of Consulting Psychology,* 17, 269-282.

Evans, Richard I. (1967) *Dialogue with Erik Erikson.* New York: Harper & Row.

Eysenck, S. B. G. (1961) Personality and pain assessment in childbirth of married and unmarried mothers. *Journal of Mental Science,* 107, 417-430.

Eysenck, S. B., and Eysenck, H. J. (1969) Scores of three personality variables as a function of age, sex, and social class. *British Journal of Social and Clinical Psychology,* 8, 69-76.

Fagot, Beverly, and Patterson, Gerald R. (1969) An *in vivo* analysis of reinforcing contingencies for sex-role behaviors in the preschool child. *Development Psychology,* 1, 563-568.

Farr, Roberta S. (1969) Personality variables and problem solving performance: An investigation of the relationships between field-dependence-independence, sex-role identification, problem difficulty and problem solving performance. *Dissertation Abstracts,* 29A, 2561-2562.

Farrell, Muriel. (1957) Sex differences in block play in early childhood education. *Journal of Educational Research,* 51, 279-284.

Faust, M. S. (1960) Developmental maturity as a determinant in prestige of adolescent girls. *Child Development,* 31, 173-186.

Feigl, Herbert. (1958) The "mental" and the "physical." In Herbert Feigl, Michael Scriven and Grover Maxwell (Eds.) *Minnesota Studies in the Philosophy of Science.* Minneapolis: University of Minnesota Press.

Fernberger, S. W. (1948) Persistence of stereotypes concerning sex differences. *Journal of Abnormal and Social Psychology,* 43, 97-101.

Feshbach, Norma D. (1969) Sex differences in children's modes of aggressive responses toward outsiders. *Merrill-Palmer Quarterly,* 15, 249-258.

Fischer, Donald G., Kelm, Harold, and Rose, Ann. (1969) Knives as aggression-eliciting stimuli. *Psychological Reports,* 24, 755-760.

Fisher, Emanuel E. (1957) *A critical evaluation of the Freudian theories of feminine psychology.* (Doctoral dissertation, New York University) Ann Arbor, Michigan: University Microfilms, No. 22, 738.

Fisher, Sarah C. (1948) Relationships in attitudes, opinions, and values among family. *University of California Publications in Culture and Society,* 2, 28-99.

Fisher, Seymour, and Osofsky, Howard. (1967) Sexual responsiveness in women: psychological correlates. *Archives of General Psychiatry,* 17, 214-226.

Fitzgerald, D., and Roberts, K. (1966) Semantic profiles and psychosexual interests as indicators of identification. *Personnel and Guidance Journal,* 44, 802-806.

Flavell, John H. (1963) *The developmental psychology of Jean Piaget.* New York: D. Van Nostrand.

Fodor, Nandor. (1949) The trauma of bearing. *Psychiatric Quarterly,* 23, 59-70.

Ford, C. S. (1945) *A comparative study of human reproduction.* New Haven: Yale University Press.

Ford, Clellan S. and Beach, Frank A. (1951) *Patterns of sexual behavior.* New York: Hoeber.

Forrest, Tess. (1966) Paternal roots of female character development. *Contemporary Psychoanalysis,* 3, 21-38.

Foundeur, M., Fixsen, C., Triebel, W. A., and White, M. A. (1957) Postpartum mental illness: controlled study. *American Medical Association Archives of Neurology and Psychiatry,* 77, 503-512.

Franck, Kate, and Rosen, L. (1949) A projective test of masculinity and femininity. *Journal of Consulting Psychology,* 13, 247-56.

Frandsen, Arden N., and Holder, James R. (1969) Spatial visualization in solving complex verbal problems. *Journal of Psychology,* 73, 229-233.

Frank, Lawrence I. (1956) The interpersonal and social aspects. In Irma H. Gross (Ed.) *Potentialities of women in the middle years.* East Lansing, Michigan: Michigan State University Press, 105-127.

Frank, Lawrence K., Harrison, Ross, Hellersberg, Elisabeth, Machover, Karen and Steiner, Meta. (1951) Personality development in adolescent girls. *Monograph of the Society for Research in Child Development,* 16.

Freedman, D. S., Freedman, R., and Whelpton, P. K. (1960) Size of family and preference for children of each sex. *American Journal of Sociology,* 66, 141-146.

Freedman, L. Z. and Ferguson, Vera M. (1950) The question of "painless childbirth" in primitive cultures. *American Journal of Orthopsychiatry,* 20, 363-372.

Freedman, Mervin B. (1967) *The college experience.* San Francisco: Jossey-Bass.

Freedman, Mervin B. (1965) The sexual behavior of American college women: An empirical study and an historical survey. *Merrill-Palmer Quarterly,* 11, 33-48.

Freud, Sigmund. (1965) *New introductory lectures on psychoanalysis.* New York: Norton. (Originally published 1933) .

Freud, Sigmund. (1962) *Civilization and its discontents.* New York: Norton. (Originally published 1930) .

Freud, Sigmund (1960) *The ego and the id.* New York: Norton. (Originally published 1923) .

Freud, Sigmund. (1956) The passing of the Oedipus-complex. In Ernest

Jones (Ed.) *Collected papers,* Vol. II. London: Hogarth Press. (Originally published 1924).

Freud, Sigmund. (1953a) Analysis of a phobia in a five-year old boy. In James Strachey (Ed.) *Standard edition of the complete psychological works of Sigmund Freud,* Vol. 10. London: Hogarth. (Originally published 1909).

Freud, Sigmund. (1953b) The aetiology of hysteria. In James Strachey (Ed.) *Standard edition of the complete psychological works of Sigmund Freud,* Vol. 3. London: Hogarth. (Originally published 1896).

Freud, Sigmund. (1953c) My views on the part played by sexuality in the aetiology of the neuroses. In James Strachey (Ed.) *Standard edition of the complete psychological works of Sigmund Freud,* Vol. 7. London: Hogarth. (Originally published 1906).

Freud, Sigmund. (1951) *Group psychology and the analysis of the ego.* New York: Liveright Publishing Co.

Freud, Sigmund. (1950a) *Female sexuality.* Collected Papers, Vol. V. London: Hogarth. (Originally published 1931).

Freud, Sigmund. (1905b) Some psychological consequences of the anatomical distinction between the sexes. *Collected papers,* Vol. V. London: Hogarth. (Originally published 1925).

Freud, Sigmund. (1938a) Three contributions to the theory of sex. In A. A. Brill (Ed.) *Basic writings of Sigmund Freud.* New York: Modern Library. (Originally published 1905).

Freud, Sigmund. (1938b) The interpretation of dreams. In A. A. Brill (Ed.) *Basic writings of Sigmund Freud.* New York: Modern Library. (Originally published 1900).

Friedan, Betty. (1963) *The feminine mystique.* New York: Dell.

Friedman, David B. (1966) Toward a unitary theory of the passing of the oedipal conflict. *Psychoanalytic Review,* 53, 38-48.

Friedman, Stanley M. (1952) An empirical study of the castration and oedipus complexes. *Genetic Psychology Monographs,* 46, pt. 1, 61-130.

Fromm, Erich, *et al.* (1968) The Oedipus complex: Comments on "The case of little Hans." *Contemporary Psychoanalysis,* 4, 178-188.

Fromm, Erich, Fernando Narváez M., y colaboradores. (1966) El complejo de Edipo. Comentarios al "análisis de la fobia de un nino de cinco años." [The Oedipus complex: Commentaries on the "Analysis of a five year old child's phobia."] *Revista de Psicoanalisis, Psiquiatria, y Psicologia,* 4, 26-33.

Fruchter, B. (1954) Measurement of spatial abilities: History and background. *Educational and Psychological Measurement,* 14, 387-395.

Gagnon, John H. (1967) Sexuality and sexual learning in the child. In John H. Gagnon and William Simon (Eds.) *Sexual deviance.* New York: Harper & Row, pp. 15-42.

Gagnon, J. H. (1965) Sexuality and sexual learning in the child. *Psychiatry,* 28, 212-228.

Ganley, Barbara D. (1968) Sex roles and differences in moral behavior. *Dissertation Abstracts,* 29, 755.

Garai, Josef E. (1970) Sex differences in mental health. *Genetic Psychology Monographs,* 81, 123-142.

Garai, Josef E. and Scheinfeld, Amram. (1968) Sex differences in mental and behavioral traits. *Genetic Psychology Monographs,* 77, 169-299.

Gardner, R. W., Jackson, D. N. and Messick, S. J. (1960) Personality organization in cognitive controls and intellectual abilities. *Psychological Issues,* 2 (Whole No. 8).

Garn, S. M. (1957) Roentgengrammetric determinations of body composition. *Human Biology,* 29, 337-353.

Garn, S. M. (1958) Fat, body size, and growth in the newborn. *Human Biology,* 30, 265-280.

Garron, David C. (1970) Sex-linked, recessive inheritance of spatial and numerical abilities, and Turner's syndrome. *Psychological Review,* 77, 147-152.

Garron, David C., and Vander Stoep, Laima R. (1969) Personality and intelligence in Turner's syndrome: A critical review. *Archives of General Psychiatry,* 21, 339-346.

Gebhard, Paul H. (1966) Factors in marital orgasm. *The Journal of Social Issues,* 22, 88-95.

Gebhard, Paul H. (1965) Situational factors affecting human sexual behavior. In Frank A. Beach (Ed.) *Sex and behavior.* New York: Wiley.

Gebhard, Paul H., Pomeroy, Wardell B., Martin, Clyde E., and Christenson, Cornelia V. (1958) *Pregnancy, birth and abortion.* New York: Wiley.

Gelford, Abraham. (1952) The relationship of the onset of pubescence to certain interpersonal attitudes in girls. *Dissertation Abstracts,* 12, 721.

Getzels, J. W., and Walsh, J. J. (1958) The method of paired direct and projective questionnaires in the study of attitude structure and socialization. *Psychological Monographs,* 72, No. 1.

Gewirtz, Jacob J., and Stingle, Karen G. (1968) Learning of generalized imitation as the basis for identification. *Psychological Review,* 75, 374-397.

Gewirtz, Jacob L. (1969) Mechanisms of social learning: Some role of stimulation and behavior in early human development. In David A. Goslin (Ed.) *Handbook of socialization theory and research.* Chicago: Rand McNally, pp. 57-212.

Gibbs, F. A. and Reid, D. E. (1942) The electroencephalogram in pregnancy. *American Journal of Obstetrics and Gynecology,* 44, 672-675.

Gill, Lois J. and Spilka, B. (1962) Some nonintellectual correlates of academic achievement among Mexican-American secondary school students. *Journal of Educational Psychology,* 53, 144-49.

Gillman, Robert D. (1968) The dreams of pregnant women and maternal adaptation. *American Journal of Orthopsychiatry,* 38, 688-692.

Glick, Ira A., Salerno, Louis J. and Royce, Jack R. (1965) Psychophysiologic factors in the etiology of preeclampsia. *Archives of General Psychiatry,* 12, 260-266.

Glover, Edward. (1956) *On the early development of the mind.* London: Imago.

Glueck, Bernard C., Jr. (1963) Early sexual experiences in schizophrenia. In Hugo Beigel (ed.) *Advances in sex research.* New York: Hoeber, pp. 248-255.

Goldberg, Susan, and Lewis, Michael. (1969) Play behavior in the year-old infant: Early sex differences. *Child Development,* 40, 21-31.

Goldstein, Alvin, and Chance, June. (1965) Effects of practice on sex-related differences in performance on Embedded Figures. *Psychonomic Science,* 3, 361-362.

Goodenough, Evelyn. (1957) Interest in persons as an aspect of sex differences in the early years. *Genetic Psychology Monographs,* 55, 287-323.

Goodenough, Florence L. (1931) *Anger in young children.* Institute of Child Welfare Monograph Series, No. 9. Minneapolis, Minnesota: University of Minnesota Press.

Gordon, E. M. (1967) Acceptance of pregnancy before and since oral contraception. *Obstetrics and Gynecology,* 29, 144-6.

Gordon, R. E. (1957) Emotional disorders of pregnancy and child bearing. *Journal of the Medical Society of New Jersey,* 54, 16-23.

Gordon, Richard E., and Gordon, Katherine K. (1967) Factors in postpartum emotional adjustment. *American Journal of Orthopsychiatry,* 37, 359-360.

Gordon, Richard E., and Gordon, Katherine K. (1960) *The Split-level trap.* United States: Bernard Geis.

Gordon, Richard E., and Gordon, Katherine K. (1959) Social factors in the prediction and treatment of emotional disorders of pregnancy. *American Journal of Obstetrics and Gynecology,* 77, 1074-1083.

Gordon, R. E., and Gordon, Katherine K. (1957) Some social psychiatric aspects of pregnancy and childbearing. *Journal of the Medical Society of New Jersey,* 54, 569-572.

Gordon, R. E., Kapostins, E. E. and Gordon, Katherine K. (1965) Factors in postpartum emotional adjustment. *Obstetrics and Gynecology,* 25, 158-166.

Goy, Robert W. (1968) Organizing effect of androgen on the behaviour of rhesus monkeys. In Richard P. Michael (Ed.) *Endocrinology and human behaviour.* London: Oxford University Press, 12-31.

Graham, David T., and Stevenson, Ian. (1963) Disease as response to life stress: I. The nature of the evidence. In Harold I. Lief, Victor F. Lief, and Nina R. Lief. (Eds.) *The psychological basis of medical practice.* New York: Hoeber.

Gray, S. W. (1959) Perceived similarity to parents and adjustment. *Child Development,* 30, 91-107.

Gray, Susan W., and Klaus, Rupert. (1956) The assessment of parental identification. *Genetic Psychology Monographs,* 54, 87-114.

Greenhill, M. H. (1946) A psychosomatic evaluation of the psychiatric and endocrinological factors in the menopause. *Southern Medical Journal,* 39, 786-794.

Greenson, R. R. (1967) Masculinity and femininity in our time. In Charles Wahl (Ed.) *Sexual problems.* Glencoe, Illinois: Free Press, pp. 39-52.

Grim, Paul F., Kohlberg, Lawrence, and White, Sheldon H. (1968) Some relationships between conscience and attentional processes. *Journal of Personality and Social Psychology,* 8, 239-252.

Grimm, Elaine R. (1969) Women's attitudes and reactions to childbirth. In G. D. Goldman and D. S. Milman (eds.) *Modern woman.* Springfield, Illinois: Charles C Thomas, 129-151.

Grimm, Elaine R. (1967) Psychological and social factors in pregnancy, delivery and outcome. In Stephen Richardson and Alan F. Guttmacher (Eds.) *Childbearing—its social and psychological aspects.* Baltimore: Williams & Wilkins, 1-52.

Grimm, Elaine R. (1962) Psychological investigation of habitual abortion. *Psychosomatic medicine,* 24, 369-378.

Grimm, Elaine R. (1961) Psychological tension in pregnancy. *Psychosomatic Medicine,* 23, 520-527.

Grimm, Elaine R., and Venet, Wanda R. (1966) The relationship or emotional adjustment and attitudes to the course and outcome of pregnancy. *Psychosomatic Medicine,* 28, 34-49.

Grinder, R. E. (1964) Relations between behavioral and cognitive dimensions of conscience in middle childhood. *Child Development,* 35, 881-91.

Grollman, Arthur. (1964) *Clinical endocrinology.* Philadelphia: Lippincott.

Group for the Advancement of Psychiatry. (1968) *Normal adolescence.* New York: Charles Scribner's Sons.

Gurin, G., Veroff, J., and Feld, Sheila. (1960) *Americans view their mental health.* New York: Basic Books.

Guze, S. B., De Long, W. B., Majerius, P. W. and Robins, E. (1959) Association of clinical psychiatric disease with hyperemesis gravidarum. *New England Journal of Medicine,* 261, 1363-1368.

Gyermik, Lasjlo, Genther, Gene, and Fleming, Noel. (1967) Some effects of progesterone and related steroids on the central nervous system. *International Journal of Neuropharmacology,* 6, 191-198.

Haan, Norma, Smith, M. Brewster and Block, Jeanne. (1968) Moral reasoning of young adults: Political-social behavior, family background, and personality correlates. *Journal of Personality and Social Psychology,* 10, 183-201.

Hall, Calvin S. (1967) Are prenatal and birth experiences represented in dreams? *Psychoanalytic Review,* 54, 157-174.

Hall, Calvin S. (1964) A modest confirmation of Freud's theory of a distinction between the superego of men and women. *Journal of Abnormal and Social Psychology,* 69, 440-42.

Hall, Calvin S. (1954) *A primer of Freudian psychology.* New York: Mentor. (Also in hardcover by World Publishing Co.)

Hall, Calvin S. and Domhoff, Bill. (1963a) Aggression in dreams. *International Journal of Social Psychiatry,* 9, 259-267.

Hall, Calvin S. and Domhoff, Bill. (1963b) A ubiquitous sex difference in dreams. *Journal of Abnormal and Social Psychology,* 66, 278-80.

Hall, Calvin S. and Lindzey, Gardner. (1957) *Theories of personality.* New York: Wiley.

Hall, Calvin S. and Van de Castle, Robert L. (1966) *The content analysis of dreams.* New York: Appleton-Century-Crofts.

Hall, Calvin S. and Van de Castle, R. L. (1965) An empirical investigation of the castration complex in dreams. *Journal of Personality,* 33, 20-29.

Hall, M., and Keith, R. A. (1964) Sex-role preference among children of upper and lower social class. *Journal of Social Psychology,* 62, 101-110.

Hall, D. E., and Mohr, G. J. (1933) Prenatal attitudes of primiparae. *Mental Hygiene,* 17, 226-234.

Halleck, Seymour L. (1967) Sex and mental health on the campus. *Journal of the American Medical Association,* 200, 684-690.

Hamburg, David A. (1966) Effects of progesterone on behavior. In R. Levine (Ed.) *Endocrines and the central nervous system.* (*Proceedings of the Association for Research in Nervous and Mental Diseases,* 43) Baltimore: Williams & Wilkins.

Hamburg, David A., and Lunde, Donald T. (1966) Sex hormones in the development of sex differences. In Eleanor E. Maccoby (Ed.) *The development of sex differences.* Stanford, California: Stanford University Press.

Hamburg, David A., Moos, Rudolf H., and Yalom, Irvin D. (1968) Studies of distress in the menstrual cycle and postpartum period. In Richard P. Michael. (Ed.) *Endocrinology and human behaviour.* London: Oxford University Press, pp. 94-138.

Hamilton, Eleanor. (1955) Emotional aspects of pregnancy: an intensive study of fourteen normal primiparae. Unpublished doctoral dissertation. New York: Columbia University.

Hamilton, Gilbert V. (1929) *A research in marriage.* New York: Albert and Charles Boni.

Hamilton, James A. (1962) *Postpartum problems.* Saint Louis: C. V. Mosby.

Hammer, Max. (1970) Preference for a male child: Cultural factor. *Journal of Individual Psychology,* 26, 54-56.

Hampson, J. L., and Hampson, Joan G. (1961) The ontogenesis of sexual behavior in man. In W. C. Young (Ed.) *Sex and internal secretions.* (3rd ed.), Baltimore: William & Wilkins.

Hanford, Jean M. (1968) Pregnancy as a state of conflict. *Psychological Reports,* 22, 1313-1342.

Hansen, E. W. (1966) The development of maternal and infant behavior in the rhesus monkey. *Behaviour,* 27, 107-149.

Harlow, H. F. (1958) The nature of love. *American Psychologist,* 13, 673-685.

Harlow, H. F., Harlow, Margaret K. and Hansen, E. W. (1963) The maternal affectional system of rhesus monkeys. In Harriet L. Rheingold (Ed.) *Maternal behavior in mammals.* New York: Wiley, pp. 254-281.

Harlow, Harry F., and Suomi, Stephen J. (1970) Nature of love—Simplified. *American Psychologist,* 25, 161-168.

Harlow, Harry F., and Zimmerman, R. R. (1959) Affectional responses in the infant monkey. *Science,* 130, 421-432.

Harris, D. B. (1959) Sex differences in the life problems and interests of adolescents, 1935 to 1957. *Child Development,* 30, 453-459.

Harris, D. B., and Teng, S. C. (1957) Children's attitudes toward peers and parents as revealed by sentence completion. *Child Development,* 28, 401-411.

Hart, H. H. (1961) A review of the psychoanalytic literature on passivity. *Psychiatric Quarterly,* 35, 331-352.

Hart, K. D. (1960) Monthly rhythm of libido in married women. *British Medical Journal,* 1, 1023-1024.

Hartley, Ruth E., Hardesty, F., and Gorfein, D. S. (1962) Children's perceptions and impression of sex preferences. *Child Development,* 33, 221-27.

Hartup, Willard W. (1963) Dependence and independence. In Harold W. Stevenson (Ed.) *Child psychology.* Chicago: University of Chicago Press.

Hartshorne, H., and May, M. A. (1928) *Studies in deceit.* New York: Macmillan.

Hartup, W. W., and Zook, Elsie A. (1960) Sex-role preferences in three and four year old children. *Journal of Consulting Psychology,* 24, 420-26.

Harvey, W. A., and Sherfey, M. J. (1954) Vomiting in pregnancy: a psychiatric study. *Psychosomatic Medicine,* 16, 1-9.

Hattendorf, K. W. (1932) A study of the questions of young children concerning sex: a phase of an experimental approach to parent education. *Journal of Social Psychology,* 3, 37-65.

Hechter, O. and Halkerston, I. D. K. (1965) Effects of steroid hormones on gene regulation and cell metabolism. *Annual Review of Physiology,* 27, 133.

Heilbrun, Alfred B., Jr. (1968) Sex-role identity in adolescent females a theoretical paradox. *Adolescence,* 3, 79-88.

Heilbrun, Alfred B., Jr. (1965a) Sex differences in identification learning. *Journal of Genetic Psychology,* 106, 185-193.

Heilbrun, Alfred B., Jr. (1965b) An empirical test of the modeling theory of sex-role learning. *Child Development,* 35, 789-799.

Heilbrun, Alfred B., Jr. (1962) Parental identification and college adjustment. *Psychological Reports,* 10, 853-854.

Heilbrun, A. B., Jr. (1960) Personality differences between adjusted and maladjusted college students. *Journal of Applied Psychology,* 44, 341-346.

Heilbrun, Alfred B., Jr., and Fromme, Donald K. (1965) Parental identification of late adolescents and level of adjustment: The importance of parent-model attributes, ordinal position, and sex of the child. *Journal of Genetic Psychology,* 107, 49-59.

Heinstein, M. I. (1963) Behavioral correlates of breast-bottle regime under varying parent-infant relationships. *Monographs of the Society for Research in Child Development,* 28.

Helper, M. M. (1955) Learning theory and self-concept. *Journal of Abnormal and Social Psychology,* 51, 184-194.

Hemphill, R. E. (1952) Incidence and nature of puerperal psychiatric illness. *British Medical Journal,* 2, 1232-1235.

Henry, C. E. (1944) Electroencephalograms of normal children. *Monograph of the Society for Research in Child Development,* 9, No. 3.

Henton, C. L. (1961) The effect of socioeconomic and emotional factors on the onset of menarche among Negro and white girls. *Journal of Genetic Psychology,* 98, 255-264.

Hertzler, A. E. (1950) Problems of the normal adolescent girl. *California Journal of Secondary Education,* 15, 114-119.

Herzberg, Frederich I. (1952) A study of the psychological factors in primary dysmenorrhea. *Journal of Clinical Psychology,* 8, 174-178.

Hetherington, E. Mavis. (1965) A developmental study of the effects of sex of the dominant parent on sex-role preference, identification, and imitation in children. *Journal of Personality and Social Psychology,* 2, 188-194.

Hetzel, B. S., Bruer, B., and Poidevin, L. O. S. (1961) A survey of relations between common antenatal complications in primiparae and stressful life situations during pregnancy. *Journal of Psychosomatic Research,* 5, 175-182.

Hill, K. T., and Sarason, S. B. (1966) The relation of test anxiety and defensiveness to test and school performance over the elementary-school years: A further longitudinal study. *Monographs of the Society for Research in Child Development,* 31.

Hirsch, Arthur H. (1967) *The love elite; the story of women's emancipation and her drive for sexual fulfillment.* New York: Julian Press.

Hoffman, M. L. (1963) Child-rearing practices and moral development: generalizations from empirical research. *Child Development,* 34, 295-318.

Hollender, Marc H., Luborsky, Lester, and Scaramella, Thomas J. (1969)

Body contact and sexual excitement *Archives of General Psychiatry,* 20, 188-191.

Hooke, J. F., and Marks, P. A. (1962) MMPI characteristics of pregnancy. *Journal of Clinical Psychology,* 18, 316-317.

Hooker, Evelyn. (1965) Gender identity in male homosexuals. In J. Money (Ed.) *Sex research.* New York: Holt, Rinehart & Winston.

Horney, Karen. (1967) *Feminine psychology.* H. Kelman (Ed.) New York: Norton.

Horney, Karen. (1939) *New ways in psychoanalysis.* New York: Norton.

Horney, Karen. (1933) The denial of the vagina. *International Journal of Psychoanalysis,* 14, 57-70.

Horney, Karen. (1932) The dread of woman. *International Journal of Psychoanalysis,* 13, 348-360.

Horney, Karen. (1926) The flight from womanhood. *International Journal of Psychoanalysis,* 7, 324-339.

Horney, Karen. (1924) On the genesis of the castration complex in women. *International Journal of Psychoanalysis,* 5, 50-65.

Horsley, J. S. (1966) The psychology of normal pregnancy. *Nursing Times,* 62, 400-402.

Hull, Clark L. (1943) *Principles of behavior.* New York: Appleton-Century-Crofts.

Hurlock, Elizabeth B. (1967) *Adolescent development.* (3rd ed.) New York: McGraw-Hill.

Hurst, John C., and Strousse, Flora (1938) The origin of emotional factors in normal pregnant women. *American Journal of Medical Science,* 196, 95-99.

Hyman, Herbert, and Sheatsley, Paul B. (1954) The scientific method. In Donald Porter Geddes (Ed.) *An analysis of the Kinsey reports on sexual behavior in the human male and female.* New York: Dutton.

Hytten, F. E. (1959) Is breast feeding best? *American Journal of Clinical Nutrition,* 7, 259-263.

Immergluck, Ludwig, and Mearini, Maria C. (1969) Age and sex differences in responses to Embedded Figures and Reversible Figures. *Journal of Experimental Child Psychology,* 8, 210-211.

Ivey, M. E., and Bardwick, J. M. (1968) Patterns of affective fluctuation in the menstrual cycle. *Psychosomatic Medicine,* 30, 336-345.

Jacobs, Betty. (1943) Aetiological factors and reaction types in psychoses following childbirth. *Journal of Mental Science,* 89, 242-256.

Jacobson, Leonard I., Kaij, L., and A. Nilsson. (1965) Post-partum mental disorders in an unselected sample: Frequency of symptoms and predisposing factors. *British Medical Journal,* 1, 1640-1643.

Jacobson, Leonard I., Berger, Stanley E., and Millham, Jim (1969) Self-esteem, sex differences, and the tendency to cheat. *Proceedings of the*

77th Annual Convention of the American Psychological Association, 4, 353-4.

Janowsky, David S., Gorney, Roderich, and Mandell, Arnold J. (1967) The menstrual cycle: psychiatric and ovarian-adrenocortical hormone correlates: case study and literature review. *Archives of General Psychiatry,* 17, 459-469.

Jansson, Bengt. (1963) Psychic insufficiencies associated with childbearing. *Acta Psychiatrica Scandinavica,* 39, Supplement, 172, 1-168.

Jansson, B., and Selldén, U. (1966) Electroenphalographic investigation of women with psychic insufficiencies associated with childbearing. *Acta Psychiatrica Scandinavica,* 42, 89-96.

Jarosz, M. (1967) Neuroses and pseudoneurotic syndromes and hypoglycemic states. *Polish Medical Journal,* 6, 1285-1291. Abstract in *Psychological Abstracts.*

Jarrahi-Zadeh, Ali, Kane, F. J., Van de Castle, R. L., Lachenbruch, P. A., and Ewing, J. A. (1969) Emotional and cognitive changes in pregnancy and early puerperium. *British Journal of Psychiatry,* 115, 797-805.

Jay, Phyllis. (1963) Mother-infant relations in langurs. In Harriet L. Rheingold (Ed.) *Maternal behavior in mammals.* New York: John Wiley, pp. 282-304.

Jeffcoate, T. N. (1965) The causes of abnormal uterine action in labour. *Australian and New Zealand Journal of Obstetrics and Gynaecology,* 5, 222-227.

Jeffcoate, T. N. (1949) Incoordinate uterine action in labor. *Transactions of the Edinburgh Obstetrical Society,* 101, 23.

Jensen, A. R. (1958) Personality. In P. R. Farnsworth (ed.) *Annual Review of Psychology.* Palo Alto, California: Annual Reviews.

Jensen, G. D., Bobbitt, R. A., and Gordon, B. N. (1968) Sex differences in the development of independence of infant monkeys. *Behavior,* 30, 1-14.

Johnson, M. M. (1963) Sex role learning in the nuclear family. *Child Development,* 34, 319-334.

Johnson, M. M. (1955) Instrumental and expressive components in the personalities of women. Unpublished doctoral dissertation, Radcliffe.

Johnson, Virginia E., and Masters, William H. (1964) Sexual incompatibility: diagnosis and treatment. In Charles W. Lloyd (Ed.) *Human reproduction and sexual behavior.* Philadelphia: Lea & Febiger.

Johnson, W. B., and Terman, L. M. (1940) Some highlights in the literature of psychological sex differences published since 1920. *Journal of Psychology,* 9, 327-336.

Jones, Ernest. (1953) *The life and work of Sigmund Freud.* New York: Basic Books.

Jones, Ernest. (1942) Psychology and childbirth. *Lancet,* 1, 695.

Jones, Mary C., and Mussen, P. H. (1963) Self-conceptions, motivations and interpersonal attitudes of early-and late-maturing girls. In R. E. Grinder (Ed.) *Studies in adolescence.* New York: Macmillan.

Kagan, J. (1969a) Continuity in cognitive development during the first year. *Merrill-Palmer Quarterly,* 15, 101-119.

Kagan, Jerome. (1969) The three faces of continuity in human development. In David A. Goslin (Ed.) *Handbook of socialization theory and research.* Chicago: Rand McNally, pp. 983-1004.

Kagan, Jerome. (1964a) The child's sex role classification of school objects. *Child Development,* 35, 1051-1056.

Kagan, Jerome. (1964b) Acquisition and significance of sex typing and sex role identity. In M. L. Hoffman and Lois W. Hoffman (Eds.) *Review of child development research.* New York: Russell Sage Foundation, pp. 137-167.

Kagan, Jerome. (1958) The concept of identification. *Psychological Review,* 65, 296-305.

Kagan, Jerome, and Freeman, Marion. (1963) Relation of childhood intelligence, maternal behaviors, and social class to behavior during adolescence. *Child Development,* 34, 899-911.

Kagan, Jerome, and Moss, H. A. (1962) *Birth to maturity.* New York: Wiley.

Kagan, Jerome, and Moss, H. A. (1960) The stability of passive and dependent behavior from childhood through adulthood. *Child Development,* 31, 577-591.

Kaij, L., Jacobson, L., and Nilsson, A. (1967) Post-partum mental disorder in an unselected sample: The influence of parity. *Journal of Psychosomatic Research,* 10, 317-325.

Kammeyer, Kenneth. (1967) Sibling position and the feminine role. *Journal of Marriage and the Family,* 29, 494-499.

Kammeyer, Kenneth. (1964) The feminine role: an analysis of attitude consistency. *Journal of Marriage and Family,* 26, 295-305.

Kane, Francis J., Lipton, Morris A. and Ewing, John A. (1969) Hormonal influences in female sexual response. *Archives of General Psychiatry,* 20, 202-209.

Kanin, Eugene, and Howard, David. (1958) Postmarital consequences of premarital sex adjustments. *American Sociological Review,* 64, 556-562.

Kann, Jules. (1950) An exploratory study of the relationship of certain psychological variables to the degree of difficulty of childbirth. Unpublished doctoral dissertation. University of Pittsburgh.

Kaplan, Arnold R. (1968) Physiological and pathological correlates of differences in taste acuity. In Steven G. Vandenberg (Ed.) *Progress in human behavior genetics.* Baltimore, Maryland: Johns Hopkins, pp. 31-66.

Kapp, F. T., Hornstein, S., and Graham, V. T. (1963) Some psychologic factors in prolonged labor due to inefficient uterine action. *Comprehensive Psychiatry,* 4, 9-18.

Karacan, I. (1968) Sleep patterns in pregnancy and postpartum. *Psychophysiology,* 5, 229-230.

Kartchner, F. D. (1950) A study of emotional reactions during labor. *American Journal of Obstetrics and Gynecology,* 60, 19-29.

Kazzaz, D. S. (1965) Attitude of expectant mothers in relation to onset of labor. *Obstetrics and Gynecology,* 26, 585-591.

Keeler, M. H., Kane, F., and Daly, R. (1964) An acute schizophrenic episode following abrupt withdrawal of Enovid in a patient with previous postpartum psychiatric disorder. *American Journal of Psychiatry,* 120, 1123-1124.

Kegel, A. H. (1952) Sexual functions of the puboccygeus muscle. *Western Journal of Surgery, Obstetrics and Gynecology,* 60, 521-524.

Kelley, K., Daniels, G., Poe, J., Easser, R., and Monroe, R. (1954) Psychological correlates with secondary amenorrhea. *Psychosomatic Medicine,* 16, 129-147.

Kessel, N., and Coppen, A. (1963) The prevalence of common menstrual symptoms. *Lancet,* 2, 61-64.

Kestenberg, Judith S. (1965) Menarche. In Sandor Lorand and Henry Schneer (Eds.) *Adolescents.* New York: Dell, pp. 19-50.

Keys, A. B., Brozěk, J., Henschel, A., Mickelson, O., and Taylor, H. L. (1950) *The biology of human starvation.* Minneapolis: University of Minnesota Press.

Kinsey, Alfred, Pomeroy, Wardell B., Martin, Clyde E. and Gebhard, Paul H. (1965) *Sexual behavior in the human female.* New York: Pocket Books.

Kirkendall, L. A. (1961a) Sex drive. In A. Ellis and A. Abardanel (Eds.) *Encyclopedia of sexual behavior.* New York: Hawthorn.

Kirkendall, Lester A. (1961b) *Premarital intercourse and interpersonal relationships.* New York: Julian Press.

Kirkpatrick, Clifford. (1959) The sociological significance of this research. In Winston Ehrmann. *Premarital dating behavior.* New York: Henry Holt, pp. 289-295.

Kitay, P. M. (1940) A comparison of the sexes in their attitudes and beliefs about women: A study of prestige groups. *Sociometry,* 3, 399-407.

Klein, Edward B., and Gould, Laurence J. (1969) Alienation and identification in college women. *Journal of Personality,* 37, 468-480.

Klein, Henriette, Potter, Howard W., and Dyk, Ruth B. (1950) *Anxiety in pregnancy and childbirth.* New York: Hoeber.

Klinger, E., Albaum, A., and Hetherington, M. (1964) Factors influencing the severity of moral judgments. *Journal of Social Psychology,* 63, 319-326.

Knobloch, G., and Pasamanick, B. (1963) Predicting intellectual potential in infancy. *American Journal of Diseases of Children,* 106, 43-51.

Koch, Helen L. (1956) Attitudes of young children toward their peers as related to certain characteristics of their siblings. *Psychological Monographs,* 70, No. 19 (Whole No. 426).

Kohlberg, L. (1969) Stage and sequence: The cognitive developmental approach to socialization. In David A. Goslin (Ed.) *Handbook of socialization theory and research.* Chicago: Rand McNally, 347-480.

Kohlberg, Lawrence. (1966) A cognitive-developmental analysis of children's sex-role concepts and attitudes. In Eleanor Maccoby (Ed.) *The development of sex differences.* Stanford, California: Stanford University Press, pp. 82-173.

Kohlberg, Lawrence. (1964) Development of moral character and moral ideology. In M. L. Hoffman and Lois W. Hoffman (Eds.) *Review of child development research.* New York: Russell Sage Foundation.

Kohlberg, L. (1963) Moral development and identification. In Harold W. Stevenson (Ed.) *Child psychology.* Chicago: University of Chicago Press, pp. 277-332.

Kohlberg, Lawrence, and Zigler, Edward. (1967) The impact of cognitive maturity on the development of sex-role attitudes in the years 4 to 8. *Genetic Psychology Monographs,* 75, 89-165.

Kohn, M. L. (1959) Social class and parental values. *American Journal of Sociology,* 64, 337-351.

Komarovsky, Mirra. (1953) *Women in the modern world, their education and their dilemmas.* Boston: Little, Brown.

Kommunist (Moscow), November, 1963, p. 82 as cited in Louis Fischer (1965) *The life of Lenin.* New York: Harper & Row, p. 555.

Kopell, B., Lunde, D., Clayton, R., Moos, R., and Hamburg, D. (1969) Variations in some measures of arousal during the menstrual cycle. *Journal of Nervous and Mental Diseases,* 148, 180-187.

Kostick, M. M. (1954) Study of transfer: Sex differences in the reasoning process. *Journal of Educational Psychology,* 45, 449-458.

Krebs, R. L. (1968) Girls—more moral than boys or just sneakier. *Proceedings of the 76th Annual Convention of the American Psychological Association,* 3, 607-608.

Kreitler, Hans, and Kreitler, Shulameth. (1966) Children's concepts of sexuality and birth. *Child Development,* 37, 363-78.

Kroger, William S. (Ed.) (1962) *Psychosomatic obstetrics, gynecology, and endocrinology.* Springfield, Illinois: Charles C Thomas.

Kroger, W. S., and De Lee, S. T. (1946) The psychosomatic treatment of hyperemesis gravidarum by hypnosis. *American Journal of Obstetrics and Gynecology,* 51, 544-552.

Kroth, Jerome A. (1968) Relationship between anxiety and menarcheal onset. *Psychological Reports,* 23, 801-802.

Kuhlen, Raymond G., and Houlihan, Nancy B. (1965) Adolescent heterosexual interest in 1942 and 1963. *Child Development,* 36, 1049-1052.

Ladner, Joyce A. (1968) On becoming a woman in the ghetto: Modes of adaptation. *Dissertation Abstracts,* 29A (6-A), 1970.

Laitman, Morris. (1958) Psychodynamic factors associated with functional infertility in married couples: a comparative study of psychological factors in a group of fertile married couples and a group of infertile married couples without medical basis for their condition. *Dissertation Abstracts,* 18, 1492.

Lamb, Wanda M., Ulett, George A., Masters, William H., and Robinson, Donald W. (1953) Premenstrual tension: EEG, hormonal and psychiatric evaluation. *American Journal of Psychiatry,* 109, 840-848.

Lampl-deGroot, Jeanne. (1933) Problems of femininity. *Psychoanalytic Quarterly,* 2, 489-518.

Landis, Carney, Landis, Agnes, and Bolles, M. Marjorie. (1940) *Sex in development.* New York: Paul Hoeber.

Landis, J. T., and Landis, Mary G. (1963) *Building a successful marriage.* (4th ed.) Englewood Cliffs, New Jersey: Prentice-Hall.

Landis, Judson T., and Landis, Mary G. (1958) *Building a successful marriage.* (3rd ed.) Englewood Cliffs, New Jersey: Prentice-Hall.

Landis, Judson T., Poffenberger, T., and Poffenberger, S. (1950) The effects of first pregnancy upon sexual adjustment of 212 couples. *American Sociological Review,* 15, 767-772.

Landy, Eugene E. (1967) Sex differences in some aspects of smoking behavior. *Psychological Reports,* 20, 575-580.

Lansdell, H. (1964) Sex differences in hemispheric asymmetries of the human brain. *Nature,* 203, 550.

Lansdell, H. (1962) A sex difference in effect of temporal-lobe neuro-surgery on design preference. *Nature,* 194, 852-854.

Lansky, Leonard M. (1968) Some comments on Ward's (1968) "Variance of sex-role preferences among boys and girls." *Psychological Reports,* 23, 649-650.

Lansky, Leonard M., and McKay, Gerald. (1969) Independence, dependence, manifest and latent masculinity-femininity: Some complex relationships among four complex variables. *Psychological Reports,* 24, 263-268.

Lansky, Leonard M., and McKay, Gerald. (1963) Sex role preferences of kindergarten boys and girls: some contradictory results. *Psychological Reports,* 13, 415-21.

Lansky, Leonard M., Crandall, V. J., Kagan, J., and Baker, C. T. (1961) Sex differences in aggression and its correlates in middle-class adolescents. *Child Development,* 32, 45-58.

Larsen, Virginia L. (1966) Stresses of the childbearing years. *American Journal of Public Health,* 56, 32-6.

Larsen, Virginia L. (1961) Sources of menstrual information: a comparison of age groups. *Family Life Coordinator,* 10, 41-43.

Larsen, Virginia L., *et al.* (1966) Attitudes and stresses affecting perinatal adjustment. Report, Mental Health Research Institute, Fort Steilacom, Washington. As cited in Grimm, 1969.

Lasagna, L., Mosteller, F., Felsinger, J. M., and Beecher, H. R. (1954) A study of the placebo response. *American Journal of Medicine,* 16, 770-779.

Lazowick, L. M. (1955) On the nature of identification. *Journal of Abnormal and Social Psychology,* 51, 175-183.

Lefkowitz, M. M. (1962) Some relationships between sex-role preference in children and other parent and child variables. *Psychological Reports,* 10, 43-53.

Leventhal, D. B., and Shemberg, K. M. (1969) Sex role adjustment and nonsanctioned aggression. *Journal of Experimental Research in Personality,* 3, 283-286.

Levin, Rachel B. (1966) An empirical test of the female castration complex. *Journal of Abnormal Psychology,* 71, 181-88.

Levin, Rachel B. (1963) The psychology of women: An empirical test of a psychoanalytic construct. *Dissertation Abstracts,* 24, 837.

Levine, Seymour. (1966) Sex differences in the brain. *Scientific American,* 214, 84-90.

Levinger, G. (1964) Task and social role specialization of husband and wife behavior in marriage. *Sociometry,* 27, 433-448.

Levitt, E. E. and Lubin, B. (1967) Some personality factors associated with menstrual complaints and menstrual attitude. *Journal of Psychosomatic Research,* 11, 267-270.

Levy, David M. (1966) *Maternal overprotection.* New York: Norton.

Levy, David M. (1942) Psychosomatic studies of some aspects of maternal behavior. *Psychosomatic Medicine,* 4, 223-227.

Levy, David M. (1940) Control-situation studies of children's responses to the difference in genitalia. *American Journal of Orthopsychiatry,* 10, 755-62.

Lewis, Michael. (1969) Infants' responses to facial stimuli during the first year of life. *Developmental Psychology,* 1, 75-86.

Lewis, M., Kagan, J., and Kalafat, J. (1966) Patterns of fixation in the young infant. *Child Development,* 37, 331-341.

Lewis, O. (1941) Manly-hearted women among the north Piegan. *American Anthropologist,* 43, 173-187.

Lewis, V. G., Money, J., and Epstein, R. (1968) Concordance of verbal and nonverbal ability in the adrenogenital syndrome. *Johns Hopkins Medical Journal,* 122, 192-5.

Liccione, John V. (1955) The changing family relationships of adolescent girls. *Journal of Abnormal and Social Psychology,* 51, 421-26.

Linton, R. (1942) Age and sex categories. *American Sociological Review,* 7, 589-603.

Lipsett, L. P., and Levy, N. (1959) Electrotactual threshold in the human neonate. *Child Development,* 30, 547-54.

Ljung, Bengt-Olov. (1965) The adolescent spurt in mental growth. *Stockholm Studies in Educational Psychology* 8. Stockholm, Sweden: Almquist & Wiksell.

Lloyd, Charles and Leathem, James H. (1964) Physiology of the female reproductive tract. In Charles W. Lloyd (Ed.) *Human reproduction and sexual behavior.* Philadelphia: Lea & Febiger, 70-91.

Locke, Harvey J. (1951) *Predicting adjustment in marriage: a comparison of a divorced and a happily married group.* New York: Henry Holt.

Loiselle, Robert and Mollenauer, Sandra. (1965) Galvanic skin response to sexual stimuli in a female population. *Journal of General Psychology,* 73, 273-278.

Lomas, P. (1959) The husband-wife relationship in cases of puerperal breakdown. *British Journal of Medical Psychology,* 32, 117-132.

Lorenz, Konrad. (1963) *Evolution and modification of behavior.* Chicago: University of Chicago Press.

Lunneborg, Patricia W. (1969) Sex differences in aptitude maturation during college. *Journal of Counseling Psychology,* 16, 463-464.

Luria, Z., Goldwasser, Miriam, and Goldwasser, Adena. (1963) Response to transgression in stories by Israeli children. *Child Development,* 34, 271-280.

Lykken, David T. (1968) Statistical significance in psychological research. *Psychological Bulletin,* 70, 151-59.

Lynn, David B. (1969a) Curvilinear relation between cognitive functioning and distance of child from parent of same sex. *Psychological Review,* 76, 236-240.

Lynn, David B. (1969b) *Parental and sex role identification: A theoretical formulation.* Berkeley, California: McCutchan.

Lynn, David B. (1962) Sex-role and parental identification. *Child Development,* 33, 555-564.

Lynn, David B. and Sawrey, W. L. (1959) The effects of father absence on Norwegian boys and girls. *Journal of Abnormal and Social Psychology,* 59, 258-62.

Lynn, Rosalie. (1962) Sex-role preference and mother-daughter fantasies in young girls. *Dissertation Abstracts,* 22, 4084.

MacArthur, R. (1967) Sex differences in field dependence for the Eskimo: Replication of Berry's findings. *International Journal of Psychology,* 2, 139-140.

MacBrayer, Caroline T. (1960) Differences in perception of the opposite sex by males and females. *Journal of Social Psychology,* 53, 309-14.

Maccoby, Eleanor E. (1968) The development of moral values and behavior in childhood. In John A. Clausen. *Socialization and society*. Boston: Little Brown, 227-269.

Maccoby, Eleanor E. (Ed.) (1966a) *The development of sex differences*. Stanford, California: Stanford University Press.

Maccoby, Eleanor E. (1966b) Sex differences in intellectual functioning. In Eleanor E. Maccoby (Ed.) *The development of sex differences*. Stanford, California: Stanford University Press.

Maccoby, Eleanor E. (1963) Woman's intellect. In Seymour M. Farber and Roger, H. L. Wilson (Eds.) *The potential of women*. New York: McGraw-Hill, pp. 24-39.

Maccoby, Eleanor E. (1959) Role-taking in childhood and its consequences for social learning. *Child Development*, 30, 239-252.

Maccoby, Eleanor E., Dowley, Edith M., Degerman, J. W., and Degerman, R. (1965) Activity level and intellectual functioning in normal preschool children. *Child Development*, 36, 761-70.

Maccoby, Eleanor E., Wilson, W. C. and Burton, R. V. (1958) Differential movie-viewing behavior of male and female viewers. *Journal of Personality*, 26, 259-67.

Macfarlane, Jean W., Allen, Lucile, and Honzik, Marjorie P. (1954) A developmental study of the behavior problems of normal children between twenty-one months and fourteen years. *University of California Publications in Child Development*, 2, 1-122.

Machotka, Pavel, and Ferber, Andrew S. (1967) Delineation of family roles. *American Journal of Orthopsychiatry*, 37, 409-410.

Mackinnon, P. C., and Mackinnon, I. L. (1956) Hazards of the menstrual cycle. *British Medical Journal*, 1, 555.

MacLean, Paul D. (1965) New findings relevant to the evolution of psychosexual functions of the brain. In John Money (Ed.) *Sex research new developments*. New York: Rinehart & Winston.

Maddison, David, and Viola, Agnes. (1968) The health of widows in the year following bereavement. *Journal of Psychosomatic Research*, 12, 297-306.

Majerius, P. W., Guze, S. B., DeLong, W. B., and Robins, E. (1960) Psychologic factors and psychiatric disease in hyperemesis gravidarum: a follow-up study of 69 vomiters and 66 controls. *American Journal of Psychiatry*, 117, 421-428.

Malcovati, P., Fornari, F., and Miraglia, F. (1965) Les angoisses primaires chez la femme lors de l'accouchement. In *1st International Congress of Psychosomatic Medicine and Childbirth*. Paris: Gauthier-Villars, pp. 81-85.

Mallick, Shahbaz K., and McCandless, B. R. (1966) A study of catharsis of aggression. *Journal of Personality and Social Psychology*, 4, 591-596.

Mandell, Arnold J., and Mandell, Mary. (1967) Suicide and the menstrual cycle. *Journal of the American Medical Association*, 200, 792-3.

Mann, Edward C. (1963) Primary dysmenorrhea. In Joe V. Meigs and Somers H. Sturgis (Eds.) *Progress in gynecology,* vol. IV. New York: Grune & Stratton, pp. 123-145.

Mann, Edward C. (1959) Habitual abortion: a report in two parts on 160 patients. *American Journal of Obstetrics and Gynecology,* 77, 706-718.

Mann, Edward C. (1957) The role of emotional determinants in habitual abortion. *Surgical Clinics of North America,* 37, 447-458.

Mann, Edward C. (1956) Psychiatric investigation of habitual abortion: preliminary report. *Obstetrics and Gynecology,* 7, 589-601.

Mann, Edward C. and Elaine R. Grimm. (1962) Habitual abortion. In William S. Kroger (Ed.) *Psychosomatic obstetrics, gynecology, and endocrinology.* Springfield, Illinois: Charles C Thomas.

Marañon, Gregorio. (1932) *The evolution of sex and intersexual conditions.* London: George Allen & Unwin.

Markham, Sylvia. (1961) A comparative evaluation of psychotic and non-psychotic reactions to childbirth. *American Journal of Orthopsychiatry,* 31, 565-578.

Marks, P. (1961) An assessment of the diagnostic process in a child guidance setting. *Psychological Monographs,* 75 (Whole No. 507).

Marmor, Judd. (1963) Some considerations concerning orgasm in the female. In Manfred F. DeMartion (Ed.) *Sexual behavior and personality characteristics.* New York: Citadel.

Maslow, A. H. (1963) Self-esteem (dominance-feeling) and sexuality in women. In Manfred F. DeMartino (ed.) *Sexual behavior and personality characteristics.* New York: Citadel, pp. 71-112.

Masters, William H. (1956) Sex steroid replacement in the aging individual. In Earl Engle and Gregory Pincus (Eds.) *Hormones and the aging process.* New York: Academic Press, pp. 49-62.

Masters, William H., and Johnson, Virginia E. (1970) *Human sexual inadequacy.* Boston: Little, Brown.

Masters, William H., and Johnson, Virginia E. (1966) *Human sexual response.* Boston: Little, Brown.

Masters, William H., and Johnson, Virginia E. (1965a) The sexual response cycle of the human female 1. Gross anatomic considerations. In John Money (Ed.) *Sex research new developments.* New York: Holt, Rinehart & Winston.

Masters, William H., and Johnson, Virginia E. (1965b) The clitoris: anatomic and clinical considerations. In John Money (Ed.) *Sex research new developments.* New York: Holt, Rinehart & Winston.

May, Robert. (1968) Fantasy differences in men and women. *Psychology Today,* 1, 42-45, 69.

McCall, J. R. (1955) *Sex differences in intelligence: A comparative factor study.* Washington: Catholic University Press.

McCammon, C. C. (1951) A study of four hundred seventy-five pregnancies in American Indian Women. *American Journal of Obstetrics and Gynecology,* 61, 1159-1170.

McCance, R. A., Luff, M. C., and Widdowson, E. E. (1937) Physical and emotional periodicity in women. *Journal of Hygiene,* 37, 571-611.

McCandless, B. R. (1961) *Children and adolescents: behavior and development.* New York: Holt, Rinehart, and Winston, p. 28.

McCandless, Boyd R., and Ali, Fahmida. (1966) Relations among physical skills and personal and social variables in three cultures of adolescent girls. *Journal of Educational Psychology,* 57, 366-372.

McCarthy, Dorothea. (1943) Language development of the preschool child. In R. G. Barker, J. S. Kounin and R. F. Wright (Eds.) *Child behavior and development.* New York: McGraw Hill.

McConnell, O. L., and Daston, P. G. (1961) Body image changes in pregnancy. *Journal of Projective Techniques,* 25, 451-456.

McDonald, F. J. (1963) Children's judgments of theft from individual and corporate owners. *Child Development,* 34, 141-50.

McDonald, Robert L. (1968) The role of emotional factors in obstetric complications: A review. *Psychosomatic Medicine,* 30, 222-237.

McDonald, Robert L. (1965) Fantasy and outcome of pregnancy. *Archives of General Psychiatry,* 12, 602-606.

McDonald, Robert L., and Christakos, A. C. (1963) Relationship of emotional adjustment during pregnancy in obstetrical complications. *American Journal of Obstetrics and Gynecology,* 86, 341-348.

McDonald, R. L., Gynther, M. D., and Christakos, A. C. (1963) Relations between maternal anxiety and obstetric complications. *Psychosomatic Medicine,* 25, 357-363.

McFate, M. Q., and Orr, F. G. (1949) Through adolescence with the Rorschach. *Rorschach Research Exchange,* 13, 302-19.

McGeorge, M. (1960) Current trends in breast feeding. *New Zealand Medical Journal,* 59, 31-41.

McGuire, Carson. (1961) Sex role and community variability in test performances. *Journal of Education Psychology,* 52, 61-73.

McKee, J. P., and Sherriffs, A. C. (1960) Men's and women's beliefs, ideals and self-concepts. In J. M. Seidman (Ed.) *The adolescent—a book of readings.* New York: Holt, Rinehart, and Winston.

McKee, J. P., and Sherriffs, A. C. (1957) The differential evaluation of males and females. *Journal of Personality,* 25, 356-371.

McNeile, L. G., and Page, E. W. (1939) Personality type of patient with toxemias of late pregnancy. *American Journal of Medical Science,* 197, 393-400.

McNeill, David, and Livson, Norman. (1963) Maturation rate and body build in women. *Child Development,* 34, 25-32.

Mead, Margaret. (1958) In J. M. Tanner and Barbel Inhelder (Eds.) *Dis-*

cussions on child development. New York: International Universities Press.

Mead, Margaret. (1955) *Male and female.* New York: The American Library of World Literature.

Mead, Margaret. (1935) *Sex and temperament in three primitive societies.* New York: Morrow.

Mead, Margaret and Newton, Niles. (1967) Cultural patterning of perinatal behavior. In Stephen Richardson and Alan F. Gutmacher (Eds.) *Childbearing–Its social and psychological aspects.* Baltimore: Williams & Wilkins, pp. 142-244.

Medinnus, Gene R. (1966) Age and sex differences in conscience development. *Journal of Genetic Psychology,* 109, 117-118.

Meehl, Paul E. (1967) Theory-testing in psychology and physics: a methodological paradox. *Philosophy of Science,* 34, 103-115.

Meiers, Robert L. (1967) Relative hypoglycemia in schizophrenic reactions. *Journal of Schizophrenia,* 1, 204-208.

Meites, Joseph, Nicoll, Charles S. and Talwalker, P. K. (1963) Lactation. In Andrew V. Nalbandov (Ed.) *Advances in neuroendocrinology.* Urbana: University of Illinois Press, pp. 238-288.

Melges, F. T. (1968) Postpartum psychiatric syndromes. *Psychosomatic Medicine,* 30, 95-108.

Mellander, B., Vahlquist, B. and Melbin, T. (1959) Breast feeding and artificial feeding. *Acta Paediatrica,* 48, suppl. 116.

Melody, George F. (1961) Behavioral implications of premenstrual tension. *Obstetrics and Gynecology,* 17, 439-441.

Meltzer, H. (1941) Sex differences in parental preference patterns. *Character and Personality,* 10, 114-128.

Michael, Richard P. (1968) Gonadal hormones and control of primate behaviour. In Richard P. Michael (Ed.) *Endocrinology and human behaviour.* London: Oxford University Press, 69-93.

Michael, Richard P. (1965) Some aspects of the endocrine control of sexual activity in primates. *Proceedings of the Royal Society of Medicine,* 58, 595-598.

Michael, W. G., Guilford, J. P., Fruchter, B., and Zimmerman, W. S. (1957) The description of spatial-visualization abilities. *Educational and Psychological Measurement,* 17, 185-199.

Miller, Alan R. (1969) Analysis of the Oedipal complex. *Psychological Reports,* 24, 781-782.

Milner, Esther. (1949) Effects of sex role and social status on the early adolescent personality. *Genetic Psychological Monographs,* 40, 231-325.

Milton, G. A. (1957) The effects of sex-role identification upon problem solving skills. *Journal of Abnormal and Social Psychology,* 55, 208-212.

Minuchin, Patricia. (1965) Sex-role concepts and sex-typing in childhood as a function of school and home environments. *Child Development,* 36, 1033-1048.

Mischel, Walter. (1966) A social-learning view of sex differences in behavior. In E. Maccoby (Ed.) *The development of sex differences.* Stanford, California: Stanford University Press.

Mitchell, Gary D. (1968) Attachment differences in male and female infant monkeys. *Child Development,* 39, 611-620.

Mitchell, Leslie H. (1966) Dominance and femininity as factors in the sex role adjustment of parents and children. *Dissertation Abstracts,* 26, 7740.

Money, John. (1968) Cognitive deficits in Turner's syndrome. In Steven G. Vandenberg (Ed.) *Progress in human behavior genetics.* Baltimore, Maryland: Johns Hopkins, 4-30.

Money, J. (1965a) Psychosexual differentiation. In J. Money (Ed.) *Sex research new developments.* New York: Holt, Rinehart and Winston.

Money, John. (1965b) Influence of hormones on sexual behavior. *Annual Review of Medicine,* 16, 67-82.

Money, John. (1964) Two cytogenetic syndromes: psychologic comparisons. I. Intelligence and specific factor quotients. *Journal of Psychiatric Research,* 2, 223-231.

Money, John. (1961) Sex hormones and other variables in human eroticism. In W. C. Young (Ed.) *Sex and internal secretions.* (3rd ed.) Baltimore: Williams & Wilkins.

Money, John, and Ehrhardt, Anke A. (1968) Prenatal hormone exposure: Possible effects on behavior in man. In Richard P. Michael (Ed.) *Endocrinology and human behaviour.* London: Oxford University Press.

Moos, R. H., Kopell, B. S., Melges, F. T., Yalom, I. D., Lunde, D. T., Clayton, R. B., and Hamburg, D. A. (1969) Fluctuations in symptoms and moods during the menstrual cycle. *Journal of Psychosomatic Research,* 13, 37-44.

Morton, J. H., Addition, H., Addison, R. G., Hunt, L. and Sullivan, J. J. (1953) A clinical study of premenstrual tension. *American Journal of Obstetrics and Gynecology,* 65, 1182-1191.

Morton, Joseph. (1962) Premenstrual tension. In William S. Kroger (Ed.) *Psychosomatic obstetrics, gynecology, and endocrinology.* Springfield, Illinois: Charles C Thomas.

Mosher, D. L., and Greenberg, Irene. (1969) Females' affective responses to reading erotic literature. *Journal of Consulting and Clinical Psychology,* 33, 472-477.

Moss, H. A. (1967) Sex, age, and state as determinants of mother-infant interaction. *Merrill-Palmer Quarterly,* 13, 19-36.

Mowrer, O. H. (1960) *Learning theory and the symbolic process.* New York: Wiley.

Mowrer, O. H. (1950) *Learning theory and personality dynamics.* New York: Ronald.

Mussen, Paul H. (1969) Early sex-role development. In D. A. Goslin (Ed.) *Handbook of socialization theory and research.* Chicago: Rand McNally, pp. 707-732.

Mussen, P., and Rutherford, E. (1963) Parent-child relations and parental personality in relation to sex-role preferences. *Child Development, 34*, 589-607.

Myrdal, Alva, and Klein, Viola. (1968) *Women's two roles: Home and work.* London: Routledge & Kegan Paul, 2nd ed.

Nelson, Edward A., Grinder, Robert E., and Mutterer, Marcia L. (1969) Sources of variance in behavioral measures of honesty in temptation situations: Methodological analyses. *Developmental Psychology,* 1, 265-279.

Nemtsova, O. L., Morachevskaia, E. V., and Andreeva, E. I. (1958) Dinamika uslovnore flektornoi deiatel'nosti pri beremennosti u zhivotnykh (Dynamics of conditioned-reflex activity during pregnancy in animals). *Zh. Vyssh. Nerv. Derat. Pavlov.* 8, 234. Abstract in *Psychological Abstracts, 33,* 309, 1959.

Neugarten, Bernice L. (1968) Adult personality: toward a psychology of the life cycle. In Bernice L. Neugarten (Ed.) *Middle age and aging.* Chicago: University of Chicago Press, 137-147.

Neugarten, Bernice L. (1956) Kansas City study of adult life. In Irma H. Gross (Ed.) *Potentialities of women in middle years.* East Lansing, Michigan: Michigan State University Press, 33-45.

Neugarten, Bernice L., and Guttman, David L. (1968) Age-sex roles and personality in middle age: A Thematic Apperception Study. In B. L. Neugarten (Ed.) *Middle age and aging.* Chicago: University of Chicago Press, 58-71.

Neugarten, Bernice L., and Kraines, Ruth J. (1965) Menopausal symptoms in women of various ages. *Psychosomatic Medicine,* 27, 266-273.

Neugarten, B. L., and Weinstein, Karol K. (1968) The changing American grandparent. In B. L. Neugarten (Ed.) *Middle age and aging.* Chicago: University of Chicago Press, 280-285.

Neugarten, Bernice L., Wood, Vivian, Kraines, Ruth J. and Loomis, Barbara. (1963) Women's attitudes toward the menopause. *Vita Humana,* 6, 140-151.

Newson, John, and Newson, Elizabeth. (1968) *Four years old in an urban community.* London: George Allen and Unwin.

Newson, John, and Newson, Elizabeth. (1963) *Infant care in an urban community.* London: George Allen and Unwin.

Newson, John and Newson, Elizabeth. (1962) Breast feeding in decline. *British Medical Journal,* No. 2, 1744-5.

Newton, Niles. (1963) Emotions of pregnancy. *Clinical Obstetrics and Gynecology,* 6, 638-668.

Newton, Niles. (1955) *Maternal emotions.* New York: Hoeber.

Newton, Niles, Foshee, D., and Newton, M. (1966) Experimental inhibition of labor through environmental disturbance. *Obstetrics and Gynecology,* 27, 371-7.

Newton, Niles, Peeler, D., and Newton, M. (1968) Effect of disturbance on labor. *American Journal of Obstetrics and Gynecology,* 101, 1096-1102.

Newton, D., Peeler, D., and Rawlins, C. (1968) Effect of lactation on maternal behavior in mice with comparative data on humans. *Lying-In: The Journal of Reproductive Medicine,* 1, 257-262.

Nielsen, Johannes. (1969) Klinefelter's syndrome and the XYY syndrome. *Acta Psychiatrica Scandinavica, Supplementum* 209.

Nilsson, A., Kaij, L. and Jacobson, L. (1967) Post-partum mental disorders in an unselected sample: The psychiatric history. *Journal of Psychosomatic Research,* 10, 327-339.

Oetzel, Roberta M. (1966) Annotated bibliography. In Eleanor E. Maccoby (Ed.) *The development of sex differences.* Stanford, Calif.: Stanford University Press.

Opum, Magnus. (1967) Sex differences in sin preferences. *Psychological Reports,* 21, 752.

Orlansky, H. (1949) Infant care and personality. *Psychological Bulletin,* 46, 1-48.

Osgood, C., Suci, G., and Tannenbaum, P. H. (1957) *The measurement of meaning.* Urbana: University of Illinois Press.

Osofsky, H. J. and Fisher, S. (1967) Psychological correlates of the development of amenorrhea in a stress situation. *Psychosomatic Medicine,* 29, 15-22.

Packard, Vance. (1968) *Sexual wilderness.* New York: David McKay.

Paffenbarger, R. S. (1964) Epidemiological aspects of parapartum mental illness. *British Journal of Preventive and Social Medicine,* 18, 189-195.

Paffenbarger, R. S. (1961) The picture puzzle of the pospartum psychosis. *Journal of Chronic Disease,* 13, 161-173.

Parker, Elizabeth. (1960) *The seven ages of woman.* Baltimore: John Hopkins Press.

Parsons, Talcott. (1964a) The father symbol. In *Social structure and personality.* Glencoe, Illinois: Free Press. (1st published in 1954).

Parsons, Talcott. (1964b) *Social structure and personality.* Glencoe, Illinois: Free Press of Glencoe.

Parsons, Talcott. (1958) Social structure and the development of personality: Freud's contribution to the integration of psychology and sociology. *Psychiatry,* 21, 321-340.

Parsons, Talcott. (1953) A revised analytical approach to the theory of social stratification. In R. Bendix and S. M. Lipset (Eds.) *Class, status, and power.* Glencoe, Illinois: Free Press, pp. 92-128.

Parsons, Talcott, and Bales, R. (1955) *Family socialization and interaction process.* Glencoe, Illinois: Free Press.

Parsons, Talcott, and Shils, Edward A. (Eds.) (1959) *Toward a general theory of action.* Cambridge, Mass.: Harvard University Press.

Patel, A. S., and Gordon, J. E. (1960) Some personal and situational determinants of yielding to influence. *Journal of Abnormal and Social Psychology,* 61, 411-18.

Paulson, M. J. (1961) Psychological concomitants of premenstrual tension. *American Journal of Obstetrics and Gynecology,* 81, 733-738.

Paulson, M. J., and Wood, K. R. (1966) Perceptions of the emotional correlates of dysmenorrhea. *American Journal of Obstetrics and Gynecology,* 95, 991-996.

Pavenstadt, E. (1965) Communication. Conference on Mental Health in Pregnancy, NIMH. Bethesda, Maryland as cited in Grimm (1969).

Pennington, V. M. (1957) Meprobamate (Miltown) in premenstrual tension. *Journal of the American Medical Association,* 164, 638.

Peskin, H. (1968) The duration of normal menses as a psychosomatic phenomenon. *Psychosomatic Medicine,* 30, 378-389.

Peterson, Esther. (1964) Working women. *Daedalus,* 93, 671-99.

Phillips, B. N. (1966) Defensiveness as a factor in sex differences in anxiety. *Journal of Consulting Psychology,* 30, 167-169.

Piaget, Jean. (1970) *American Psychologist,* 25, 65-79.

Piret, Roger. (1965) *Psychologie différentielle des sexes.* Paris: Presses Universitaires de France.

Piskin, V. (1960) Psychosexual development in terms of object and role preferences. *Journal of Clinical Psychology,* 16, 238-240.

Pleshette, N., Asch, S. S., and Chase, J. (1965) A study of anxieties during pregnancy, labor, the early and late puerperium. *Bulletin of the New York Academy of Medicine,* 32, 436-456.

Poffenberger, S., Poffenberger, T., and Landis, J. T. (1952) Intent toward conception and the pregnancy experience. *American Sociological Review,* 17, 616-620.

Pohlman, Edward H. (1969) *Psychology of birth planning.* Cambridge, Massachusetts: Shenkman.

Popenoe, Paul. (1961) Premarital experience no help in sexual adjustment after marriage. *Family Life,* 21, 1-2.

Porteus, Barbara D., and Johnson, R. C. (1965) Children's responses to two measures of conscience development and their relation to sociometric nomination. *Child Development,* 36, 703-11.

Protheroe, Colin. (1969) Puerperal psychoses: A long term study, 1927-1961. *British Journal of Psychiatry,* 115, 9-30.

Pugh, T. F., Jerath, B. K., Schmidt, W. M., and Reed, R. B. (1963) Rates of mental disease related to childbearing. *New England Journal of Medicine,* 268, 1224-8.

Rabban, M. (1950) Sex-role identification in young children in diverse social groups. *Genetic Psychological Monographs,* 42, 81-158.

Rabe, Claire F. (1963) A study of sexual attitudes as revealed by symbols in dreams. Research Report No. 2, Institute of Dream Research. (M. A. thesis Western Reserve University, 1949).

Rado, S. (1965) A critical examination of the concept of bisexuality. In Judd Marmor (Ed.) *Sexual inversion.* New York: Basic Books.

Rado, S. (1933) Fear of castration in women. *Psychoanalytic Quarterly,* 2, 425-75.

Rainwater, Lee. (1966) Some aspects of lower class sexual behavior. *Journal of Social Issues,* 22, 96-108.

Rainwater, Lee. (1965) *Family design, marital sexuality, family size and family planning.* Chicago: Aldine.

Rakoff, Abraham E. (1963) Discussant. In Andrew V. Nalbandov (Ed.) *Advances in neuroendocrinology.* Urbana, Illinois: University of Illinois Press.

Rangell, Leo. (1955) The role of the parent in the oedipus complex. *Bulletin of the Menninger Clinic,* 19, 9-15.

Read, G. D. (1944) *Childbirth without fear.* New York: Harper.

Rebelsky, Freda G., Alinsmith, W., and Grinder, R. E. (1963) Resistance to temptation and sex differences in children's use of fantasy confession. *Child Development,* 34, 955-62.

Rebus, B. M. (1965) Prostrannstvennoe voobrazhenie kak odna izivazhnykh sposobnosteĭ k tekhnicheskomu tvorchestvu. (Spatial visualization as an important component of creativity in the field of engineering.) *Voprosy Psikhologii,* 5, 36-49. Abstract in *Psychological Abstracts.*

Reevy, William R. (1963) Vestured genital apposition and coitus. In Hugo Beigel (Ed.) *Advances in sex research.* New York: Hoeber. Pp. 27-32.

Reik, Theodore. (1960) *Sex in man and woman.* New York: Noonday Press.

Reiss, Ira. (1967) *The social context of premarital sexual permissiveness.* New York: Holt, Rinehart and Winston.

Reiss, Ira L. (1962) Sociological studies of sexual standards. In George Winokur (Ed.) *Determinants of human sexual behavior.* Springfield, Illinois: Charles C Thomas, pp. 101-141.

Reiss, Ira L. (1960) *Premarital sexual standards in America.* Glencoe, Illinois: Free Press.

Rempel, H., and Signoi, E. I. (1964) Sex differences in self-rating of conscience as a determinant of behavior. *Psychological Reports,* 15, 277-78.

Reynolds, Evelyn. (1969) Variations of mood and recall in the menstrual cycle. *Journal of Psychosomatic Research,* 13, 163-166.

Rheingold, Harriet, and Eckerman, Carol O. (1970) The infant separates himself from his mother. *Science,* 168, 78-83.

Rheingold, Joseph. (1964) *The fear of being a woman: A theory of maternal destructiveness.* New York: Grune & Stratton.

Ribeiro, A. L. (1962) Menstruation and crime. *British Medical Journal,* 1, 640.

Richey, Marjorie H., and Fichter, James J. (1969) Sex differences in moralism and punitiveness. *Psychonomic Science,* 16, 185-186.

Riffatorre, Birgitte B. (1965) Determination of pregnancy depression and its relation to marital status and group affiliation in a single ethnic group. *Dissertattion Abstracts,* 25, 5390.

Riley, Matilda W., Foner, Anne, Hess, Beth, and Toby, Marcia L. (1969) Socialization for the middle and later years. In David A. Goslin (Ed.) *Handbook of socialization theory and research.* Chicago: Rand McNally, 951-982.

Ringrose, C. A. D. (1961a) Psychosomatic influences in the genesis of toxemia of pregnancy. *Canadian Medical Association Journal,* 84, 647-651.

Ringrose, C. A. D. (1961b) Further observations on the psychosomatic character of toxemia of pregnancy. *Canadian Medical Association Journal,* 84, 1064-5.

Riopelle, A. J. and Rogers, C. M. (1965) Age change in chimpanzees. In A. M. Schrier, H. F. Harlow and F. Stollnitz (Eds.) *Behavior of nonhuman primates.* New York: Academic Press, 449-462.

Robertson, G. G. (1946) Nausea and vomiting of pregnancy. *Lancet,* 2, 336-341.

Robertson, W. D. (1961) Breast feeding practices: some implications of regional variations. *American Journal of Public Health,* 51, 1035-1042.

Robin, A. A. (1962) The psychological changes of normal parturition. *Psychiatric Quarterly,* 36, 129-150.

Rogers, W. C. (1962) The role of endocrine allergy in the production of premenstrual tension. *Western Journal of Surgery,* 70, 100-102.

Róheim, Géza. (1950) The Oedipus complex, magic and culture. In Géza Róheim (Ed.) *Psychoanalysis and the social sciences.* New York: International Universities Press. Vol. II, pp. 173-228.

Rokeach, M. (1943) Studies in beauty: I. The relationship between beauty in women, dominance and security. *Journal of Social Psychology,* 17, 181-189.

Romney, A. Kimball. (1965) Variations in household structure as determinants of sex-typed behavior. In Frank A. Beach (Ed.) *Sex and Behavior.* New York: Wiley.

Roper, Elmo. (1946) Women in America. The Fortune Survey, Part 1. *Fortune Magazine,* August 1946.

Rosenberg, Benjamin G., and Sutton-Smith, B. (1964) Ordinal position and sex-role identification. *Genetic Psychological Monographs,* 70, 297-328.

Rosengren, W. R. (1962a) Social status, attitudes toward pregnancy and child-rearing attitudes. *Social Forces,* 41, 127-134.

Rosengren, W. R. (1962b) Social instability and attitudes toward pregnancy as a social role. *Social Problems,* 9, 371-378.

Rosengren, W. R. (1961) Social sources of pregnancy as illness or normality. *Social Forces,* 39, 260-267.

Rosenkrantz, Paul, Vogel, Susan, Bee, Helen, Broverman, Inge, and Broverman, Donald M. (1968) Sex-role stereotypes and self-concepts in college students. *Journal of Consulting and Clinical Psychology,* 32, 287-295.

Rosenthal, Irene. (1963) Reliability of retrospective reports of adolescence. *Journal of Consulting Psychology,* 27, 189-198.

Rosenthal, R., Mulry, R. L., Persinger, G. W., Vikan-Kline, Grothe, Linda, and Grothe, Mardell. (1964) Emphasis on experimental procedure, sex of subjects and the biasing effects of experimental hypotheses. *Journal of Projective Techniques and Personality Assessment,* 28, 470-73.

Rothbart, Mary K., and Maccoby, Eleanor E. (1966) Parents' differential reactions to sons and daughters. As cited in Oetzel (1966).

Rowell, Thelma E. (1967) Female reproductive cycles and the behavior of baboons and rhesus macaques. In Stuart A. Altmann (Ed.) *Social communication among primates.* Chicago: University of Chicago Press.

Rubin, Isadore. (1966) Sex after forty—and after seventy. In Ruth Brecher and Edward Brecher (Eds.) *An analysis of human sexual response.* Boston: Little Brown, pp. 251-266.

Rubin, Reva. (1967a) Attainment of the maternal role. 1. Processes. *Nursing Research,* 16, 237-245.

Rubin, Reva. (1967b) Attainment of the maternal role. 2. Models and referrants. *Nursing Research,* 16, 242-6.

Rudy, Arthur J. (1965) Sex-role perceptions in early adolescence. *Dissertation Abstracts,* 26, 6174-5.

Rutherford, Eldred E. (1969) A note on the relation of parental dominance as a decision maker in the home to children's ability to make sex-role discriminations. *Journal of Genetic Psychology,* 114, 185-191.

Rutherford, Eldred E. (1965) Familial antecedents of sex role development in young children. *Dissertation Abstracts,* 25, 4252-3.

Ryle, A. (1961) Psychological disturbances associated with 345 pregnancies and 137 women. *Journal of Mental Science,* 107, 279-286.

Sadow, L., Gedo, J., Miller, J., Pollock, G., and Sabshin, M. (1968) The process of hypothesis change in three early psychoanalytic concepts. *Journal of the American Psychoanalytic Association,* 16, 245-273.

Salber, E. J., Stitt, P. G., and Babbott, J. G. (1959) Patterns of breast feeding in a family health clinic. *New England Journal of Medicine,* 260, 310-315.

Salerno, Louis J. (1962) Psychophysiologic aspects of toxemia. In William S. Kroger (Ed.) *Psychosomatic obstetrics, gynecology and endocrinology.* Springfield, Illinois: Charles C Thomas, pp. 104-114.

Salerno, L. J. (1958) Psychophysiologic aspect of toxemias of pregnancy. *American Journal of Obstetrics and Gynecology,* 76, 1268-74.

Sanchez-Hidalgo, E. (1952) The feeling of inferiority in the Puerto Rican female. *Rev. Asoc. Maestros,* 11, 170-171. Abstract in *Psychological Abstracts.*

Sandström, C. I. and Lundberg, I. A. (1956) A genetic approach to sex differences in localization. *Acta Psychologica,* 12, 247-253.

Sandström, C. I. (1953) Sex differences in localization and orientation. *Acta Psychologica,* 9, 82-96.

Sanford, R. N. (1955) The dynamics of identification. *Psychological Review,* 62, 106-117.

Santrock, John W. (1970) Paternal absence, sex typing and identification. *Developmental Psychology,* 2, 264-272.

Sapir, Selma G. (1966) Sex differences in perceptual motor development. *Perceptual and Motor Skills,* 22, 987-992.

Schachter, S. (1964) In P. H. Leiderman and D. Shapiro (Eds.) *Psychobiological approaches to social behavior.* Stanford, California: Stanford University Press.

Schaefer, Leah C. (1969) Frigidity. In George D. Goldman and Donald S. Milman (Eds.) *Modern woman.* Springfield, Illinois, Charles C Thomas, 165-177.

Scheinfeld, Amram. (1944) *Women and men.* New York: Harcourt Brace.

Schneirla, T. C., Rosenblatt, Jay S., and Tobach, Ethel. (1963) Maternal behavior in the cat. In Harriet L. Rheingold (Ed.) *Maternal behavior in mammals.* New York: John Wiley, pp. 122-168.

Schoeppe, A. (1953) Sex differences in adolescent socialization. *Journal of Social Psychology,* 38, 175-185.

Schofield, Michael. (1965) *The sexual response of young people.* London: Longmans, Green and Co.

Scott, Eileen, Illsley, R. and Biles, M. E. (1965a) A psychological investigation of primigravidae, III. Some aspects of maternal behaviour. *Journal of Obstetrics and Gynaecology of the British Empire,* 63, 494.

Scott, E. and Thomson, A. M. (1956b) A psychological investigation of primigravidae, IV. Psychological factors in the clinical phenomena of labor. *Journal of Obstetrics and Gynaecology of the British Empire,* 63, 502-508.

Scriven, Michael. (1959) The experimental investigation of psychoanalysis. In Sidney Hook (Ed.) *Psychoanalysis, scientific method and philosophy.* New York: New York University Press.

Seager, C. P. (1960) A controlled study of postpartum mental illness. *Journal of Mental Science,* 106, 214-230.

Sears, Robert R. (1965) Development of gender role. In Frank A. Beach (Ed.) *Sex and behavior.* New York: Wiley.

Sears, Robert R. (1963) Dependency motivation. In M. R. Jones (Ed.) *Nebraska Symposium on Motivation.* Lincoln: University of Nebraska Press, pp. 25-64.

Sears, Robert R. (1957) Identification as a form of behavioral development. In D. B. Harris (Ed.) *The concept of development.* Minneapolis: University of Minnesota Press, pp. 149-161.

Sears, Robert R. (1943) *Survey of objective studies of psychoanalytic concepts.* New York: Social Science Research Council.

Sears, Robert R., Maccoby, E. E., and Levin, H. (1957) *Patterns of child rearing*. Evanston, Illinois: Row, Peterson.

Sears, Robert R., Pintler, M. H., and Sears, P. S. (1946) Effect of father separation on preschool children's doll play aggression. *Child Development,* 17, 219-243.

Sears, Robert R., Rau, Lucy, and Alpert, Richard. (1965) *Identification and child rearing.* Stanford, California: Stanford University Press.

Sears, Robert R., Whiting, J. W. M., Nowlis, V., and Sears, P. S. (1953) Some child rearing antecedents of aggression and dependency in young children. *Genetic Psychology Monographs,* 47.

Sears, Robert R. and Wise, G. W. (1950) Relation of cup feeding in infancy to thumb-sucking and the oral drive. *American Journal of Orthopsychiatry,* 20, 123-138.

Selye, Hans. (1956) *The stress of life.* New York: McGraw-Hill.

Seward, Georgene H. (1956) *Psychotherapy and cultural conflict.* New York: Ronald Press.

Seward, Georgene H. (1946) *Sex and the social order.* New York: McGraw-Hill.

Seward, Georgene H. (1944) Psychological effects of the menstrual cycle on women workers. *Psychological Bulletin,* 41, 90-102.

Seward, Georgene H., Wagner, Philip S., Heinrich, Jerome F., Block, Saul K., and Myerhoff, H. Lee. (1965) The question of psychophysiologic infertility: some negative answers. *Psychosomatic Medicine,* 27, 533-545.

Sewell, W. H. (1952) Infant training and the personality of the child. *American Journal of Sociology,* 58, 150-159.

Shader, Richard I., DiMascio, Alberto, and Harmatz, Jerold. (1968) Characterological anxiety levels and premenstrual libido changes. *Psychosomatics, 9,* 197-198.

Shaffer, John. (1962) A specific cognitive deficit observed in gonadal aplasia (Turner's syndrome). *Journal of Clinical Psychology,* 18, 403-406.

Shainess, N. (1966) Psychological problems associated with motherhood. In S. Arieti (Ed.) *Handbook of American psychiatry,* vol. 2. New York: Basic Books, pp. 47-65.

Shainess, N. (1961) A re-evaluation of some aspects of femininity through a study of menstruation: A preliminary report. *Comprehensive Psychiatry,* 2, 20-26.

Shanan, J., Brzezinski, H., Sulman, F., and Sharon, M. (1965) Active coping behavior, anxiety and cortical steroid excretion in the prediction of transient amenorrhea. *Behavioral Science,* 10, 461-465.

Sher, Monroe A. and Lansky, Leonard M. (1968) The It Scale for Children: Effects of variations in the sex-specificity of the It figure. *Merrill-Palmer Quarterly,* 14, 322-330.

Sherfey, Mary Jane. (1966) The evolution and nature of female sexuality in relation to psychoanalytic theory. *Journal of the American Psychoanalytic Association,* 14, 28-128.

Sherman, Julia A. (1967) Problem of sex differences in space perception and aspects of intellectual functioning. *Psychological Review,* 74, 290-299.

Shock, Nathan. (1953) Some physiological aspects of adolescence. In Jerome Seidman (Ed.) *The adolescent.* New York: Dryden.

Shope, David. (1968) A comparison of orgastic and nonorgastic girls. *Journal of Sex Research,* 4, 206-219.

Shope, David F., and Broderick, Carlfred B. (1967) Level of sexual experience and predicted adjustment in marriage. *Journal of Marriage and Family,* 29, 424-427.

Shorr, E. (1942) Problems of mental adjustment at the climacteric. *Public Health Report.* Washington Supplement No. 168, 125-137.

Shuttleworth, F. K. (1959) A bisocial and developmental theory of male and female sexuality. *Marriage and Family Living* 22, 163-170.

Shuttleworth, Margaret. (1954) An investigation of the relationship between certain psychological factors and childbirth. *Dissertation Abstracts,* 14, 716.

Siebert, Lawrence A. (1966) Superego sex differences. *Dissertation Abstracts,* 26, 7441-7442.

SIECUS (Sex Information and Education Council of the United States) (1970) *Sexuality and man.* New York: Charles Scribner's Sons.

Simon, William, and Gagnon, John H. (1969a) On psychosexual development. In David A. Goslin (Ed.) *Handbook of socialization theory and research.* Chicago: Rand McNally, 733-752.

Simon, W. and Gagnon, John H. (1969b) *Trans-action,* 6, 9-18.

Simpson, Margarete. (1935) Parent preferences of young children. New York: Bureau of Publications, Teachers College, Columbia University.

Siñán Dominguez Laws, Ruth. (1965) Estudio psicológico de la agresión, desgracias, actos amistosos y buena suerte, en los sueños de un grupo de niños mexicanos. [Psychological study of aggression, misfortunes, friendly acts, and good luck in the dreams of a group of Mexican children.] *Archivos Panameños de Psicologia,* 1, 281-351. Abstract in *Psychological Abstracts.*

Skaggs, E. E. (1940) Sex differences in moral attitudes. *Journal of Social Psychology,* 11, 3-10.

Smith, Anthony J. (1950a) Menstruation and industrial efficiency, I, Absenteeism and activity level. *Journal of Applied Psychology,* 34, 1-5.

Smith, Anthony J. (1950b) Menstruation and industrial efficiency, II, Quality and quantity of production. *Journal of Applied Psychology,* 34, 148-152.

Smith, M. E. (1962) The values most highly esteemed by men and women in *Who's Who* suggested as one reason for the great difference in representation of the two sexes in those books. *Journal of Social Psychology,* 58, 339-344.

Smith, S. (1939) Age and sex differences in children's opinions concerning sex differences. *Journal of Genetic Psychology,* 54, 17-25.

Smith, S. M. (1954) Discrimination between electroencephalograph recordings of normal females and normal males. *Annals of Eugenics,* 18, 344-350.

Smith, W., and Powell, E. K. (1956) Response to projective material by pre- and post-menarcheal subjects. *Perceptual and Motor Skills,* 6, 155-158.

Soichet, Samuel. (1959) Emotional factors in toxemia of pregnancy. *American Journal of Obstetrics and Gynecology,* 77, 1065-1073.

Sontag, L. W. (1947) Physiological factors and personality in children. *Child Development,* 18, 185-189.

Sopchak, A. L. Parental "identification" and "tendency toward disorders" as measured by the MMPI. *Journal of Abnormal and Social Psychology,* 47, 159-165.

Southam, A. L. and Gonzaga, F. P. (1965) Systemic changes during the menstrual cycle. *American Journal of Obstetrics and Gynecology,* 91, 142-157.

Spence, Kenneth W. and Spence, Janet T. (1966) Sex and anxiety differences in eyelid conditioning. *Psychological Bulletin,* 65, 137-142.

Spencer, Thomas D. (1967) Sex-role learning in early childhood. In Willard W. Hartup and Nancy L. Smothergill (Eds.) *The young child: Reviews of research.* Washington, D. C.: National Association for the Education of Young Children.

Spencer-Booth, Yvette. (1968) The behaviour of group companions towards rhesus monkey infants. *Animal Behaviour,* 16, 541-557.

Spero, Jeannette R. (1969) A study of the relationship between selected functional menstrual disorders and interpersonal conflict. *Dissertation Abstracts,* 29A, 2905-2906.

Spuhler, J. N. (1967) Behavior and mating patterns in human populations. In J. N. Spuhler (Ed.) *Genetic diversity and human behavior.* Chicago: Aldine, pp. 241-268.

Srole, Leo, Langner, Thomas S., Michael, Stanley T., Opler, Marvin K., and Rennie, Thomas A. C. (1962) *Mental health in the metropolis.* New York: McGraw-Hill.

Stafford, Richard E. (1963) An investigation of similarities in parent-child test scores for evidence of hereditary component. Unpublished dissertation, Princeton University.

Stafford, R. E. (1961) Sex differences in spatial visualization as evidence of sex-linked inheritance. *Perceptual and Motor Skills,* 13, 428.

Stagner, Ross and Drought, Neal. (1935) Measuring children's attitudes toward their parents. *Journal of Educational Psychology,* 26, 169-176.

Stein, Aletha H. (1969) The influence of social reinforcement on the achievement behavior of fourth-grade boys and girls. *Child Development,* 40, 727-736.

Stein, Aletha H., and Smthells, Jancis. (1969) Age and sex differences in children's sex-role standards about achievement. *Developmental Psychology,* 1, 252-259.

Steinman, Anne. (1963) A study of the concept of feminine role of 51 middleclass American families. *Genetic Psychology Monographs,* 67, 275-352.

Stephens, William N. (1961) A cross-cultural study of menstrual taboos. *Genetic Psychology Monographs,* 64, 385-416.

Stern, K., and Prados, M. (1946) Personality studies in menopausal women. *American Journal of Psychiatry,* 103, 358-368.

Stevenson, Ian, and Graham, David T. (1963) Disease as response to life stress: II. Obtaining the evidence clinically. In Harold I. Lief, Victor F. Lief, and Nina R. Lief (Eds.) *The psychological basis of medical practice.* New York: Hoeber, pp. 137-154.

Stewart, D. B., and Scott, E. M. (1953) The assessment of efficiency in labor; psychological factors related to labor. *Edinburgh Medical Journal,* 60, 49-58.

Stoller, Robert J. (1968) *Sex and gender.* New York: Science House.

Stone, C. P., and Barker, R. G. (1939) The attitudes and interests of premenarcheal and postmenarcheal girls. *Journal of Genetic Psychology,* 54, 27-71.

Straus, Murray A. (1967) The influence of sex of child and social class on instrumental and expressive family roles in a laboratory setting. *Sociology and Social Research,* 52, 7-21.

Strean, Herbert S. (1967) A family therapist looks at "Little Hans." *Family Process,* 6, 227-234.

Strodtbeck, F. L., and Mann, R. D. (1956) Sex differentiation in jury deliberation. *Sociometry,* 19, 3-11.

Survey Research Center (no date-circa 1954) *Adolescent girls.* Ann Arbor: Institute for Social Research, University of Michigan.

Sutherland, H., and Stewart, I. (1965) A critical analysis of the premenstrual syndrome. *Lancet,* 1, 1180-1183.

Sutton-Smith, Brian, and Rosenberg, B. G. (1969) Modeling and reactive components of sibling interaction. In John P. Hill (Ed.) *Minnesota symposia on child psychology.* Minneapolis: University of Minnesota Press, pp. 131-152.

Sutton-Smith, B., Rosenberg, B. G., and Morgan, E. F. (1963) Development of sex differences in play choices during preadolescence. *Child Development,* 34, 119-126.

Swanson, Ethel, and Foulkes, David. (1967) Dream content and the menstrual cycle. *Journal of Nervous and Mental Disorders,* 145, 358-363.

Swenson, Clifford H. (1967) Sexual behavior and psychopathology; a test of Mowrer's hypothesis. *Journal of Clinical Psychology,* 18, 406-409.

Tanner, J. M. (1963) The course of children's growth. In R. E. Grinder (Ed.) *Studies in adolescence.* New York: Macmillan, pp. 417-432.

Tanner, J. M. (1962) *Growth at adolescence.* (2nd ed.) Springfield, Illinois: Charles C Thomas.

Tanner, J. M. (1961) *Education and physical growth.* London: University of London Press.

Tanner, J. M. and Inhelder, Bärbel (Eds.) (1958) *Discussions on child development.* New York: International Universities Press.

Taylor, H. C., Jr. (1949a) Vascular congestion and hyperemia: Part I. Physiologic basis and history of the concept. *American Journal of Obstetrics and Gynecology,* 57, 211-227.

Taylor, H. C., Jr. (1949b) Vascular congestion and hyperemia: Part II. The clinical aspects of the congestion-fibrosis syndrome. *American Journal of Obstetrics and Gynecology,* 57, 637-653.

Taylor, H. C., Jr. (1949c) Vascular congestion and hyperemia: Part III. Etiology and therapy. *American Journal of Obstetrics and Gynecology,* 57, 654-668.

Taylor, Howard P. (1962) Nausea and vomiting of pregnancy: hyperemesis gravidarum. In William S. Kroger (Ed.) *Psychosomatic obstetrics, gynecology and endocrinology.* Springfield, Illinois: Charles C Thomas.

Terman, L. M. (1963) Correlates of orgasm adequacy. In Manfred F. De Martino (Ed.) *Sexual behavior and personality characteristics.* New York: Citadel Press.

Terman, L. M. (1938) *Psychological factors in marital happiness.* New York: McGraw Hill.

Terman, L. M., and Miles, Catherine C. (1936) *Sex and personality.* New York: McGraw-Hill.

Terman, L. M., and Tyler, Leona E. (1954) Psychological sex differences. In L. Carmichael (Ed.) *Manual of child psychology.* (2nd ed.) New York: Wiley.

Tetlow, C. (1955) Psychoses of childbearing. *Journal of Mental Science,* 101, 629-639.

Theiner, Eric C. (1965) Differences in abstract thought process as a function of sex. *Journal of General Psychology,* 73, 285-290.

Thomas, C. L., and Gordon, J. E. (1959) Psychosis after childbirth: ecological aspects of a single impact stress. *American Journal of Medical Science,* 238, 363-388.

Thomas, Paula I. (1966) Sub-cultural differences in sex role preference patterns. *Dissertation Abstracts,* 26, 6894-6895.

Thomason, Bruce. (1955) Marital sexual behavior and total marital adjustment: a research report. In Jerome Himelhoch and Sylvia Fleis Fava (Eds.) *Sexual behavior in American society.* New York: Norton.

Thompson, Clara. (1949) Cultural pressures in the psychology of women. In P. Mullahy (Ed.) *Study of interpersonal relations.* New York: Hermitage Press.

Thompson, Clara. (1943) Penis envy in women. *Psychiatry,* 6, 123-126.

Thompson, Clara. (1942) Cultural pressures in the psychology of women. *Psychiatry,* 5, 331-339.

Thompson, L. J. (1942) Attitudes of primiparae as observed in a prenatal clinic. *Mental Hygiene,* 26, 243-256.

Tintera, John W. (1967) Endocrine aspects of schizophrenia: Hypoglycemia of hypoadrenocorticism. *Journal of Schizophrenia,* 1, 150-181.

Tobin, S. M. (1957) Emotional depression during pregnancy. *Obstetrics and Gynecology,* 10, 677-681.

Tod, E. D. M. (1964) Puerperal depression. *Lancet,* 2, 1264-1266.

Tonks, C. M., Rack, P. H. and Rose, M. J. (1968) Attempted suicide and the menstrual cycle. *Journal of Psychosomatic Research,* 11, 319-323.

Torghele, John R. (1957) Premenstrual tension in psychotic women. *Lancet,* 77, 163-170.

Treadway, C. Richard, Kane, Francis J., Jarrahi-Zadeh, Ali, and Lipton, Morris A. (1969) A psychoendocrine study of pregnancy and puerperium. *American Journal of Psychiatry,* 125, 1380-1386.

Tryon, C. M. (1944) The adolescent peer culture. *Yearbook of the National Society for the Study of Education,* 43, 217-239.

Tulkin, Steven R., Muller, John P., and Conn, Lake L. (1969) Need for approval and popularity: Sex differences in elementary school students. *Journal of Consulting and Clinical Psychology,* 33, 35-39.

Tuma, E., and Livson, N. (1960) Family socioeconomic status and adolescent attitudes to authority. *Child Development,* 31, 387-399.

Tupper, Carl, Moya, F., Stewart, L. C., Weil, R. J., and Gray, J. D. (1957) The problem of spontaneous abortion. I. A combined approach. *American Journal of Obstetrics and Gynecology,* 73, 313-321.

Topper, C., and Weil, R. J. (1962) The problem of spontaneous abortion. IX. The treatment of habitual aborters by psychotherapy. *American Journal of Obstetrics and Gynecology,* 83, 421-424.

Tylden, Elizabeth. (1968) Hyperemesis and physiological vomiting. *Journal of Psychosomatic Research,* 12, 85-93.

Tyler, Leona E. (1965) *The psychology of human differences.* New York: Appleton-Century Crofts.

Udry, J. Richard, and Morris, Naomi M. (In Press) The effect of contraceptive pills on the distribution of sexual activity in the menstrual cycle. *Nature.*

Udry, J. Richard, and Morris, Naomi M. (1968) Distribution of coitus in the menstrual cycle. *Nature,* 220, 593-596.

Vener, Arthur M., and Snyder, Clinton A. (1966) The preschool child's awareness and anticipation of adult sex roles. *Sociometry,* 29, 159-168.

Von Felsinger, J. M. (1948) The effect of ovarian hormone on learning. Unpublished dissertation. Yale University.

Wall, W. D. (1948) Happiness and unhappiness in the childhood and adolescence of a group of women students. *British Journal of Psychology,* 38, 191-208.

Wallach, Edward F., and Garcia, Celso R. (1968) Psychodynamic aspects of oral contraception: A review. *Journal of the American Medical Association,* 203, 927-931.

Wallerstein, J. A., and Wyle, C. I. (1947) Our law-abiding law-breakers. *Probation,* 25, 107-112.

Wallin, Paul. (1960) A study of orgasm as a condition of women's enjoyment of intercourse. *Journal of Social Psychology,* 51, 191-198.

Walster, Elaine, Aronson, Vera, Abrahams, Darcy, and Rottmann, Leon. (1966) The importance of physical attractiveness in dating behavior. *Journal of Personality and Social Psychology,* 4, 508-516.

Walters, R. H., and Demkow, Lillian. (1963) Timing of punishment as a determinant of response inhibition. *Child Development,* 34, 207-214.

Ward, William D. (1969) Process of sex-role development. *Developmental Psychology,* 1, 163-168.

Ward, William D. (1968) Variance of sex-role preference among boys and girls. *Psychological Reports,* 23, 467-470.

Ward, William D., and Furchak, Andrew F. (1968) Resistance to temptation among boys and girls. *Psychological Reports,* 23, 511-514.

Washburn, T., Medearis, D., and Childs, B. (1965) Sex differences in susceptibility to infections. *Pediatrics,* 35, 57-64.

Watson, A. S. (1959) A psychiatric study of idiopathic prolonged labor. *Obstetrics and Gynecology,* 13, 598-602.

Watson, John S. (1969) Operant conditioning of visual fixation in infants under visual and auditory reinforcement. *Developmental Psychology,* 1, 508-516.

Waxenberg, Sheldon E. (1969) Psychotherapeutic and dynamic implications of recent research on female sexual functioning. In George D. Goldman and Donald S. Milman (Eds.) *Modern woman: Her psychology and sexuality.* Springfield, Illinois: Charles C Thomas, pp. 3-29.

Waxenberg, Sheldon E. (1963) Some biological correlatives of sexual behavior. In George Winokur (Ed.) *Determinants of human sexual behavior.* Springfield, Illinois: Charles C Thomas, pp. 52-75.

Weaver, Frances J. (1969) Selected aspects of father-daughter interaction and daughter's instrumentalness in late adolescence. *Dissertation Abstracts,* 29 (10-A) 3690-3691.

Weil, R. J., and Stewart, Lucille. (1957) The problem of spontaneous abortion. III. Psychosomatic and interpersonal aspects of habitual abortion. *American Journal of Obstetrics and Gynecology,* 73, 322-327.

Weil, R. J., and Tupper, C. (1960) Personality, life situation and communication: a study of habitual abortion. *Psychosomatic Medicine,* 22, 448-455.

Weiler, H. (1959) Sex ratio and birth control. *American Journal of Sociology,* 65, 298-299.

Weinlander, Albertina A. (1966) Sex differences in scores on the Structured-Objective Rorschach Test. *Psychological Reports,* 18, 839-842.

Weinstein, Eugene A., and Geisel, Paul N. (1960) An analysis of sex differences in adjustment. *Child Development,* 31, 721-728.

Weiss, Edward, and English, O. Spurgeon. (1957) *Psychosomatic Medicine,* 3rd ed. Philadelphia: Saunders.

Weiss, Robert S., and Samuelson, Nancy M. (1958) Social roles of American women: their contribution to a sense of usefulness and importance. *Marriage and Family Living,* 20, 358-366.

Wenner, Naomi K. (1966) Dependency patterns in pregnancy. In Jules H. Masserman (Ed.) *Sexuality of women.* Scientific proceedings of the tenth annual spring meeting of the American Academy of Psychoanalysis. New York: Grune & Stratton, 94-104.

Werdelin, I. (1961) *Geometrical ability and the space factors in boys and girls.* Lund, Sweden: University of Lund.

Werts, Charles E., Gardiner, S. M., Mitchell, Karen, Thompson, J. and Oliver, G. (1965) Factors related to behavior in labor. *Journal of Health and Human Behavior,* 6, 238-242.

Westley, William A., and Epstein, Nathan B. (1969) *The silent majority.* San Francisco: Jossey-Bass.

Westoff, C. F., Potter, R. G., Jr., Sagi, P. C., and Mishler, E. G. (1961) *Family growth in metropolitan America.* Princeton, New Jersey: Princeton University Press.

Westoff, C. F., Potter, R. G., Jr., and Sagi, P. C. (1963) *The third child.* Princeton, New Jersey: Princeton University Press.

Whalen, R. E. (1968) Differentiation of the neural mechanisms which control gonadotropin secretion and sexual behavior. In Milton Diamond (Ed.) *Perspectives in reproduction and sexual behavior.* Bloomington: Indiana University Press.

Whelpton, P. K., Campbell, A. A., and Petterson, J. (1966) *Fertility and family planning in the United States.* Princeton, New Jersey: Princeton University Press.

White House conference on child health and protection, section III. (1936) *The young child in the home. A survey of 3,000 American families.* New York: Appleton-Century.

White, R. (1959) Motivation reconsidered: The concept of competence. *Psychological Review,* 66, 297-333.

Whiteman, P., and Kosier, K. P. (1964) Development of children's moralistic judgments: age, sex, I. Q. and certain personal-experiential variables. *Child Development,* 35, 843-50.

Whiting, J. (1966) as reported in Roy G. D'Andrade. Sex differences and cultural institutions. In Eleanor E. Maccoby (Ed.) *The development of sex differences.* Stanford, California: Stanford University Press.

Whiting, John W. M. (1960) Resource mediation and learning by reasoning. In Ira Iscoe and Harold W. Stevenson (Eds.) *Personality development in children.* Austin: University of Texas Press.

Wickham, M. (1958) The effects of the menstrual cycle on test performance. *British Journal of Psychology,* 49, 34-41.

Wilson, Glenn D. (1967) Social desirability and sex differences in expressed fear. *Behavior Research and Therapy,* 5, 136-137.

Wilson, G. D. (1966) An electrodermal technique for the study of phobia. *New England Medical Journal,* 85, 696-698.

Wilson, R. A., and Wilson, T. A. (1963) Fate of the non-treated postmenopausal woman: A plea for the maintenance of adequate estrogen from puberty to the grave. *Journal of the American Geriatric Society,* 11, 347-362.

Winch, Robert F. (1951) Further data and observations on the oedipus hypothesis: the consequence of an inadequate hypothesis. *American Sociological Review,* 16, 784-795.

Winch, Robert F. (1950) Some data bearing on the oedipus hypothesis. *Journal of Abnormal and Social Psychology,* 15, 481-489.

Winokur, George, and Werboff, Jack. (1956) The relationship of conscious maternal attitudes to certain aspects of pregnancy. *Psychiatric Quarterly Supplement,* 30, 61-73.

Winston, S. (1932) Birth control and the sex-ratio at birth. *American Journal of Sociology,* 38, 225-231.

Wisdom, John. (1953) *Philosophy and psychoanalysis.* New York: Philosophical Library.

Witkin, Herman A. (1969) Social influences in the development of cognitive style. In David A. Goslin (Ed.) *Handbook of socialization theory and research.* Chicago: Rand McNally.

Witkin, Herman A. (1949) Sex differences in perception. *Transactions of the New York Academy of Science,* 12, 22-26.

Witkin, Herman A. (1948) The effect of training and of structural aids on performance in three tests of space orientation. Report No. 80. Washington: Division of Research, Civil Aeronautics Association.

Witkin, Herman A., Dyk, R. B., Faterson, H. F., Goodenough, D. R., and Karp, S. A. (1962) *Psychological differentiation.* New York: Wiley.

Witkin, Herman A., Lewis, Helen B., Herzman, M., Machover, Karen, Meissner, Pearl B., and Wapner, S. (1954) *Personality through perception.* New York: Harper.

Wolpe, J. and Rachman, S. (1963) Psychoanalytic evidence: A critique based on Freud's case of Little Hans. In Stanley Rachman (Ed.) *Critical essays on psychoanalysis.* London: Pergamon Press, 198-220.

Woolever, C. (1963) Daily plasma progesterone levels during menstrual cycle. *American Journal of Obstetrics and Gynecology,* 85, 981-8.

Woodside, Maya. (1948) Orgasm capacity among two hundred English working-class wives. *Marriage Hygiene,* 1, 134-137.

Wright, Benjamin, and Taska, Shirley. (1966) The nature and origin of feeling feminine. *British Journal of Social and Clinical Psychology,* 5, 140-149.

Wylie, Ruth C. (1961) *The self concept: A critical survey of pertinent research literature.* Lincoln: University of Nebraska Press.

Yalom, Irvin D., Lunde, Donald T., Moos, Rudolf B., and Hamburg, David A. (1968) "Postpartum blues" syndrome: a description and related variables. *Archives of General Psychiatry,* 18, 16-27.

Yarrow, Marion R., Campbell, John D., and Burton, Roger V. (1968) *Child rearing: An inquiry into research and methods.* San Francisco: Jossey-Bass.

Young, William, Goy, Robert W., and Phoenix, Charles H. (1964) Hormones and sexual behavior. *Science,* 143, 212-218.

Zarrow, M. X. (1961) Gestation. In William C. Young (Ed.) *Sex and internal secretions.* Baltimore: William & Wilkins.

Zeldith, Morris. (1955) Role differentiation in the nuclear family: A comparative study. In Talcott Parsons and Robert F. Bales. *Family, socialization and interaction process.* Glencoe, Illinois: Free Press.

Zemlick, Maurice J. (1952) Maternal attitudes of acceptance and rejection during and after pregnancy. Doctoral dissertation. St. Louis: Washington University.

Zemlick, Maurice J. and Watson, Robert I. (1953) Maternal attitudes of acceptance and rejection during and after pregnancy. *American Journal of Orthopsychiatry,* 23, 570-584.

Zilboorg, Gregory. (1957) The clinical issues of postpartum psychopathological reactions. *American Journal of Obstetrics and Gynecology,* 73, 305-312.

Zilboorg, Gregory. (1928) Post-partum schizophrenias. *Journal of Nervous and Mental Disease,* 68, 370-383.

Zuckerman, Marvin, Nurnberger, John I., Gardiner, Sprague H., Vandiveer, James M., Barrett, Beatrice H. and den Breeijen, Arie. (1963) Psychological correlates of somatic complaints in pregnancy and difficulty in childbirth. *Journal of Consulting Psychology,* 27, 324-329.

INDEX